Double Visions
Double Visions
Visions

Women and Men
in Modern and Contemporary Irish Fiction

James M. Cahalan

 Syracuse University Press

Permission to reprint material from the following sources is gratefully acknowledged: Simon and Schuster for a version of the chapter "Gender" in James M. Cahalan, *Liam O'Flaherty: A Study of the Short Fiction,* 41–52; *Colby Quarterly* for versions of the Cahalan articles "Forging a Tradition: Emily Lawless and the Irish Literary Canon," 27:27–39, and "Female and Male Perspectives on Growing Up Irish in Edna O'Brien, John McGahern, and Brian Moore," 31:55–73; *Éire-Ireland* for a version of the Cahalan article " 'Humor with a Gender': Somerville and Ross and *The Irish R.M.*," 28.3:87–102; and *Notes on Modern Irish Literature* for a version of the Cahalan article " 'The guilty forgiving the innocent': Stanislaus, Shaun, and Shem in *Finnegans Wake,*" 6:5–11. Acknowledgment is also due to the Crawford Municipal Art Gallery, Cork, for their kind permission and assistance in the reproduction of Charles Vincent Lamb's, *Quaint Couple.*

The paper used in this publication meets the minimum requirements of American National Standard for Information Sciences—Permanence of Paper for Printed Library Materials, ANSI Z39.48-1984. ∞™

Library of Congress Cataloging-in-Publication Data

Cahalan, James M.
    Double visions : women and men in modern and contemporary Irish fiction / James M. Cahalan. — 1st ed.
        p.   cm. — (Irish studies)
    Includes bibliographical references (p.   ) and index.
    ISBN 0-8156-2804-8 (pbk. : alk. paper)
    1. English fiction—Irish authors—History and criticism.
2. Women and literature—Ireland—History—20th century.   3. English fiction—20th century—History and criticism.   4. Feminism and literature—Ireland—History.   5. Man-woman relationships in literature.   6. Gender identity in literature.   7. Sex role in literature.   8. Men in literature.   I. Title.   II. Series: Irish studies (Syracuse, N.Y.)
PR8807.W6C35   1999
823′.9109353—dc21   99-20984

*To the people from whom I first
learned about gender differences:
my mother, father, sister, and brothers*

James M. Cahalan is professor of English at Indiana University of Pennsylvania and the author of *Modern Irish Literature and Culture: A Chronology, Liam O'Flaherty: A Study of the Short Fiction, The Irish Novel: A Critical History,* and *Great Hatred, Little Room: The Irish Historical Novel* (Syracuse University Press).

Contents

Preface

This book takes up comparative readings of fiction by Irish women and men, exploring a series of "double visions" that one gains by reading the works of these women and men together, rather than separately as has usually been the case in studies of Irish fiction. In *Feminist Visions of Gender Similarities and Differences,* the psychologist Meredith M. Kimball argues that "feminist theories and politics will be richer and stronger, and that each of us will provide a better criticism of our own work if we engage in practicing double visions. . . . The major goal of practicing double visions is to resist the choice of either connections and similarities or differences as more true or politically valid than the other" (1995, 11). Of course, one can identify similarities between some of the experiences of women and men only after recognizing the differences that distinguish and define them. Within the Irish tradition, in his poem "The Double Vision of Michael Robartes," William Butler Yeats describes, among other strange visions, a Sphinx figure that is part woman and part lion—suggesting the intersections of the female and the male, often of interest in his work, as explored in Elizabeth Butler Cullingford's book *Gender and History in Yeats's Love Poetry* (1993).

Let me summarize how this book about Irish women and men came to be, since that background is part of the story that I have to tell and the analysis that I advance in the following chapters. My first book, *Great Hatred, Little Room: The Irish Historical Novel* (1983), dealt with a fairly male-dominated subgenre across two centuries, but I was struck even then by how much the points of view on Irish history in the novels of women writers such as Iris Murdoch and Eilís Dillon differed from those of their male compatriots. My second book, *The Irish Novel: A Critical History* (1988), examined the works of a great many authors and also assessed the impact on the field of feminist and other recent critical approaches; in that book, given an immense subject and limited space, I found myself often suggesting further directions for needed research, a few of which I have followed myself in my own subsequent work. A quick sketch in that book of Emily Lawless, for example, led me to publish an article about her work in 1991, the same year that my book *Liam O'Flaherty: A Study of the Short Fiction* appeared. The fact that the upper-class, Anglo-Irish Protestant Lawless and the proletarian, Catholic-Gaelic O'Flaherty wrote about the Aran Islands in almost diametrically opposite ways occurred to me at that time, but the fuller significance of this contrast, as developed in chapter 2, dawned on me only gradually.

Next, and quite similarly, I conducted separate projects on the feminist collaborators Somerville and Ross and on male sibling rivalry in Joyce. Yet again, it occurred to me only later how opposite these intimate family relationships (the subject of chapter 3) were in female versus male terms. Struck by the need to compare parallel works by women and men, in the mid-1990s I researched the bildungsromans, or novels about coming of age, by Edna O'Brien, John McGahern, and Brian Moore (as further developed in chapter 4). Most recently, in 1997, I explored the "Troubles" novels of Jennifer Johnston, Bernard MacLaverty, Julia O'Faolain, and William Trevor (chapter 5). I noticed in each case many of the same kinds of male/female differences and patterns that I had already found in Lawless versus O'Flaherty and in Somerville and Ross versus Joyce. In the meantime, I had also been reading a lot of feminist criticism in general, particularly for the bibliographic essay that I wrote for my co-edited book *Practicing Theory in Introductory College Literature Courses* (1991), and also studying Irish women's (and men's) history and literature for my reference book *Modern Irish Literature and Culture: A Chronology* (1993).

In short, the ongoing research that led to this book was inductive rather than deductive; without planning to do so, I realized that I had found recurrent gender features and contrasts running through the several different Irish fiction writers on whom I had been working. Rather than select these writers according to a predetermined thesis that I then applied to them, I developed the model for gender studies outlined in my introductory chapter largely out of my earlier, distinct studies of the writers and their works themselves. One might object that I was a slow learner, and I would not disagree. However, I also feel that my findings are more compelling because of their inductive basis. The patterns described in this book really are to be found in these particular authors' works (although many of these features may also be found in the works of a great many other writers, perhaps even in other periods, from other countries). I did not choose these writers in order to push a set thesis onto them.

It was also almost entirely accidental how my own research happened to follow the chronology of these fiction writers themselves. I worked first on Lawless and O'Flaherty, and next on Somerville and Ross, followed by Joyce—with these authors writing at the turn of the century and during the early twentieth century. Then I studied the 1960s bildungsromans by O'Brien, McGahern, and Moore, and lastly I turned to the late-twentieth-century "Troubles" novels of Johnston, MacLaverty, O'Faolain, and Trevor. As I note in my introduction, it is also coincidental that in every major pair of fiction authors under consideration in this book, the women's books happen to have been published earlier than the men's books, allowing me to be chronologically consistent in discussing the women first in each case.

Although for the most part the pairings of authors and contrasts of texts in this book dawned on me inductively, almost taking me by surprise, I should clarify that in some cases I have deliberately paired works that seem to me especially comparable. On the one hand, all of the fiction writers that I examine merit close study, or I would not have included them. On the other hand, a couple of novels were included not because they are their authors' best works, but rather because they were the most similar, in their basic content, to the novels with which I compare and contrast them. My intention is to compare and contrast women and men writing fairly similar kinds of fiction, in each case, to see how similar material looks through the lens of gender—rather than to contrast very different types of writing, in which other kinds of differences would more frequently complicate the picture. Liam O'Flaherty published several novels better than *The Black Soul,* and his short stories (also treated in chapter 2) represent his best work, but I also include *The Black Soul* because as a study of an isolated protagonist on the Aran Islands, its content is closest to Emily Lawless's *Grania.* Similarly, Jennifer Johnston has published several novels better than *Shadows on Our Skin,* but like Bernard MacLaverty's *Cal,* it is a narrative of an adolescent boy caught in the Troubles of County Derry, and I have therefore selected it for close comparison with *Cal* in chapter 5. I make no attempt in this book to survey these authors' works beyond the particular ones that I have chosen for close comparison—having already written such a survey in *The Irish Novel: A Critical History,* to which I refer readers looking for such an approach.

For much the same reason, because I wanted to isolate particularly parallel pairs of authors and texts, the specific perspectives on gender vary somewhat from chapter to chapter. The most common pattern involves mostly women writing about women versus men writing about men—in the cases of Lawless versus O'Flaherty, Somerville and Ross versus Joyce, and Edna O'Brien versus John McGahern and Brian Moore. However, in chapter 3 I am interested even more in the contrasts found in the careers of the authors themselves—Somerville and Ross in contrast to Joyce—than in their fictional characters, though their characters certainly reflect their authors' lives. Also, in chapter 5, I complicate the plot by focusing both on Johnston's and MacLaverty's novels about adolescent males and on novels by Julia O'Faolain and William Trevor that concentrate simultaneously on both female and male protagonists. Again, I have not attempted nor do I have the space to be comprehensive here: I do not attempt to work male sibling rivalry through all of Joyce's writings, for example, and I mention but do not concentrate on Johnston's several novels about women. Centering this book on a dozen authors and a specific set of texts, I do not claim that these particular examples emerge as easily formulaic for all of Irish fiction, though I do believe that they are suggestive of the parallels and contrasts one can find in many other authors and works.

I want to thank several individuals and institutions who helped make this book possible. Jonathan Allison of the University of Kentucky encouraged the project, and Nancy Holmes made a suggestion that helped me improve my chapter outline. Two hard-working graduate assistants at Indiana University of Pennsylvania (IUP)—Mohammed El Nahal and Rebecca Steinberger—contributed crucial assistance in a variety of ways. I am also thankful to my IUP graduate students in the doctoral courses that helped me develop my thinking. Professor Ann Owens Weekes of the University of Arizona read the manuscript thoroughly and made helpful, specific suggestions, as did IUP Professor Lea Masiello (for whose personal and familial as well as academic support I am, as always, very grateful). Professor Philip O'Leary of Boston College wrote to me about about Irish Gaelic prose during the Free State period, and Professor Patricia Haberstroh of Lasalle University made useful suggestions in phone conversations. IUP Professor of Psychology Maureen C. McHugh (our former Director of Women's Studies) steered me to some important recent sources concerning the psychology of women. Esther Beers provided crucial secretarial assistance.

At Syracuse University Press, I am especially thankful for the consistent support of Cynthia Maude-Gembler, Acquisitions Editor, and Sanford Sternlicht, Irish Studies Series Editor. It was mighty nice of Colleen O'Sullivan of the Crawford Municipal Art Gallery in Cork to phone me internationally and speed to me the transparency of the Charles Lamb painting that graces the cover of this book, and also very thoughtful of Andrew Haggerty at the University of Miami to suggest another painting that helped me think of the one by Lamb. I thank my home institution for an IUP Faculty Senate Fellowship and a sabbatical award, both of which hastened the completion of this book, as did a grant from the Faculty Professional Development Council of the Pennsylvania State System of Higher Education. IUP's interlibrary loan department performed yeoman service, as always.

More generally, I express my thanks to the officers and my fellow members of the American Conference for Irish Studies (ACIS) and the International Association for the Study of Irish Literatures (IASIL), at whose conferences I developed my thinking in this book over several years, as I also did in my articles for journals (listed on my ackowledgments page) whose editors and guest editors likewise earned my debts of gratitude: Marilyn Throne, George O'Brien, and Douglas Archibald at the *Colby Quarterly*; Thomas Dillon Redshaw and James Rogers at *Éire-Ireland*; and Edward Kopper at *Notes on Modern Irish Literature*.

Indiana, Pennsylvania   James M. Cahalan
August 1998

Double Visions

1

Introduction

Critical and Cultural Contexts

This book is about Irish women and men—both the actual authors of books of fiction, and their fictional characters who reflect life in Ireland as lived by real men and women. In the chapters that follow, I compare and contrast selected works by a deliberately gender-balanced critic's dozen of modern and contemporary writers: Emily Lawless, Liam O'Flaherty, Somerville and Ross, James Joyce, Edna O'Brien, John McGahern, Brian Moore, Jennifer Johnston, Bernard MacLaverty, Julia O'Faolain, and William Trevor. I also examine the works of a few other authors more briefly, such as Kate O'Brien's *The Land of Spices* (as contrasted with Joyce's *A Portrait of the Artist as a Young Man*), Seamus Deane's *Reading in the Dark,* and also several recent Irish films. For the most part, however, I limit my gaze here to a relatively small group of authors and texts that I feel particularly invite comparison, partly because I want to look closely at a few especially interesting (and representative) examples rather than survey the field, and partly because I have already surveyed this field more widely in the past.

(In)famously, Freud asked, what do women want? I wonder, what do Irish women and men want? And I try to find some of the answers in the fiction of these particular Irish women and men. I want to bring gender issues to bear on both women and men. For far too long, Irish women writers have tended to be largely segregated (and often marginalized) as "women writers," whereas generally Irish male writers have been regarded simply as "writers"—as if gender were not everywhere in their works, too. Joyce is the only male Irish fiction writer who has received ample feminist attention; the critical tunnel vision (feminist and otherwise) on Joyce has tended to shut down parallel study of other Irish authors. Feminist critics of Irish fiction usually write either about Joyce or about a woman novelist such as Kate O'Brien—not about John McGahern or Bernard MacLaverty. Whereas feminist analysis of Joyce or O'Brien has a great deal to teach us, do we not also have much to learn about gender issues in McGahern, MacLaverty, and other male fiction writers? To not ask questions about gender in their works is, paradoxically, both to neglect important aspects of the fiction of these men and to privilege them. For to pretend that they are simply "writers," not also men, is to participate in a falsely "universalizing" patriarchy whose characteristics extend far beyond Ireland. As Elaine Showalter notes, "In an essay in *Signs* in 1981, Myra Jehlen argued that feminist criticism should also draw attention to the gender of male discourse. By developing a history of women's writing, she pointed out, feminist criticism had demonstrated that the assumed universality of the literary canon was a patriarchal myth, and that what was usually called 'literature' was in fact 'men's writing' " (1989, 5). Jehlen criticized a feminist tendency to "conflate feminist thought with thinking about women," and advocated a new feminist rereading of "everything, thereby finding a way to engage the dominant intellectual systems directly and organically: locating a feminist terrestrial fulcrum" (1981, 577).

I intend to steer a middle course between the opposite poles represented by two insightful books on gender and major male writers, Sandra Gilbert and Susan Gubar's *The War of the Words* (1988) and Declan Kiberd's *Men and Feminism in Modern Literature* (1985). Gilbert and Gubar focus on the misogynist proclivities found in male writers; Kiberd, on androgynous impulses. For example, Gilbert and Gubar highlight Joyce's derisive parody, in the "Nausicaa" chapter of *Ulysses,* of what he described as the "namby pamby marmalady drawersy style" of female romances (146), whereas Kiberd concentrates on Leopold Bloom's many androgynous tendencies, seeing them as rooted in Joyce's own affirmation of the feminine within himself (171–203). Both views are valid, and their contradictory nature points to the many ways of reading Joyce— and other writers—as well as to the fact that gender is an issue fraught with many tensions and contradictions. I feel that in this particular case, Gilbert and Gubar are too quickly dismissive of Joyce, while Kiberd goes too far in the opposite, too generous direction, whereas his more recent, postcolonial study *Inventing Ireland* (1995) is slightly more gender-balanced. Both misogyny and androgyny can be found in Joyce, who is neither simply a misogy-

nist pig nor an androgynous angel. Male writers—and female writers—are not necessarily either villains or victors.

I feel supported in my approach by several feminist writers on
Irish literature. In their introduction to the collection of essays
Gender in Irish Writing (1991), for example, Toni O'Brien Johnson
and David Cairns complain that "studies of Ireland's literatures in
which gender has been foregrounded remain few," and they note
their contributors' new determination "to include the masculine and
attend to the construction of the dynamics of gender" (1). Although
most feminist studies of Ireland focus on women, most of the essays
in *Gender in Irish Writing* are about men, so much so that the book
as a whole falls short of gender balance in the opposite direction. In
Irish Women Writers, an Uncharted Tradition (1990), Ann Owens Weekes
deplores critics' "failure to recognize the possibility of real differences
between women's and men's depictions of women" (3), while she
focuses her book entirely on women novelists.

Most specifically, and in line with my inductive experience as
outlined in my preface, I read Katie Donovan's Raven Arts Press
pamphlet *Irish Women Writers: Marginalised by Whom?* (1988) only
in October 1997, while researching this introduction.[1] I was stirred
to find this Irish woman writer advocating the kind of critical
agenda that I had been following. Donovan argues that "isolating
women writers into a single category has the self-defeating effect of
further marginalising them from the literary mainstream" (5), and
that instead we should compare and contrast the works of both
women and men together, focusing on "the thematic alignment of
male and female writers, contrasted with their divergence of narrative" (37). She asks, "How can we reach any conclusion about the
Irish woman writer's merits if we examine her in isolation, as though
comparison with her male peers might be an exercise too rigorous
for her slender talents to endure? If Irish women writers are to be
recalled and examined with more credit and understanding than
they currently receive, they must be taken from the outhouse and
ushered into the centre of the Irish literary tradition" (7).

In her essay, Donovan mentions some of the same writers that
I examine—Somerville and Ross, Kate and Edna O'Brien (no relation), Joyce—and even pairs up two of the same novels, Johnston's

---

1. I am grateful to my colleague and friend Professor Patricia Haberstroh for
suggesting that I read Donovan's essay.

Shadows on Our Skin and MacLaverty's *Cal,* though her brief comparison leads her to views almost opposite to the ones that I advance in my chapter about them. Such gender-balanced comparisons and contrasts of female and male writers have been few and far between, in studies not only of Irish literature, but in literary criticism in general. Another work exemplifying the kind of approach that I want to pursue in this book, though in a different field, is Marcellus Blount's essay "Caged Birds: Race and Gender in the Sonnet" (1990), in which he compares and contrasts four African American poets: Henrietta Cordelia Ray and Paul Laurence Dunbar in the nineteenth century and Claude McKay and Gwendolyn Brooks in the twentieth century.

Irish Women Writers is the title of both Weekes's book and Donovan's essay, even though both are specifically about novels and short stories, not poetry or plays. This equation of literature with fiction perhaps reflects these two Irish natives' sense that for Irish women, at least until recently, fiction has been *the* genre, within which, as Nuala O'Faolain puts in in her essay on "Irish Women and Writing in Modern Ireland" (1985), "The novel is the necessary form of communication between sister and sister" (131). Despite the example of Lady Augusta Gregory, female playwrights have been few and far between in Irish theatres dominated by men, and the renaissance of Irish women's poetry, celebrated in Patricia Haberstroh's book *Women Creating Women: Contemporary Irish Women Poets* (1996) has come into its full force only within the past twenty years or so, whereas even a prolific poet such as Katharine Tynan was submerged within the earlier renaissance dominated by Yeats. Even one of the most successful contemporary women poets, Nuala Ní Dhomhnaill, agrees with Joyce Carol Oates that she would rather be viewed as a poet writing among women and men, not as just a "woman poet" or "feminist": "When people say to me, 'Are you a "postfeminist"?',", Donovan cites Ní Dhomhnaill as answering, "I think, who the hell cares? I don't want to be used and taken for a feminist" (quoted in Donovan 1988, 6). As noted in chapter 5, Jennifer Johnston and Julia O'Faolain have also found feminism too limiting in their own careers. Edna O'Brien has seldom been regarded as a feminist, even though she is the novelist who has done perhaps more than anyone else to encourage the entire current generation of Irish women novelists with the notion that they, too, can write honestly about their experiences and also sell books. At the same time, she recognizes just how crucial gender is, remarking as recently as 1997, "I do not see into male sensibility as clearly as into female. This is not unusual; very few writers have made the gender leap."

All of the fiction writers, both female and male, whose books I discuss in the following chapters have been commercially successful; even the most neglected one, Emily Lawless, sold well during her own period, with her novel *Hurrish* (1886) so well known that it was praised by the British prime minister, Gladstone. The best-selling novelists within my critic's dozen—Joyce, Edna O'Brien, O'Flaherty, Somerville and Ross—represent a gender-balanced subset of the writers under consideration here. I am interested in reception, so I have chosen authors with generally strong sales records as well as critical response. In *Women Creating Women,* Haberstroh argues that whereas on the one hand Donovan advocates moving women writers into the mainstream to join men, on the other hand "one can also argue that an isolating spotlight gets women into print, where they eventually have the chance to sink or swim on their own merits" (1996, 8), and Haberstroh cites others who agree with her. My feeling is that the seeming difference of opinion here between Donovan and Haberstroh really depends more on genre than on gender, and attending to genre may remove the disagreement: Donovan is writing about prose fiction, and Haberstroh about poetry. Donovan is right that women have excelled (and sold well) in prose fiction, and should be compared with men in the "mainstream"; Haberstroh is correct that women have been severely underrepresented in poetry and deserve special attention. It is sometimes difficult to generalize about literature as a whole; fiction and poetry require different means of assessment for different kinds of writers and in view of divergent marketing patterns. A number of Irish fiction writers have made livings from their craft, whereas not many Irish poets have been able to do so, simply because fiction generally sells better than poetry.

As Donovan notes, "It is to fiction that Irish women writers have made their largest contribution. . . . With its open form and straightforward chronology, the novel could be written on the sly, picked up quickly and dropped again when the writer's privacy was invaded, just like a letter" (1988, 7–8). Long before Edna O'Brien, Maria Edgeworth wrote *Castle Rackrent* (1800), often described as the first Irish novel—and a big influence not only on subsequent Irish novelists but, with its use of an oral style and an unreliable narrator, on the likes of Mark Twain. Recent research has delved back into Irish fiction even before Edgeworth, with Siobhan Kilfeather (1986), for example, working on Mary Davys, a neglected Irish novelist, essayist, and contemporary of Swift. And in her essay "Women as Writers: Dánta Grá to Maria Edgeworth" (1985), Eiléan Ní Chuilleanáin traces a rich vein of Irish women writers in other genres, in Irish as well as in English, from Renaissance times up to Edgeworth.

Edgeworth was followed by other well-known women novelists such as Sydney Owenson (Lady Morgan), Somerville and Ross, and Elizabeth Bowen—and a number of not so well-known authors. Janet Madden-Simpson borrows Daniel Corkery's phrase "the hidden Ireland," which he coined to refer to the Gaelic poets of the eighteenth century, to describe the treatment of women writers within an Irish critical tradition dominated by men, in the introduction to her anthology *Women's Part: An Anthology of Short Fiction by and about Irishwomen 1890–1920* (1984), which includes such writers as Jane Barlow, Evelyn Conlon, George Egerton, M. E. Francis, and Katharine Tynan. In her introduction, "Anglo-Irish Literature: The Received Tradition," Madden-Simpson notes how the comparatively liberal reading list of Irish literature handed to her (and to me, her classmate) at University College, Dublin in 1975 was male-dominated.[2] Whereas Madden-Simpson's anthology included some of the largely forgotten writers of the turn of the century, the editors of *Territories of the Voice: Contemporary Stories by Irish Women Writers* were able to celebrate the " 'great wave' of contemporary Irish women's writing" (DeSalvo, D'Arcy, and Hogan 1989, xi), adding, "Almost all of the stories were written after 1960, the date that Janet Madden-Simpson marks as the beginning of contemporary Irish women's literature, a time when 'currents of feminine revolt' increasingly came to the surface" (xii). Nuala

2. In another essay, "Womanwriting: The Arts of Textual Politics," Madden-Simpson wrote "of a 'lost' Irish feminist foremother, Sarah Grand. Grand's novel, *The Beth Book* (1897), subtitled *A Study of the Life of a Woman of Genius,* sold 20,000 copies in the week following its publication, and is now available in the Virago Modern Classics series. It contained 'sustained critiques of such issues as marriage, the education of girls, the physical and social degradation of women, the rights of women to work and the possibility of restructuring society,' and its use of stream-of-consciousness as a literary technique predates that of James Joyce by several years" (quoted in DeSalvo, D'Arcy, and Hogan 1989, 17). Madden-Simpson's focus on Grand as a feminist pioneer is similar to my own on Grand's contemporary, Lawless.

Archer notes that contemporary Irish women writers "manifest a 'full array of feminisms' " (quoted in DeSalvo, D'Arcy, and Hogan 1989, xviii).

As Rosemary Mahoney writes in her book *Whoredom in Kimmage: Irish Women Coming of Age* (1993), "A book about Irish women would also have to be a book about Irish men, for . . . the women often seemed to be engaged in a response to men" (xv). What about me, a man, writing this book? Can a man be a feminist? Can men understand women (as well as men)? These questions have been much debated in recent years. Annette Kolodny believes that yes, "Men can . . . learn to apprehend the meanings encoded in texts by and about women—just as women have learned to become sensitive readers of Shakespeare and Milton, Hemingway and Mailer" (1980, 464). Writing about Joyce, Hélène Cixous notes, "Maybe a man would have had something to say about female or 'feminine' writing" (1987, 2).

In contrast, Stephen Heath speaks for most of the contributors to the collection of essays *Men in Feminism* (1987) when he announces, "Men's relation to feminism is an impossible one" (1). He notes that he feels uncomfortable writing about women, yet recalls that he has learned much from women's perceptive writings about men, and thus feels encouraged that he can write instructively about women—but must keep in mind that "all this reversing would be fine were it not that the two sides are neither equal nor symmetrical" (13). More sharply and humorously, in "Critical Cross-Dressing; Male Feminists and the Woman of the Year," Elaine Showalter criticizes well-known male theorists such as Jonathan Culler who believe that they can take up feminism, like the latest critical garb, and all too easily "read like a woman." A man might do best to give up on high notions of calling himself a feminist, and instead take the clear, direct advice of Alice Jardine, who answers the question of what women want (of such men) in her essay in the same book: "Read women's writing," she suggests, and "recognize your debts to feminism in writing" (1987, 60).

My book is an attempt to "re-vision" Irish fiction, in which I heed the advice of Irish writers such as Ann Owens Weekes and Katie Donovan, and also listen to Adrienne Rich, as cited by Joseph A. Boone and Michael Cadden in their introduction to *Engendering Men: The Question of Male Feminist Criticism* (1990): "Re-vision—the act of looking back, of seeing with fresh eyes, of entering an old text from a new critical direction—is for us more than a chapter in cultural history. . . . We need to know the writing of the past, and know it differently than we have ever known it; not to pass on a tradition but to break its hold over us (3)."To '[see] with fresh eyes,' " Boone and Cadden add, is a project "in which both men and women can—indeed must—participate if we are to create a nonsexist future" (3).

I also want to respond to the admonition of Stephen Heath: "We should take seriously at last the 'hetero' in heterosexuality, which means the heterogeneity in us, on us, through us" (1987, 22). To be heterogeneous is to be *different;* to be men and women is to be different. I should note that for the most part, my focus in this book is on heterosexual relationships in Irish fiction, though students of homosexual relationships may be interested in my chapter comparing and contrasting the platonic female-to-female careers of Somerville and Ross with the male-to-male sibling rivalry found in Joyce's life, and also in my much briefer treatment of *The Crying Game* in my conclusion. Ann Owens Weekes (1998) has written about lesbianism in Irish fiction, although only in 1997 have Irish studies conferences begun to include papers on topics such as "Male Homoeroticism in Irish Literary History" (American Conference for Irish Studies [ACIS], April 1997) and, indeed, "Irish Men's Fiction" (New England Regional ACIS meeting, November 1997). In the past, a panel devoted entirely to fiction by Irish men would have been entitled simply "Irish Fiction," with their gender erased. Things are changing.

Gender differences are not necessarily simple or natural. As Joyce scholar Bonnie Kime Scott notes, "Gender is a category constructed through cultural and social systems. Unlike sex, it is not a biological fact determined at conception. Sociology has long discussed sex roles, the term *roles* calling attention to the assigned rather than determined nature of gender" (1990, 2). Onto our biological identities have been grafted complex, socialized patterns of behavior—patterns that are not independent of other key distinctions, such as those involving race and class. As Heath puts it,

> The relation of sex to identity is not immediate, we are constructed as gendered individuals in a complex psycho-sexual history; 'male' and 'female,' 'masculinity' and 'femininity' are positions, places, terms of identification; we are unfinished, sexually heterogeneous, however much the orders of heterosexual law constrain and define; woman and man do not exist only men and women with all the shared experience that race and class can cut across

much more decisively at many points, in many situations. . . . Sexual
difference also cuts across race and class. (1987, 27–28)

Or as Showalter stresses, "all reading and writing by men as well
as by women is marked by gender. Talking about gender, moreover,
is a constant reminder of the other categories of difference, such as
race and class, that structure our lives and texts" (1989, 2–3). She
notes that "although feminist critics recognize that the meaning of
gender needs to be interpreted within a variety of historical, national, racial, and sexual contexts, they maintain that women writers are not free to renounce or transcend their gender entirely" (4).
In delineating the differences between women and men in Irish
fiction, I will need to refer often to history, politics, and class, as
well as to gender—to try to explain, for example, why Julia
O'Faolain, a middle-class Catholic, presents a view of the world
that is comparable to yet divergent from that of William Trevor, an
upper-class Protestant.

The unmistakable differences between Irish women's and men's
careers and fictional treatments of similar material are outlined in
the rest of this book in very specifically biographical and Irish
contexts, but they also have much broader cultural explanations.
These writers and their works are subject to male/female differences
long analyzed by social scientists and linguists. In *Male and Female:
A Study of the Sexes in a Changing World* (1949), Margaret Mead was
one of the first anthropologists to explicate gender differences in
cultural terms. Patricinio Schweickart summarizes decades of subsequent research succinctly and accurately:

> The works of Jean Baker Miller, Nancy Chodorow, and Carol
> Gilligan suggest that men define themselves through individu-
> ation and separation from others, while women have more flexible
> ego boundaries and define and experience themselves in terms of
> their affiliations and relationships with others. Men value au-
> tonomy, and they think of their interactions with others princi-
> pally in terms of procedures for arbitrating conflicts between
> individual rights. Women, on the other hand, value relation-
> ships, and they are most concerned in their dealings with others
> to negotiate between opposing needs so that the relationship can
> be maintained. (1986, 209)

To skeptics who react against this body of research (such as men
who respond, "I value relationships too!"), I have often suggested

the following litmus test: The next time someone else does something bad to you at work, compare your reaction to that of your spouse or significant other when something similarly threatening happens to them. Men tend to want to throw down the gauntlet and even look for revenge, whereas women more often are interested in avoiding conflict and healing the rift. Noting that women tend to value connection whereas men tend to prefer freedom, Deborah Tannen cites faculty survey results in *The Chronicle of Higher Education,* which indicated that women said they wanted to become university faculty to teach and "join a faculty," whereas men did so because they wanted independence (1990, 40–41). Such differences are rooted in childhood, when boys tend to play in larger hierarchical groups with leaders, while girls are more often in small groups or pairs with a best friend (Tannen 1990, 43–44).

In an insight particularly relevant to my chapter on novels about coming of age, Nancy Chodorow has observed that separation from one's mother is a major developmental issue in adolescence for both males and females, and her conclusions about this process are much more gender-balanced and therefore useful to me than Freud's: "Because of their mothering by women, girls come to experience themselves as less separate than boys, as having more permeable ego boundaries. Girls come to define themselves more in relation to others." (1978, 93). Or as famously expressed by Oscar Wilde in *The Importance of Being Earnest,* "All women become like their mothers. That is their tragedy. No man does. That's his" (1895, 50).

Chodorow elaborates her analysis in ways helpful to an understanding of the differences between female and male writers and characters:

> Women's mothering, then, produces asymmetries in the relational experiences of girls and boys as they grow up, which account for crucial differences in feminine and masculine personality, and the relational capacities and modes which these entail. Women and men grow up with personalities affected by different boundary experiences and differently constructed and experienced inner object-worlds, and are preoccupied with different relational issues. Feminine personality comes to be based . . . more on retention and continuity of external relationships. . . . Boys come to define themselves as more separate and distinct, with a greater sense of rigid ego boundaries and differentiation. The basic feminine sense of self is connected to the world, the basic masculine sense of self is separate. (169)

These patterns can have crucial adult consequences, even for women who did not marry, yet assumed considerable household responsibilities, such as Somerville and Ross. Chodorow notes that the activities of women tend to "have a nonbounded quality. They consist, as countless housewives can attest and as women poets, novelists, and feminist theorists have described, of diffuse obligations. Women's activities in the home involve continuous connections to and concern about children and attunement to adult masculine needs, both of which require connections to, rather than separateness from, others" (179).

I should note that the distinction made by Chodorow (and others) between women's connectedness and men's separateness is neither a definitive one nor an argument that has been accepted free of controversy and disagreement. There are occasional examples of gender interaction in Irish fiction, moreover, that run counter to this distinction—as in Somerville and Ross's *The Real Charlotte* (1894), where Charlotte Mullen feels herself caught in bitter rivalry with (more than connectedness to) her younger relative, Francie Fitzgerald. Among feminist psychologists themselves, Janis S. Bohan (1993) has criticized Chodorow's model in *The Reproduction of Mothering* as "essentialist," as not equally applicable to all women, and failing to take into account the experiences of women who are not mothers or were not raised by their own mothers. Among feminist literary theorists and critics, French poststructuralism and other developments of recent years have opened up debate about the relative value of connectedness versus autonomy and have called into question solid or simple distinctions between women and men. Diana T. Meyers criticizes Chodorow for not taking into account "any conception of the self that includes oppositional capacities" (1992, 141), and favors Julia Kristeva's "more complex view" according to which she is able to "reject the association of agency with masculinity and thus reconstrue femininity." Meyers argues that "while psychoanalytic feminism has offered important insights regarding women's potential as agents as well as proposals for realizing this potential, . . . this school of thought has thus far remained too much in the grip of the gender bifurcation Freud codified to supply an account of the individual agent and human interaction that is altogether satisfactory from a feminist point of view" (136). Hélène Cixous speaks for a number of feminist theorists when she writes, "I reproach myself for using the words *men* and *women*. We have difficulties nowadays with these words. . . . Please use as many quotation marks as you need to avoid taking these terms too literally" (1987, 1).

"Male" and "female" are certainly not terms to be discarded, however; they constantly impress themselves upon us. I want to read Irish fiction in the spirit of Cixous—as "determined particularly by sexual difference" (1987, 2). Because I am especially interested in Irish culture and the authors' lives out of which their fictions were created, I find myself continually returning to issues that are rooted in the socialization of gender. I am not convinced that poststructuralist critiques of the works of Chodorow, Gilligan, and Miller have removed their validity. Feminist psychologist Meredith M. Kimball, whose advocacy of "double visions" has inspired me—and reinforced the title of my book (as noted in my preface)—counters Bohan by noting that Chodorow herself has critized "essentialism." Miller adds that "to argue that all statements about difference are essentialist does not get us very far" (1995, 16). The considerable evidence that many behavioral differences between women and men are more constructed by their experiences in the world than innate in their biology does not make these differences any less important or pervasive. And to recognize that women and men share many human similarities in their experiences of the world, and that often distinctions of class and race and language are also crucial, is not to deny the many differences that remain between women and men, which often cut across or work together with the other kinds of differences. We do well to practice the kinds of "double visions" that Kimball recommends, not only in our understanding of human beings, but in our analyses of the literary works that humans have created.

Even earlier than these other scholars, Margaret Mead found extensive gender differences in cultures remote from those of many of her readers. For the social scientist wanting to demonstrate distinct male and female gender roles, perhaps no better laboratory than Ireland can be found. As anthropologist Nancy Scheper-Hughes writes, "Although all societies are characterized by sexual asymmetry to some extent, one would be hard put to find a society in which the sexes are as divided into opposing alien camps as they are in any small Irish village of the west. A general rule can be said to be observed: wherever men are, women will not be found, and vice versa" (1979, 104). In the traditional Irish farmhouse," explains Scheper-Hughes, "women's world is the kitchen . . . , while men keep to the barn and the fields" and "quickly flee to the pub, since men generally feel more comfortable socializing with each other outside the home" (104).

Having spent a fair bit of time on Inis Meáin (the middle Aran Island off Galway) between 1976 and 1992, I can testify to the truth of these observations. When I stayed with a family there, I was an oddball much more because I was a vegetarian who prepared some of my own food in the kitchen than because I was an American; the islanders were used to American visitors, but not to men who cooked or did any other work in the kitchen, which was completely and utterly the province of women and girls. At least in the 1970s, the pub on Inis Meáin still had the two traditionally separated halves: a "bar" restricted to men, and a "lounge" for women as well as men. I focus on the Aran Islands in my next chapter, through the fiction of Lawless and O'Flaherty.

Although such extreme gender distinctions have now softened among the younger generation in Dublin and elsewhere in Ireland, the fact that what Scheper-Hughes observed in rural Ireland is also to be found in the cities is reflected, as we shall see, in a novel such as Johnston's *Shadows on Our Skin*. The mother of Johnston's Derry protagonist scrubs the house from top to bottom on Saturdays (her "day off" from her paying job), while the father limits himself to his bedroom and the pub. Scheper-Hughes was by no means the first anthropologist to write about these issues. The patriarchal nature of Irish society was described in Conrad Arensberg's classic (if male-dominated) study, *The Irish Countryman* (1937). Arensberg examined the tenacious cultural conventions of Irish peasant society; for example, he described the Irish countryman's willingness to send a wife who did not have children back to her parents and allow his brother to marry and live on the family farm (in exchange for a "large fortune") so that children could be produced and "the identity of land and family . . . preserved for another generation" (91).[3]

3. In *Inis Beag: Isle of Ireland* (1969), John C. Messenger confirmed Arensberg's findings: "Inheritance in the island is patrilineal, and before a man can marry, his father or widowed mother must 'pass on' the property to him. . . . When a man is without sons, he most commonly wills the land to a brother's son or arranges to have a man wed his daughter and 'marry in' to the household" (72). However, more recently there have been changes in such patterns. Chris Curtin and Anthony Varley noted in 1987 that bachelorhood has become more acceptable in such rural communities, rather than considered the disastrous deviance it once was, with now "a widespread appreciation that the reasons compelling people to stay single are often very real" (303).

Enormous gender distinctions, much to the disadvantage of women, are indeed very old and quite pervasive in Ireland, and they are profoundly rooted in mythology, history, and the interactions of fiction, fact, and folklore. In *The Great Queens: Irish Goddesses from the Morrígan to Cathleen ní Houlihan* (1991), Rosalind Clark notes that "although early Irish society was male-dominated, women had a prominent role in the literature" (2). Clark adds that "since Irish women warriors in literature never find it necessary to assume a disguise, we may suppose that they might have been an accepted, though very minor, part of Irish society at one time" (27), and concludes that "we might postulate that the feminine, or women, once had a more powerful role, perhaps in a pre-Celtic society now forgotten. When we consider Celtic literature and society, it is certain at least that the goddesses, such as the Morrígan, had great power in pagan times which they lost with the advent of Christianity" (194). Similarly, in his 1984 Field Day pamphlet *Myth and Motherland,* Richard Kearney notes that pre-seventeenth-century bardic poetry spoke of *an t-atharda* (Fatherland), and speculates "that the change from fatherland to motherland has much to do with dispossession: 'The more colonially oppressed the Irish became in historical reality the more spiritualized became the mythic ideal of the Motherland' " (18).

Such notions were most famously celebrated in Irish literature in Yeats's play *Cathleen ni Hoolihan* (1902), in which his Poor Old Woman comes lamenting her four lost green fields and entices a young man to walk away from his impending wedding to help her regain her lands, at which point she becomes a beautiful young woman with the "walk of a queen" (231). We might expect that the tradition of the dispossessed woman would speak even more poignantly to such women writers as Emily Lawless and Somerville and Ross. Like Yeats, they were members of an Ascendancy on the decline, but they were also women who were either shunted aside (as was Lawless by Yeats) or chose to remain aloof from Yeats's Celtic Revival (as did Somerville and Ross). Moreover, it is now well known that *Cathleen ni Hoolihan* was virtually coauthored by Lady Augusta Gregory, who brilliantly injected Irish-English, "Kiltartan" dialect into the play, yet was willing to let Yeats take all the credit in the billing of the play.

The tradition of the Poor Old Woman, or *an tsean bhean bhocht,* was centuries old. As Catherine Nash writes,

The symbolic representation of Ireland as female derives from the sovereignty goddess figure of early Irish tradition, the personification of this goddess in the figures of Irish medieval literature, and the allegorization of Ireland as woman in the 18th-century classical poetic genre, the aisling, following colonial censorship of the expression of direct political dissent. (1994, 229)

It is indeed telling and significant that while colonial powers such as England and the United States were personified as men—John Bull and Uncle Sam—Ireland, a country colonized for eight centuries, was mythologized as a woman, confirming the Asian Ashis Nandy's observation that "the history of western colonization is the history of feminization" (quoted in St. Peter 1994, 152). In 1882 Lady Gregory met an Anglo-Irishman who assured her that the Celtic countries and Italy were female and "that it was necessary for male countries like England to 'take the female countries in hand' " (Innes 1993, 9). The double-edged trope of colonizer as male and colonized as female is part of Orientalism as elucidated by Edward Said.[4]

The tradition of personifying Ireland as a woman was originally a native one, with partly liberatory and perhaps even feminist overtones, as championed in aislings (vision-poems) in the Irish language by women as well as by men. Similarly, there is a long tradition in the Irish novel, from at least the time of John Banim's *The Boyne Water* ([1826] 1976), of sending an English male hero out to fall in love with an Irish female heroine, with such novelists aiming both to extend the metaphor and capture an audience that numbered more English than Irish readers in the nineteenth century. As we shall see, William Trevor reverses this pattern of gender and nationality by telling the story of how three generations of English women fell in love with Irish men, in *Fools of Fortune* (1983).

Beginning at least as early as the time of Spenser, native images of Ireland as a woman were appropriated and rewritten by English

4. In "The Myth of Sovereignty: Gender in the Literature of Irish Nationalism" (1994), Joseph Valente reminds us that Said "famously demonstrated how Western anthropologists, ethnographers, explorers, poets and politicians of the nineteenth century constructed the Oriental as irrational, sensual, available, supine and enigmatic as opposed to the lucid, accurate, energetic and decisive Westerner. But many of these same manichean disjunctions were taken to inform the relationship between imperial Britain and its nearest ward, Ireland" (189).

and Anglo-Irish male colonialists into terms of righteous dispossession. As Siobhan Kilfeather notes,

> In Spenser's writings we begin to see an image of Ireland personified as a woman that merges with accounts of particular Irish women until the ideas of Ireland and of woman begin to have imposed upon them contradictory expectations, on the one hand of martyred innocence, and on the other hand of devious promiscuity and barbarism. Protestant Irish writers pick up these metaphors and recreate Ireland as a weak woman, a victim. Swift's *Story of an Injured Lady* is an allegory in which Ireland, the "injured lady," is seduced by England, and eventually supplanted by her rival, Scotland. In adopting the figure of Ireland as a woman, the Protestant Irish were able to employ race and gender as similar means of categorizing inferiority. They thus transformed themselves from enemies of Ireland (and of the native Irish) into its guardians. When Henry Grattan made his most famous speech on Irish nationhood at the opening of the newly independent parliament in 1782, he created a role for himself as father of his country by creating an image of Ireland as a dependent daughter: "I found Ireland on her knees, I watched over her with paternal solicitude." (1986, 11–12)

Perhaps the single most influential reiteration of such sexist, imperialistic attitudes at the beginning of the modern period was Matthew Arnold's in his 1891 tome *On the Study of Celtic Literature*: "No doubt the sensibility of the Celtic nature, its nervous exaltation, have something feminine in them" (quoted in Innes 1993, 9). Arnold's pronouncement was parrotted by other literary critics, such as Ernest Renan in 1897: "If it be permitted us to assign sex to nations as to individuals we should have to say without hesitance that the Celtic race . . . is an essentially feminine race" (quoted in Cairns and Richards 1988, 46).

Such attitudes were by no means limited to literary critics or begun by Arnold; they took much more virulent forms in the British popular press. As C. L. Innes writes in the most extensive study of this whole subject, *Woman and Nation in Irish Literature and Society 1880–1935* (1993), "Cartoons in *Punch* . . . depict Ireland as a virginal maiden, threatened by Fenians and other Irish radicals and sorely in need of rescue by paternal John Bull" (12). Lord Acton made the link between oppression of women and the Irish as clear as possible; Joseph Valente reports Acton's suggestion "that the edifying effects of British subjugation somehow compensate[d] the Celts for the 'rich treasure' they offered up on the altar of historical development, much as the edifying tutelage of a Victorian husband was held to compensate a woman for the 'treasure of her sex,' which she offered up on the altar of matrimony" (1994, 191). As Valente argues, "the gendered allegory of ethno-racial supremacism serves to naturalize both colonial subjugation and the continued subordination of women" (192).

Given the prevalence of such attitudes and the power of the British Empire, it comes as no surprise that female Irish subjugation was not merely a theory or an allegory, but a pervasive practice. Theorists were also practitioners, as in the case of Arnold, concerning whom Innes reports that "it is not at all surprising that Arnold opposed Home Rule for the Irish in 1886 on the grounds that the Irish were not capable of ruling themselves and were generally 'insubordinate, idle and improvident' " (15). For British colonial politicians of the time, actions spoke louder than words. "The nexus of the ideological modalities of Orientalism and Gaelophobia," writes Valente, "finds its personification in the prominent and formidable figure of Arthur 'Bloody' Balfour, who was charged on the one hand with justifying British sovereignty in Egypt, which he did in terms of the superior knowledge and rationality of the Anglo-Saxon, and on the other with administering British sovereignty in Ireland, which he did via the brute force of the Coercion Bills" (1994, 189).

Among the more depressing features of Irish women's history is the fact that after 1922, the new, ironically named Irish "Free State" continued the oppression of women in some ways even more effectively than had the British Empire. This was the case even though women had contributed a great deal to the struggle for independence that led to the Free State. In the 1880s, Anna Parnell and her Ladies' Land League did much to involve Irish women in politics, showing how they could challenge the British state and would not be easily intimidated—even though they were threatened with a British proclamation that "Where any females are assembled . . . such meeting is illegal" (quoted in Innes, 116)—and widening women's activism beyond "charity" work into direct action. At the turn of the century, Maud Gonne, far from merely the subject of Yeats's love poems, was another key feminist and nationalist leader. In 1900, together with the Countess Constance Markiewicz and Francis Sheehy-Skeffington (Joyce's friend), Gonne founded Inghinidhe na Éireann (Daughters of Ireland), which became

Cumann na mBan (Society of Women) in 1913, with a constitution devoted to regaining "for the women of Ireland the rights that belonged to them under the old Gaelic civilization, where sex was no bar to citizenship" (quoted in Sawyer 1993, 98). But when they tried to team up with male nationalists by attending their meeting, "those women who attended the inaugural meeting of Cumann na mBan had to observe proceedings from a special gallery (rather like the 'cage' from which Anna Parnell and her friends had had to view the proceedings of the House of Commons), and only once did their feminist ears hear an encouraging phrase—as Patrick Pearse spoke of the need to defend 'the rights common to Irish men and Irish women' " (80). As Weekes sagely notes, when speaking of wronged, old Ireland, Pearse's famous Easter 1916 Proclamation spoke traditionally of Ireland as "her" in the past tense, but when describing a futuristic, free country, he called Ireland "it" (1990, 15). Ireland was a wronged woman waiting to be freed, but that did not mean that the Republic would be governed by women or even free for women.

The Dublin Women's Suffrage Association had been founded in 1876 and grew into the Irish Women's Suffrage and Local Government Association in 1901, and the Royal University of Ireland Act had opened university examinations to women in 1879, though equality for women in universities or anywhere else in Ireland would be a long time in coming. Among the novelists I consider, Somerville and Ross were active in the suffrage movement, serving respectively as president and vice-president of the regional branch of the suffrage association in Munster. The Free State gave Irish women the vote, but little else. The Anglo-Irish War of 1919–21 concluded with the infamous treaty that partitioned Ireland between a twenty-six-county Free State and the six-county, Protestant-majority Northern Ireland within the United Kingdom—not only provoking the IRA to continue through the rest of the century the struggle to unite Ireland, but also creating separate laws between the conservative Free State and the more liberal United Kingdom. Yet things began with promise in the Free State: "Five years before the United Kingdom Parliament granted voting rights for women between the ages of 30 and 21, Irish women in this age bracket cast their votes in a Free State election" (Sawyer 1993, 98). However, women soon encountered a rigid, narrowly conservative moral code in the Free State that made life difficult for women (and for many men as well), with the banning of numerous books and films, according to a newly puritanical,

Catholic-dominated, antifemale, antisexual ethos. As Weekes puts it, "Women [were] no more free in the Ireland of the rebel Eamon de Valera than they were in that of Queen Victoria" (22).

It was as if now that she were "free," the Poor Old Woman was twisted, by the men who controlled the Free State, into a caricature of herself. As Christine St. Peter succintly summarizes the situation, "Postcolonial Ireland has been involved in its own exercise of neocolonialism, suppressing the differences within the new country" (1994, 158). St. Peter quotes Indian political philosopher Ashis Nandy's explanation that in postcolonial times, even long after national liberation, the former colonials " 'tend to observe or to impose strictly differentiated gender roles in order to assert the masculinity and right to power of the (male) subjects,' power that had been denied them previously" (152–53). Catherine Nash similarly explicates the Free State in gender terms: "while the idea of 'woman' remained the embodiment of national spirit and the allegorical figure for the land of Ireland, this land now became the domain of the overtly masculine. The west of Ireland was redefined as Gaelic, masculine, wholesome, pragmatic, and Catholic in contrast to the femininity and natural spirituality associated with the Celtic. This denial of the female was also linked to the control of sexuality by Catholicism" (1994, 236). Although the best novelists and other authors struggled valiantly against the censorship and moral dictates of the Free State, in some cases Irish literature reinforced a male-dominated nationalism, as Joseph Valente notes: "In nationalist texts such as Yeats's *Cathleen ni Hoolihan,* Pearse's *The Singer,* Maude Gonne's *Dawn,* and Lennox Robinson's *Patriots,* real women are not presented; instead we have Ireland presented as a mythical woman in order to encourage a revolutionary but ultimately masculinist state" (1994, 196).

The effects of the reactionary Free State were even more extreme on prose writing in Irish than on prose in English. At the turn of the century, Máire de Buitléir (Mary E. Butler) wrote a series of pamphlets under the title *Irishwomen and the Home Language,* making it "quite clear from the outset that the place for nationalist woman was not with the men in the public arena" but "in the kingdom of her home" (quoted in Ap Hywel 1991, 24) where, as Butler wrote elsewhere, "It is their pleasant, their charming duty, to make their homes worthy of Irish-Ireland" (quoted in Ap Hywel 1991, 28). Although the prose writings of numerous women are cited in Philip O'Leary's book *The Prose Literature of the*

Gaelic Revival, 1881–1921 (1994), there is much less prose in Irish by women to be found after 1921, again underscoring Free State retrenchment. Whereas in my other books on Irish fiction I have been able to include extended discussions of fiction in the Irish language, here I cannot really do so (except for some of O'Flaherty's stories that were published in Irish as well as in English). This is simply because, lamentably, there are no significant female novelists in Irish to include. An examination of Alan Titley's voluminous 1991 survey of *An tÚrscéal Gaeilge* (The Gaelic novel) reveals that of the some 160 novels (1901–90) listed at the back of his book, a grand total of five novels (3 percent) were published by four little-known women: Úna Ní Fhaircheallaigh, Úna Bean Uí Dhiosca, Nóra Ní Shéaghdha, and Siobhán Ní Shúilleabháin (the only one writing since 1945). This is the case even though the idea of a "woman's voice" is so strong in Irish fiction, as drawn partly from the country's powerful oral tradition, that one of its most celebrated (male) practitioners, Séamus Ó Grianna, adopted the female pseudonym of "Máire," and Liam O'Flaherty credited his mother as his own earliest model and chief inspiration as a storyteller. Nuala Ní Dhomhnaill now leads a revival of poetry in Irish for women (and men too), and a number of novels in Irish have appeared in recent years, but women seem to be almost entirely absent from the writing of fiction in Irish.

Sexism was inscribed directly into the Irish constitution of 1937, which recognized the "special status" of the Catholic Church in the Republic of Ireland, banned divorce, and asserted that a woman's place was in the home. Although censorship and many other conservative aspects of the Free State greatly relaxed beginning in the late 1950s, change regarding issues key to gender relationships—such as divorce and birth control—have been much longer in coming and in some cases have not yet occurred. In fact, one reason why the partition of Ireland between the Republic of Ireland and Northern Ireland is likely to continue is that even many of the northern Catholics who oppose Protestant hegemony and British rule in the six counties are unlikely to want to give up the liberal laws of the United Kingdom surrounding these issues in favor of the Republic's restrictive statutes governing these matters.

For many women in the Republic, it remains a long-standing tradition to travel to England to have abortions that are illegal in the twenty-six Irish counties, and this tradition is even more encouraged by recent election results indicating that a majority of the Republic's voters want to continue the two-faced practice of prohibiting abortions in the Republic but not preventing women from traveling to the United Kingdom to obtain them legally there. The Republic of Ireland remains virtually unique in the free world as a country in which abortion is still illegal in all cases. During the 1980s citizens voted against both divorce and abortion by two-to-one margins, although finally in November 1995, after a heated campaign, the ban on divorce was lifted by the narrowest margin of any national ballot in the history of the Republic. In 1979, the Irish parliament did legalize contraception—but only for married couples and only with a medical prescription.

More positively, the last two presidents of Ireland have been women—Mary Robinson and Mary McAleese—although for readers not familiar with Irish politics it needs to be clarified that the president is not the executive head of state (a role assigned instead to the *taoiseach* or prime minister), but rather a more ceremonial yet symbolically important figure. In fall 1992, Sinéad O'Connor outraged many (but pleased some) by tearing up a photograph of Pope John Paul II while appearing on the U.S. *Saturday Night Live* television show, as a symbol of rejection of the Catholic Church's control of moral issues for women in Ireland. Rosemary Mahoney noted in 1993 that "the birth rate—still the highest in Europe—is declining, more people are using contraception than ever before, and the number of births out of wedlock has risen from one in sixty ten years ago to one in ten" (307).

In literature, matters have improved recently for women perhaps more than in any other walk of life in Ireland. Louise DeSalvo, Kathleen Walsh D'Arcy, and Katherine Hogan remember having to search everywhere for books of fiction by Irish women in the late 1970s, although Julia O'Faolain's *No Country for Young Men* (1980) subsequently received much attention, and since then a writer such as Maeve Binchy has joined Edna O'Brien at the top of the international bestseller charts, and Irish women's books in general have become more widely available, though they remain much more difficult to obtain in the United States than in Ireland or Britain (1989, xiii–xiv).[5] In the early 1980s, feminist presses such as Arlen

5. As DeSalvo, D'Arcy, and Hogan note, "Readers interested in the relationship between Irish women's fiction and the changing shape of the lives of women in Ireland will want to read books such as Jenny Beale's *Women in Ireland: Voices of Change* [1987]; Margaret MacCurtain and Donncha O'Corrain's *Women in Irish Society* [1978]; Ailbhe Smyth's *Women's Rights in Ireland* [1982]; . . . and Andrew Rynne's *Abortion: The Irish Question* [1982]" (1989, xix).

House and Attic Press in Dublin and Virago in London began publishing novels by Irish women and reprinting older, neglected works. There were other good signs such as the short-fiction series by Irish women authors in *The Irish Times* throughout the summer of 1991. Although writing for such a relatively small market as Irish readers will perhaps always remain a challenge, things have never been better for authors of Irish fiction, both women and men, than they are now.

Within such contexts as the ones that I have been tracing in this introduction—both gender issues in general and Irish conditions in particular—the fiction writers that I discuss in the rest of this book have lived, worked, and published. As Nuala O'Faolain notes, a good date by which to mark "the birth of modern Ireland"—and thus modern Irish fiction—is 1891, with the death of Parnell (1985, 128). The first novel that I examine, Emily Lawless's *Grania,* was published in 1892. To date modern Irish literature from the death of Parnell is to recognize the significance of gender to our period, since as is well known, Parnell died soon after the infamous scandal about his relationship with a married woman, Kitty O'Shea, the wife of one of his followers. Ireland divided between those who turned against the Protestant Parnell, as dominated by the Catholic Church, and those who remained loyal to him. A bitter campaign was fought in 1890 that resulted in the loss of Parnell's control of the Irish parliamentary party, and which many felt broke Parnell's heart. With the death of this formerly "uncrowned king of Ireland," who had brought the country closer to Home Rule than was ever the case again until after 1916, Ireland plunged into a period of division and depression that lasted until well after the turn of the century. The fact that the beginning of modern Irish literature is dated from the death of a man ruined by his violation of a conservative Irish moral code about gender relations is itself highly suggestive about the cultural world in which Irish writers have had to operate.

In each of my body chapters, I have deliberately selected for comparison and contrast the thematically parallel fictions of women and men with comparable (which is not to say similar) careers: the portraits of life on the Aran Islands by Emily Lawless and Liam O'Flaherty; feminist collaboration versus male sibling rivalry in the careers and comic (and other) writings of Somerville and Ross and

James Joyce; coming of age for women versus men, as reflected in the bildungsromans of Edna O'Brien, John McGahern, and Brian Moore; and the "Troubles" (of both the 1920s and the 1970s) as experienced differently by women and men in novels by Jennifer Johnston, Bernard MacLaverty, Julia O'Faolain, and William Trevor. I also make some briefer links in my conclusion to a few other writers and filmmakers. My chapters are arranged both thematically and chronologically. It is quite coincidental that in every chief pairing in this book—Lawless versus O'Flaherty, Somerville and Ross versus Joyce, O'Brien versus McGahern and Moore, Johnston versus MacLaverty, and O'Faolain versus Trevor—the books that I examine by women were published before the books by the men, so my female-male sequencing is consistent in terms of both chronology and gender. However, I move from chapters contrasting two sets of radically different authors—Lawless versus O'Flaherty and Somerville and Ross versus Joyce—to chapters in which the contrasts are perhaps not so complete; the bildungsromans discussed in chapter 4 and the "Troubles" novels examined in chapter 5 do share a number of common features. This shift is reinforced by the fact that although the novels that I treat in chapters 4 and 5 are in each case closely contemporaneous, Lawless wrote quite a bit earlier than O'Flaherty, and Somerville and Ross earlier than Joyce—further extending these contrasts between Victorian women and modernist men.

This group of writers is also interesting in terms of social class—as intertwined with religion, as is typically the case in Ireland, where "religion," rather than being really concerned with doctrinal differences, operates more as a marker of social caste, like skin color in many other countries. In my next two chapters, I contrast upper-class Protestant women (Lawless and Somerville and Ross) with working-class (O'Flaherty) and lower-middle-class (Joyce) Catholic men. Then I shift to a trio of writers all from middle-class, Catholic backgrounds: O'Brien, McGahern, and Moore. My final body chapter is focused on two pairs of writers representing opposite class relationships: an upper-class Protestant woman (Johnston) and a middle-class Catholic man (MacLaverty), and then a middle-class Catholic woman (O'Faolain) and an upper-class or upper-middle-class Protestant man (Trevor). Are the contrasts among these writers' works due to gender or to class and religion? Such differences depend on all of these factors, all intertwined, almost always. At the same time, some gender differences cut across class and religion; some features link women from very different backgrounds and men even from opposite ends of the social scale. The cultural backgrounds of Emily Lawless and Edna O'Brien, for example, were very different, but Lawless's *Grania* and O'Brien's *The Country Girls* share many similar gender patterns; each concentrates on the close relationship of two women, for instance. Liam O'Flaherty and William Trevor could not be much more different in respect to class (and personality), yet O'Flaherty's *The Black Soul* and Trevor's *Fools of Fortune* both deal with alienated male protagonists who feel alone in the world even in the company of the women they think they love. I will return to the question of how class distinctions complicate gender differences in the chapters that follow and in my conclusion.

Let me briefly outline my four body chapters. First, I contrast the Aran Islands fiction of Emily Lawless and Liam O'Flaherty, in perhaps my most bifurcated chapter, because these two writers were opposites in almost every respect. Lawless was an upper-class Protestant visitor to Inis Meáin, the middle island and the most isolated Irish-speaking place in Ireland, and was not an Irish speaker. O'Flaherty was a native of Inis Mór, the big island, who grew up speaking both Irish and English in a large, poor family, and who returned to the island, for a time, looking for solace after wandering the world as a young man. Lawless's family was rather repressed and effete; O'Flaherty came from a family of rebels and storytellers. Lawless was a quiet person who became a neglected writer; O'Flaherty was an often angry character whom others tended to either love or hate, and he was determined to confound society whenever possible and make a defiant mark on the world. These great differences are reflected in the fiction of these authors. The protagonists of both Lawless's *Grania* (1892) and O'Flaherty's *The Black Soul* (1924) are lonely people on a beautiful if harsh island, but they are lonely for almost opposite reasons: Grania, because she is a victimized woman who cannot overcome her bleak situation; O'Flaherty's autobiographical antihero, because he is shell-shocked, angry at the world and other people, and does not fit in on the island. I want to examine these writers at their best, and so although I contrast these two novels and also cite Lawless's shorter works about Inis Meáin, I spend more time on *Grania,* her best novel and arguably the first Irish feminist novel, and on several of O'Flaherty's short stories (the genre in which he did most of his best work).

In my chapter contrasting Somerville and Ross with Joyce, I am perhaps even more concerned with their careers than with their books, though along with other works I do give special attention to the stories of *The Irish R. M.* (1928 [1898–1915]) and to *Finnegans Wake* (1939), which are both very funny books that are also most connected to the aspects of these authors' careers that most interest me here. Somerville and Ross were the two most closely collaborative major writers of whom I am aware, not only in Irish literature but in any literature in the English language, of any period since the Middle Ages. These two cousins wrote completely together, handing the pen back and forth, and even after the death of Violet Martin ("Ross"), Edith Somerville believed that she could still draw inspiration from her cousin and insisted on signing virtually all of her remaining books, over more than three decades, with both of their names. In pointed contrast, James Joyce carried on an epic sibling rivalry with his younger brother Stanislaus during his entire career. The more conscientious if not so creative Stanislaus often helped out his famous brother, monetarily and otherwise, becoming, in the words of the title of his memoir, *My Brother's Keeper*. Yet James gave Stanislaus little credit for his help, writing him out of the pages of his books (as when Stanislaus had thought that *A Portrait of the Artist as a Young Man* would be dedicated to him, but it was not). This absence remained the case until their stormy relationship spilled over into the pages of *Finnegans Wake,* in which Stanislaus is addressed directly and sardonically as "Stainusless." Somerville and Ross were all about feminist collaboration, whereas James Joyce, male egotist, wanted only his own name in the spotlight. This is my most detailed chapter, not only because Somerville and Ross and Joyce are the most major writers treated in this book, but also because this is my most compelling case of female-male differences, as played out in these authors' very lives as well as in their writings.

Edna O'Brien's *The Country Girls Trilogy* (1986 [1960–64]), John McGahern's *The Dark* (1965), and Brian Moore's *The Emperor of Ice Cream* (1965) are particularly worthy of attention in terms of gender studies concerned with the socialization of women and men, as these bildungsromans concentrate on how their autobiographical protagonists grew up during the middle part of the century. O'Brien's three novels are very different indeed from the two by McGahern and Moore; I include Moore's novel to show how the pattern discovered in McGahern's very short, rural novel is continued in Moore's urban one. The rural settings of O'Brien's *The Country Girls* (the first novel in her trilogy) and McGahern's *The Dark* are strikingly similar, and both protagonists are dominated by violent fathers, but

O'Brien's young girl reacts very differently than does McGahern's young boy. We move on to urban settings in Moore's *The Emperor of Ice Cream* (Belfast) and in O'Brien's *The Lonely Girl* (Dublin) and *Girls in Their Married Bliss* (London). Again, throughout these novels we find women pulling together and men pulling apart. The relationship that runs through O'Brien's whole trilogy, unifying it, is the friendship between Kate and Baba, two young girls who become young women. *The Country Girls Trilogy* can be more aptly described as a "double-bildungsroman," in the tradition of Kate O'Brien's *The Land of Spices,* which similarly interweaves the stories of two women. These novels contrast with Joyce's *Portrait,* that most celebrated and quintessential Irish male bildungsroman, with all of its attention riveted on a single male, as is also the case in *The Dark* and *The Emperor of Ice Cream.*

Jennifer Johnston's *Shadows on Our Skin* and Bernard MacLaverty's *Cal* are both about Catholic boys in County Derry struggling to fashion lives for themselves in the midst of the northern "Troubles" of the 1970s. In each case the boy becomes enamored of an older woman and strives to escape the violent IRA, with close compatriots threatening to draw him back into that violence. These two novels tell very similar stories, but in very different ways much marked by the gender of each author. Julia O'Faolain's *No Country for Young Men* and William Trevor's *Fools of Fortune* make up another pair of novels that are strikingly parallel, and each achieved considerable popular as well as critical success. Each is concerned with the Troubles of both the 1920s and 1970s, and how the older generation comes back to haunt the current one. These complex works show how history repeats itself, focusing on recurrent relationships. O'Faolain tells the story of the Irish Grainne O'Malley and the American James Duffy, who have an affair, much as an American man and Irish woman did in the earlier generation. When Willie Quinton and Marianne Woodcombe fall in love in Trevor's novel, they are actually members of the third generations of these Irish and English families to do so. These two novels are more subtle and complicated, but once again gender differences play key roles in them.

In my conclusion I indicate, much more briefly, how female and male versions of the "Troubles" have been continued in two more recent novels, Edna O'Brien's *The House of Splendid Isolation* (1994) and Seamus Deane's *Reading in the Dark* (1996), as well as in several films. I then synthesize my overall conclusions about the fictions discussed in my body chapters and suggest a few other female-male pairings in Irish literature deserving of further study.

We can learn much about both the authors and their characters, about Irish women and men, in these works of fiction. What *do* Irish women and men want?

2

The Aran Islands Through Female and Male Eyes

Emily Lawless and Liam O'Flaherty

Two Irish fiction writers could not be much more different than Emily Lawless (1845–1913) and Liam O'Flaherty (1896–1984). Lawless was an upper-class, Protestant, Ascendancy woman who wrote long, Victorian novels, was critized by Yeats, and has been mostly ignored ever since then. O'Flaherty was a working-class man from a generation later with a Catholic, peasant, Irish-speaking background, whose best work was short fiction in a modernist mode and who became one of the most celebrated of twentieth-century fiction writers. Lawless and O'Flaherty were so dissimilar that the fact that their careers and writings were vastly divergent seems a foregone conclusion, and the question arises, why even bother to compare them here? First, the contrasts between their careers and works are illustrative of gender distinctions in Irish fiction in general. Their fiction is so steeped in gender issues—with Lawless emerging as an early feminist or protofeminist, and O'Flaherty often guilty of the most flagrant misogyny—that these distinctions cut across even the several other differences between these writers. In her essay *Irish Women Writers: Marginalised by Whom?* (1988), Katie Donovan begins by differentiating the Anglo-Irish "first Irish novelist" Maria Edgeworth from William Carleton, the Gaelic peasant who became one of the most important Irish fiction writers of the nineteenth century, by focusing on the "private" Edgeworth versus the "public" Carleton. Lawless and O'Flaherty are their cultural and literary grandchildren: as I note below, Lawless published a biography of Edgeworth, and no twentieth-century Irish writer is more similar to Carleton than O'Flaherty.[1]

1. Both Carleton and O'Flaherty were Gaelic-speaking, peasant novelists, "spoiled priests" who sought literary success, championed themselves and achieved

Another reason to link Lawless and O'Flaherty is that they share at least one key subject: the Aran Islands as both a real, naturalistic setting and a symbolic site for the delineation of typically lonely and isolated women and men. Both writers were also close observers of animals and the natural world of these islands. Although both authors wrote many books set in other locations on the mainland of Ireland, in each case their best work was about these beautiful, stark islands off the west coast of Galway: Lawless's novel about life on Inis Meáin (the small middle island, usually Anglicized as "Inishmaan"), *Grania* (1892), and O'Flaherty's many short stories about his native Inis Mór (the westernmost, big island), which he typically disguises thinly as "Inverara."

Thus, we begin with the sharpest of contrasts—not only because these two writers were so unlike each other, but also because their common fictional settings were among the places where, as Nancy Scheper-Hughes and others have observed, gender differences are at their most extreme within a country where such distinctions are generally unmistakable. The Aran Islands are perhaps best known to readers of Irish literature through John Millington Synge's celebrated one-act tragedy *Riders to the Sea* (1903), a folk drama set on Inis Meáin, in which a mother and her daughters face the deaths by drowning of all of the men in their family. Synge's play is a marvelous one, but it reinforces a view of Irish women as passive, and was championed by Irish nationalists perhaps partly for that reason, unlike a play such as *The Playboy of the Western World* (1907), which presented gender relationships in an unconventional way and was greeted with riots by nationalists.

Lawless wrote about Inis Meáin several years before her fellow Anglo-Irish writer, Synge, and as a native of Inis Mór, O'Flaherty wrote with a much more intimate knowledge of life on these islands than either Synge or Lawless had. For example, O'Flaherty echoes Synge's play at one point in his novel *The Black Soul* (1924a), yet speaks from his own boyhood experience: "The sound of racing hoofs suggested to her her lover's death. That sound is the harbinger of death in Inverara in winter" (52). O'Flaherty was a native speaker of Irish, with his knowledge of the Irish language always permeating his writing in English, whereas Lawless knew little Irish and wrote *Grania* in standard English. I take up some of the

popular and critical acclaim but, never forgetting their early days of poverty, often wrote far below their potential in search of fast money.

ramifications of this linguistic contrast between these two authors in the rest of this chapter.

Because I want to connect Lawless and O'Flaherty on the common ground of the Aran Islands, I focus entirely on their fiction set there. For this reason (and also because I feel that it is a better and more important novel), I focus on *Grania* even though Lawless's novel *Hurrish* (1886) attracted more attention during her own period. I begin my discussion of O'Flaherty with *The Black Soul,* even though *Skerrett* (1932) was a better Inis Mór novel, because *The Black Soul* offers closer parallels to *Grania.* Then I spend more time on several of O'Flaherty's Inis Mór stories, some of which are his very best works. I necessarily do not take up here many other aspects of O'Flaherty's life and works, but have dealt with several of them elsewhere at some length.[2]

Emily Lawless was a pioneer among Irish women writers. The work of twentieth-century writers such as Kate O'Brien and Jennifer Johnston would be unimaginable if Lawless had not come before. Yet during her time Lawless was the victim of critical neglect and scorn. Only recently has there been seen a flickering of interest in her work, and feminist attention to her work has been slow in coming. An important part of opening up the Irish literary canon is recognition of the valuable contributions of a writer such as Lawless, especially in *Grania,* a study of a strong, victimized peasant woman of the Aran Islands. Here I want to outline the cultural and critical difficulties that Lawless faced, introduce the view of gender (as often linked to a strong interest in the natural world) found in several of her works, assess her relationship to Edgeworth and Synge, and then advance a close reading of *Grania.*

Lawless struggled to establish a voice and a name as an Irish fiction writer during one of the most difficult periods for any kind of Irish writer—the late nineteenth century. This period came after the Great Hunger (1845–51), which was nearly as devastating for

2. I have written about O'Flaherty's powerful historical novel *Famine* (1937a), which also drew on his upbringing on Inis Mór (Cahalan 1983, 133–53); about his novels in general (Cahalan 1988, 186–91); about the bilingualism, politics, naturalism, and criticism of his short fiction (Cahalan 1991b); and about his life, work, and reception in general (Cahalan 1997, 344–48).

Irish culture as it was for the Irish people; before the rise to fame of W. B. Yeats and his Irish Renaissance; and in the shadows of the Victorian era, when the novels of Dickens, Thackeray, George Eliot, and other celebrated English writers cast the efforts of Irish fiction writers into deep, debilitating shadows. As a writer of fiction, other prose, and poetry, Lawless operated at a disadvantage not only as a Victorian Irishwoman, but also as a member of the Anglo-Irish Ascendancy who neither sought out nor was accepted by Yeats and the other members of the (mostly Ascendancy) Irish Literary Revival movement. Yeats held up the peasant writer William Carleton as his romanticized model of what an Irish fiction writer should be, and his pronouncements were tremendously influential on the formation of the Irish literary canon. It was therefore devastating to Lawless's reputation when Yeats declared in 1895 that she was "in imperfect sympathy with the Celtic nature" (quoted in Brewer 1983, 121), even though as a matter of fact her best fiction portrayed the Irish peasantry much more realistically than Yeats was ever able to do.

Yeats did include Lawless's historical novels *With Essex in Ireland* (1890) and *Maelcho* (1894) in his listing of the "Best Irish Books." His selection of these books, however, suggests that his treatment and that of other early critics of Lawless was similar to their abuse of her fellow Irish Victorian Charles Lever. "They got hold of the wrong Lever" (Jeffares 1980, 104), A. Norman Jeffares concludes in view of the stereotyping of Lever as narrowly Anglo-Irish despite the wide range of his work. They also got hold of the wrong Lawless, regarding her as a "mere historian" rather than a fiction writer of any importance. As far as we can tell, Yeats ignored *Grania*, the sketches in *Traits and Confidences* (1897), and most of her other prose, focusing only on her historical novels and her history *The Story of Ireland* (1887).

Lawless was condescended to much as were the great turn-of-the-century fiction-writing duo Somerville and Ross who, like Lawless, stood aloof from the Literary Revival movement, as we shall see in my next chapter, and instead modeled themselves on precursors such as Edgeworth, in particular. Very much enamored of Yeats's cultural and literary views as well as of his writing, Ernest Boyd subtitled his chapter on prose fiction in his influential book *Ireland's Literary Renaissance* (1922) "The Weak Point of the Revival," grudgingly surveying Lawless's work but finding it of negligible significance. As Janet Madden-Simpson stresses, too often "Ireland is thought of as a country with an impressive literary tradition from which come great male artists" (1984, 1). This is largely true even of John Wilson Foster's otherwise innovative study of Lawless's period, *Fictions of the Irish Literary Revival: A Changeling Art* (1987), which seeks to overcome Boyd's dismissal of the supposed "Weak Point of the Revival" and open up the canon well beyond Yeats and Synge. Highlighted in its table of contents are twenty-two male fiction writers, including at least eight lesser-known talents, but Foster treats in detail only two women—the already well-known Lady Gregory along with Eleanor Hull as the only noncanonical woman. Foster mentions Lawless only in passing, seeming to accept Synge's dismissal of her work (104). It is noteworthy that Joyce (who was critical of Yeats's Revival) appears to refer to her, in masculinized form, in *Finnegans Wake* when he writes of "a whippingtop for Eddy Lawless" (1939, 210, lines 32–33).

In her time Emily Lawless was well known enough that as he prepared his arguments in favor of Irish Home Rule, the British prime minister William Gladstone praised her novel *Hurrish,* the story of a peasant family feud set amidst the Land League struggles in County Clare. Gladstone stated that Lawless had presented to her readers "not as an abstract proposition, but as a living reality, the estrangement of the people of Ireland from the law." Yet Irish nationalists were much less hospitable. The *Nation* accused her of grossly exaggerating the violence of peasants, on whom she looked down from "the pinnacle of her three-generation nobility," and called *Hurrish* "slanderous and lying from cover to cover." Even though Lawless had painted her peasant hero Hurrish O'Brien and his sister-in-law Ally as saintly, the nationalist reviewers attacked her more negative characterizations of Hurrish's bloodthirsty mother and his foolish, bigoted neighbors the Bradys—thereby condemning the same kind of vivid, realistic portrayals of peasant life in Lawless that they had earlier praised in Carleton (Brewer 1983, 122–23).

Although it was not guilty of these misplaced charges, *Hurrish* was a sentimental novel in which Lawless remained a long way from exploring her own identity, by a writing about a male peasant, and it is unfortunate that Lawless's reputation remained attached to this novel. In fact, Lawless explored herself and her position in respect to Ireland and Irish nationalism much more compellingly

and truly in *Grania,* significantly positioning the novel and its
female protagonist offshore, on Inis Meáin, separated from the
rest of Ireland, populated by people who view themselves as quite
different from the Irish of the mainland. Self and nation, for Lawless, became competing, conflicting notions. She could find herself
only on an island of her own.

Lawless's reputation has been a long time recovering or even
emerging from such early dismissals and attacks. Lawless's poetry
was collected and republished in 1965, with one poem ("After
Aughrim") more recently included in *Ireland's Women: Writings Past
and Present,* edited by Katie Donovan, A. Norman Jeffares, and
Brendan Kennelly (1994, 409–10). The reprinting of several of her
books at the end of the 1970s in the nineteenth-century Irish fiction
series edited by Robert Lee Wolff and published by Garland, together with a couple of dissertations and useful and appreciative
articles in the 1980s by Betty Webb Brewer and Elizabeth Grubgeld,
indicated a slight revival of interest in Lawless. Still applicable
today is Madden-Simpson's point that at the turn of the century,
"The urgent problem of national identity at this crucial period of
Irish history swamped the 'woman question' and sapped its vitality" (1984, 12). Seamus Deane and the other editors of the massive
three-volume *Field Day Anthology of Irish Writing* (1991) included
a small excerpt only from *Hurrish* (3: 1027–33), along with a short
biographical note assessing Lawless only in terms of nationalism,
not gender (3: 1216).

In a useful survey of her career, Brewer's main concern is to show
that Lawless made a valuable contribution to Irish literary nationalism, and Grubgeld's article on *Grania* focuses on Lawless's reputedly
bleak Victorian treatment of the land. Lawless's lifelong interest in
the geology and plant life of County Clare (where she spent summers
since childhood), the Aran Islands, and the west of Ireland in general
has been rightly noted by the few commentators on her work. *Grania*
is a novel that closely links the barren setting of Inis Meáin with the
tragic victimization of its female protagonist. The connection between the novel's setting and its clear feminism, however, seems to
have escaped critics. This is surprising, because *Grania* was the most
clearly feminist (or at least protofeminist) nineteenth-century Irish
novel since those of Sydney Owenson at the beginning of the century,
and given that Lawless published a biography of Edgeworth (1904)
in which she attacked her oppression at the hands of her patriarchal

father, Richard Lovell Edgeworth.[3] In *Anglo-Irish Literature: A Review of Research* (1976), James Kilroy noted the irony that this study of one Irish novelist by another was published in an "English Men of Letters" series—completely missing or ignoring the equal if not greater irony that the two women were thereby classified as "*Men* of Letters."

Her father having died when she was fourteen, Lawless was raised by her mother (to whom she was very close) along with her eight siblings. The fact that her father and two of her sisters committed suicide suggests that a perhaps partly genetic melancholy was yet another obstacle that Lawless had to overcome.[4] Wolff notes that she "began to write in the early 1880s under friendly prompting from the successful and enormously prolific Scottish novelist Mrs. Oliphant" (1979, vi). Raised by her mother, prompted to write by Oliphant, and inspired throughout her career by the example of Edgeworth, Lawless clearly experienced female tradition and mentorship as central shaping influences. A chronological survey of her works indicates that she became more attentive to gender as she went along. It also suggests that her abiding interest in the natural world—the chief aspect of her work, along with her pursuit of Irish history, that has been critically noted previously—is not separate or divergent from her attention to gender, but rather closely intertwined with it. We can therefore identify aspects of her work that look ahead to ecofeminism, which opposes patriarchal domination of the natural world as well as male oppression of women.[5]

From the beginning of her career, Lawless insisted that the

3. I found only two glimmers of feminism in criticism on Lawless previous to my own 1991 article. One was Brewer's mention that the key to *Grania* is "the complex psychology of its heroine. . . . Though rooted in nature, the context in which Grania struggles to understand herself—particularly herself as a woman— is relational" (1983, 124). The other was Grubgeld's remark in her article on Lawless's poetry that "another reason for her obscurity may lie in the unfortunate disregard for women's writing which has characterized much study of Irish literature" (1986, 35).

4. Grubgeld (1987) takes the fact that Lawless contended in her later years with her mother's unexpected death in 1895 as well as her own worsening health, resultant exile to England, and heroin addiction as crucial to her experience, arguing that disillusionment and the contrast between happy childhood and unhappy maturity are central themes in her work.

5. In recent years, "ecocriticism has become an established field of study" (1993, 4), as Cheryll Burgess Glotfelty stresses in the first issue of a journal founded in response to such approaches, *ISLE: Interdisciplinary Studies in Literature and Environment,* and also as reported by Karen J. Winkler in 1996 in *The*

natural world should be understood on its own terms, scientifically, rather than romantically misperceived from the outside. As she wrote in her early essay on the west of Ireland, "Iar-Connaught: A Sketch," "all acquaintanceship with scenery may be said to come under one or other of two heads: to be either extrinsic or intrinsic—the point of view . . . of the tourist and that of the native" (1882b, 319). Clearly she felt herself to be a native rather than a tourist. Lawless's story in *Traits and Confidences* entitled "An Entomological Adventure" is an undoubtedly autobiographical account of a young girl's bug-hunt in the middle of the night, capturing simultaneously the sensitivity and imagination of girlhood and her own early desire to be a naturalist: "The very sonorousness of the name was worth anything; a name which you secretly rolled round and round in your mouth, and applied to yourself as you walked about the house. What dignity, what majesty lay in its syllables— En-to-mo-lo-gist! Could anything be more entrancing?" (1897, 11– 12). In an Irish literary canon much celebrated for stories of boyhood—by Carleton, O'Flaherty, Joyce, Frank O'Connor, and others—but not much known for stories of girlhood, this one is interesting and valuable.

Lawless's most in-depth scrutiny of nature from her particularly female perspective comes in *A Garden Diary* (1901). Exiled for health reasons by this time of her life to Surrey in England, "a tall, almost angular" woman in an "almost, shapeless gardening hat" (quoted in Wolff 1979, xiv), Lawless found solace in her garden. Concerning this work she remarked that "a good deal of it . . . is an attempt to lift the small natural history problem into a region where all Nature and Life (including our own) become, as it were, one" (quoted in Brewer 1983, 127)—thus joining her interest in the natural world with her own inner life. She sought to memorialize the rocky Burren region of her beloved County Clare in her English garden "by three or four tiers of stones . . . pretend[ing] that fragments of lime rubbish are slabs of limestone" (1901, 126).

Chronicle of Higher Education. However, ecofeminism and other ecological approaches to literary texts have remained largely the province of U.S. critics focusing on U.S. texts, with few exceptions, such as Jonathan Bate's *Romantic Ecology: Wordsworth and the Environmental Tradition* (1991). There is a need for much more such attention to women writers of Ireland, England, and other countries. While my discussion here is not primarily ecofeminist, it is informed by this approach and suggests its relevance and potential in respect to Irish women writers.

Interweaving descriptions of her garden and her own private thoughts, in *A Garden Diary* Lawless attacks the patriarchal notion that the natural world can be owned:

> How slight an excrescence this whole business that we call ownership really is; how strong, how deeply rooted the state of things which it has momentarily superseded. Let the so-called owner relax his self-assertiveness for ever so short a period. . . . Let him saunter along in the woods after dusk. . . . Let him . . . merely lean out of his window after dusk, amid the thickening shadows, and he must be of a remarkably unimpressionable turn of mind if the sense of his own shadowiness, his own inherent transitoriness, is not the clearest, strongest, and most convincing of all his sensations. (42, 43)

The fact that Lawless's earliest novels seem comparatively conventional and conservative in their portraits of women suggests that she came only slowly to the feminist insights of *Grania* and that she did so partly by attending to the natural world, as reflected in some of her other works. In *A Chelsea Householder* (1882a) and *A Millionaire's Cousin* (1885), Lawless seems out of her depth in the milieu of polite English society. Both are conventional romances with the obligatory happy ending of the genteel marriage. It was a radical departure for Lawless to write about peasant life in County Clare in *Hurrish* (1886). Yet her stereotyped, mostly male characters in that novel are quite conventional. The women in *Hurrish* linger mostly at the margins of the novel. One thought put into the mind of the villainous Maurice Brady about his fiancée, however, clearly foreshadows *Grania:* "That *Alley* should also have espoused that side of the quarrel had not even occurred to him. She was *his* property, not Hurrish's; what he did, she must think right; what he thought, she must think also; were they not all but man and wife?" (1886, 2:133). The story "Namesakes" in *Plain Frances Mowbray, and Other Tales* (1889) looks ahead even more clearly to *Grania*. It concerns the visit of a middle-class Irishman raised in England, Maurice O'Sullivan, to his family home in County Kerry, where he meets a beautiful young mother who has been abandoned by her husband. Maurice is struck not only by the fact that she is also named O'Sullivan, but by the desperate nature of her plight. He interviews another peasant about the young woman's missing husband:

"And where do you suppose he is now?"
"The Lard knows! Trapsed off t' England for the harvestin', most loike."
"Gone to England! Leaving her here all alone?"
"Trath, yes, sor; 'tis little they think of that." (1889, 305)

The young woman disappears before Maurice can speak to her a second time. Her plight is viewed from the outside, whereas in *Grania* Lawless sought to expose the plight of a peasant woman from her own point of view.

Maria Edgeworth (1904) was Lawless's other major feminist or protofeminist work. It sheds light not only on Lawless's views of gender, but also on her own place in Irish literary history, for clearly she saw Edgeworth as her literary mother. Both were Ascendancy Irishwomen who identified strongly with their country, writing about its history and its people, especially the peasantry. Both of their mothers died when they were young and both of them chose not to marry, devoting themselves instead to their roles as writers and caretakers of the land (Edgeworth on her County Longford family estate and Lawless in her garden). Both had a strong didactic streak. Even more than any of her novels, Lawless's sketches in *Traits and Confidences* are clearly indebted to Edgeworth; this is particularly clear in "Mrs O'Donnell's Report," an anecdotal account of Ascendancy family fortunes narrated by a female Thady Quirk. Neither Edgeworth nor Lawless has been examined much in a feminist light; more feminist attention to their work seems overdue.[6] Historians of women's literature in Ireland would do well to

---

6. Since my 1991 article, no further studies of Lawless have been published, except for brief references to her work such as in Margaret Kelleher's *The Feminization of Famine* (1997, 5, 114, 130, cited later in this chapter), and C. L. Innes's inclusion of her in a list of Anglo-Irish writers who "spoke to both the Anglo-Irish desire for identity and belonging, and the English desire for the exotic, for self-definition in opposition to 'the other' " (1993, 29). Only a few essays have begun to focus on gender issues in Edgeworth (though not particularly her Irish writings), such as those by Laurie Fitzgerald, Julie Shaffer, Gary Kelly, and Katie Donovan. Kathryn Kirkpatrick introduces the latest edition of Edgeworth's *Castle Rackrent* with an increased attention to the relevance of Edgeworth's unusual, difficult status as a woman who helped oversee her father's

return to Lawless's biography of Edgeworth as a key source for the reconstruction of this tradition.[7]

Lawless asserts at the end of *Maria Edgeworth* that "it has been the woman that has been . . . shown . . . rather than the author" (1904, 213). She portrays Richard Lovell Edgeworth, her father, as the chief impediment to Edgeworth's success. He subjected her to a succession of three stepmothers, two of whom were sisters and the last of whom was younger than Maria herself. When he moved his family back to his estate in Ireland in 1782, Lawless tells us,

> Mr. Edgeworth arrived on this occasion preceded or accompanied, in true patriarchal fashion, by menservants and by maidservants, by a brand-new wife, by two quite separate sets of children by two previous wives, and—a detail which even the patriarchs themselves do not seem to have found necessary—his circle was further enlarged by two unmarried sisters of his late and of his present wife, two Miss Sneyds, who from that time forward until after his own death, thirty-five years later, were to find their permanent home under his roof. . . . An autocrat he was, and had every intention of being. Wives, sisters-in-law, daughters, tenants, and the like, were all regarded by him as so many satellites, revolving gently, as by a law of nature, around the pedestal upon which he stood alone, in a graceful or commanding attitude. (1904, 37–38)

Far from having a room of her own in which to write, "All Maria Edgeworth's books were written at her own corner of the table in the library—which was the common living room of the house—amid the talk of the family and the lessons of the children" (116). Nonetheless she persisted and became the first great Irish novelist, serving as a model for later writers such as Lawless and Somerville and Ross. Edgeworth's *Castle Rackrent* (1800), in particular, gave permission to subsequent writers to enter the minds of their protagonists, as

---

Irish estate, noting that "her ambivalence works itself out in *Castle Rackrent* through the negative examples of landlords; while their satiric treatment is in the service of a more responsible landlordism, the *effect* of their portrayal is to kill off the patriarchs in the narrative, which results in increased prosperity for the novel's women" (1995, xix–xx).

7. Another such connection may be found in *The Wild Irish Girl* (1806) by Sydney Owenson (Lady Morgan), whose peasant heroine Glorvina (though much more romanticized than the more realistically portrayed Grania) is in some ways a precursor of *Grania*.

Edgeworth did with her unforgettable narrator, Thady Quirk, and as Lawless did with her Grania O'Malley.

At one point in *Maria Edgeworth,* writing a decade after *Grania,* Lawless offers an aside that seems relevant to both *Grania* and *Hurrish,* her two novels about peasant life. Her remarks here could also be applied to O'Flaherty and his conviction that he himself had "the characteristics of a low-born Irish peasant" (1934, 45):

> All peasants are difficult and elusive creatures to portray, but perhaps an Irish peasant . . . is the most elusive and the most difficult upon the face of the earth. Any one who has ever tried to fling a net over him knows perfectly well in his or her own secret soul that the attempt has been a failure—at best that entire realms and regimens of the subject have escaped observation. (1904, 88)

The description and celebration of Irish peasant life became one of the chief goals of Anglo-Irish Literary Revival writers such as Yeats, Lady Gregory, John Synge, and Douglas Hyde. Lawless, so modest and self-critical in the remark cited above, wrote as realistically as she could of Irish peasant life a decade or more before the Revival writers, who tended to ignore or even scorn her work.

Synge owed a particular debt to *Grania,* which was published six years before his first trip to Inis Meáin in 1898. He recorded his debt only in a footnote in a long-unpublished notebook that he kept in conjunction with his book *The Aran Islands,* linking it immediately to a pointed criticism of Lawless's novel: "I read *Grania* before I came here [to Inis Meáin] and enjoyed it, but the real Aran spirit is not there. . . . To write a real novel of the island life one would require to pass several years among the people, but Miss Lawless does not appear to have lived here. Indeed it would be hardly possible perhaps for a lady [to stay] longer than a few days" (quoted in Foster 1987, 102–3 n. 1). He went on to fault the accuracy of her description of the burning of kelp in the novel. Yet the most interesting facet of Synge's criticism here is his focus on her status as "a lady." One source for Synge's own play about the drowning of Inis Meáin islanders, *Riders to the Sea,* could very well be *Grania.* The differences are more striking, however. Synge's heroine is a romanticized, remote emblem of the tragedy of the sea that takes her men from her—a symbol more than a life-and-blood character, despite the realistic trappings of Synge's stage scenery and speeches. In contrast, we get close to Grania, entering her consciousness in a way that we have come to associate with twentieth-century novels. Moreover, she is strong, active, and goes to sea herself rather than passively await news of her seagoing men as does Synge's Maurya. It is worth noting that Synge's chief friend and correspondent on Inis Meáin was Máirtín MacDonagh, whereas the people there in whom Lawless was most interested appear to have been female, as can be seen also in several of her Aran poems in her collection *With the Wild Geese* (1902). Both the debt owed in Synge's work to Lawless and her own distinct contributions have gone unrecognized.

Grania—which was ignored by Yeats, Gladstone, and other well-known early commentators in favor of *Hurrish,* the historical novels, and other male-centered works—has been evaluated by Brewer and other more recent commentators as Lawless's best novel.[8] One of its strengths is that Lawless consciously abandoned in it the heavy-handed Hiberno-English dialogue typical of nineteenth-century Irish fiction and exemplified in the passage above from "Namesakes." She explained this decision in the novel's opening note of dedication "To M. C.," "who helped out its meagre scraps of Gaelic": The brogue "might surely be dispensed with, as we both agreed, in a case where no single actor of the tiny stage is supposed to utter a word of English" (n.p.). Since Inis Meáin was (and still is) Irish-speaking, there was no point in trying to write in any of the varieties of English as spoken in rural Ireland. Unlike O'Flaherty, a native speaker, Lawless could not attempt to "translate" from this very different language. Douglas Hyde and John Synge—and O'Flaherty—wrote in an Irish English that sought to capture the flavor of the Irish language; since she did not know Irish, in *Grania* Lawless wrote mostly in standard English. In addition to allowing Lawless to avoid an awkward and inaccurate Hiberno-English, it appears that her use of standard English also helped her to sympathetically enter the mind of her female protagonist. Rather than get caught up in the trappings of Hiberno-English speech as in "Namesakes," in which the victimized peasant woman and indeed peasant life in general seem much more remote, Lawless is able to imagine Grania's reactions to her experiences through the medium of her own standard English language.

8. Swinburne did praise *Grania* as "unique in pathos, humor . . . and truthfulness" (quoted in Brewer 1983, 125).

Grania's experiences are the difficult ones of a woman living on the small, bleak, rocky, poor island of Inis Meáin, the most "primitive" of the three Aran Islands. Crisscrossed everywhere by makeshift but centuries-old stone walls that appear to have been constructed mostly to get the rocks off the ground, Inis Meáin has very little arable land; even today the islanders depend for their existence primarily on fishing and public welfare ("the dole"). Only about three hundred people live there year-round, and most children are forced to emigrate to Dublin, England, or America. Marriage opportunities are obviously rare and often unromantic. During the time described by Lawless, the harsh matrimonial practices of rural Ireland examined by anthropologists such as Conrad Arensberg certainly applied on Inis Meáin. As Lawless herself stresses in *Grania,* love is "seldom talked of there, and apparently in consequence seldom felt. Marriage being largely matters of barter . . . the topic loses that predominance which it possesses in nearly every other community in the world" (1892, 78).

Even today under the best of circumstances, a woman's life on Inis Meáin is not an easy one, as I myself witnessed during two summers on the island—a romantic place for the visitor but a difficult one for its proud, hard-working residents. The middle-aged "woman of the house" (or *bean an tí*) where I first stayed looked twenty years older than she actually was; she worked hard from dawn to bedtime, cooking and cleaning with the aid of no electricity and with only very spartan supplies available at the shop when shipped in intermittently from the "mainland," though since then electricity and an airplane service have come to the island. Hard rural housework was no one's province in her large family but her own, except for some summer help from her daughters who lived and worked in Dublin for most of the year.

As Peggy O'Dowd, the noted storyteller and oldest inhabitant of the island, tells her friends about Grania's planned marriage, " 'Tis eight days in the week she'll find herself working for all her money if she means to keep a roof over her head and Murdough Blake under it. . . . Mark my words, women, so she will, so she will!" (1892, 93–94). Grania's sister similarly warns her, "Men is a terrible trouble, Grania, first and last. What with the drink and the fighting and one thing and another, a woman's life is no better than an old garron's down by the sea shore once she's got one of them over her driving her the way he chooses" (133). Grania later observes an old, broken-down *bean an tí* on fair day outside Galway, in one of the central epiphanies in the novel:

> Staring at her in the dusk of that miserable hearth Grania seemed to see herself a dozen years later; broken down in spirit; broken down in health; grown prematurely old; her capacity for work diminished; with a brood of squalid, ill-fed children clamouring for what she had not to give them; with no help; with Honor long dead; without a soul left who had known her and cared for her when she was young; with shame and a workhouse on the mainland—deepest of all degradation to an islander—coming hourly nearer and nearer. (243)

Lawless devotes close attention to Grania's consciousness and to physical descriptions of the island in a novel whose plot is very simple and spare. Happy to be taken fishing on her father's boat and looking up to Murdough Blake as both a big-brother figure and future husband, as a young girl Grania O'Malley is raised by her half-sister Honor after her father becomes a drunkard, following her mother's early death, and then dies himself. Grania grows into a strong young woman, but she then has to take care of Honor, who gets consumption. The conclusion of the novel comes when Grania tries to go by boat in a storm to the neighboring big island of Inis Mór for a priest for the dying Honor and dies in the attempt. Murdough has refused to go with her.

This novel is dominated by the character of Grania and the setting of the bleak island on which she lives, with the two directly linked: "This tall, red-petticoated, fiercely handsome girl was decidedly a very isolated and rather craggy and unapproachable sort of island" (64). The full title of the novel is *Grania (The Story of an Island)*, underscoring the identification of protagonist with place. As closely identified as Grania is with the island, it seems symbolically appropriate that her death comes when she tries to leave the island, perhaps suggesting that in doing so she loses her self. A cultural reading of the novel, however, is more compelling than a symbolic one, for Grania's destruction finally seems inevitable given the economic, patriarchal, and physical forces against which she must struggle throughout the book.

Grania's situation emerges in even sharper relief if compared to that of her namesake, the late-sixteenth-century leader Gráinne (often called "Grace") O'Malley, the "Sea-Queen," whom Lawless most likely had in mind in naming her protagonist. The historical Gráinne

O'Malley was identified with such islands as Clare Island off Mayo, dominated the Connemara region of western Ireland during her heyday, and met with Queen Elizabeth in England in 1576 after submitting to English rule (Doherty and Hickey 1989, 18). This "Sea-Queen" was no doubt a significant source for Lawless—yet it is significant that although English hegemony was the key framework for the historical person, Lawless chooses to leave England out of her novel, instead focusing on her protagonist's plight in terms of issues tied to gender and the natural world. We shall return to this issue and to the "Sea-Queen" in chapter 5, for the protagonist of Julia O'Faolain's *No Country for Young Men* is also named Gráinne O'Malley. However, as we shall see, unlike the historical "Sea-Queen" and Lawless's protagonist, O'Faolain's Gráinne O'Malley "does not capitulate," as Ann Owens Weekes notes, "in order to restore the 'order' derived from male principles" (1986, 91).

O'Faolain also makes more conscious use of the ancient mythical Grania, who in Irish legend ran off with her lover, Diarmuid, but was tricked by Fionn MacCool into living with him instead in order to protect her children. Lady Augusta Gregory—who was championed by Yeats, in contrast to his dismissal of Lawless, and who was crucial to the Literary Revival and to Yeats's work—also wrote about this Grania. She explained that whereas Yeats and Synge had each focused plays on the similar mythical character Deirdre, she preferred Grania, because "Grania had more power of will" (quoted in Innes 1993, 155). Yet Gregory never allowed her three-act play *Grania,* written during 1910–11, to be performed during her lifetime, because it was so thoroughly linked "to her own secret history" (Innes 155)—a decision similar to the listing of *Cathleen ni Hoolihan* as written solely by Yeats, even though it seems clear that Gregory coauthored that play. As with O'Faolain, one expects that Gregory probably had read Lawless's *Grania,* and it is striking how all three authors were drawn to this character.

For her own Grania O'Malley, Lawless tells us, "Inishmaan was much more than home, much more than a place she lived in, it was practically the world. . . . It was not merely her own little holding and cabin, but every inch of it that was in this peculiar sense hers. It belonged to her as the rock on which it has been born belongs to the young seamew. She had grown to it, and it had grown to her" (63). The island and the ocean can be sunny and life-giving when young Grania goes fishing with her father or experiences early happiness with Murdough, but later "the rain came down in sheets, and in sheets it swept over the surface" (171), and Grania declares to her sister, "God help us! What are we brought into it for at all, at all, I sometimes wonder, if there's to be nothing for us but trouble and trouble and trouble? 'Tis bad enough for the men, but, it's worse a hundred times for the women!" (179). The pious Honor's answer is that Inis Meáin is merely a testing ground for heaven: "What were any of us, and women specially, sent into the world for, except to save our souls and learn to bear what's given to us to bear? . . . To bear and bear, that's all she's got to do, so she has, till God sends her rest—nothing else" (179–80). As we shall see, in his fictional representations of island life, the anticlerical and even more thoroughly naturalistic O'Flaherty will admit of no such possibility of otherworldly escape.

As developed through such exchanges, Grania's relationship with her sister is the most important one in Lawless's novel, in accordance with women's tendency to place great significance on such familial relationships and friendships with other women. This pattern is found not only in the lives of real women such as Somerville and Ross, as we shall see, but also in their novels. Somerville and Ross's *The Real Charlotte* (1894), Kate O'Brien's *The Land of Spices* (1941), and Edna O'Brien's *The Country Girls Trilogy* (1986a) all are narratives similarly focused on the relationship of two women. Rather than concentrate on a single male protagonist, as the men's novels do, these women's novels tell the double stories of two women, two protagonists in a double plot. In *Grania* Honor's patience and piety contrast with Grania's more worldly passions. Grania loves Honor but does disagree with her stoic attitude: "It is all very well for you, Honor, a saint born, wanting nothing and caring for nothing, only just the bit to keep you alive and the spot to pray on. But all women are not made like that" (180). This distinction is similar to the differences between Charlotte Mullen and Francie Fitzgerald in Somerville and Ross's *The Real Charlotte* (1894) and between Kate Brady and Baba Brennan in Edna O'Brien's *The Country Girls Trilogy* (1986a), to which we will turn in my next two chapters.

Throughout her works Lawless herself appears torn between religious belief and naturalistic despair, and in this novel she seems to play out her ambivalence through Grania and Honor. On the one hand Grania tells Honor, "The priests may tell all they will of heaven, but what is it to me? just *gosther* [empty talk]!" (181). On the other hand, Lawless ends the novel by suggesting that after the sisters' death, "upon that threshold, perhaps—Who knows?—Who can tell?—they met" (355). It is tempting to hypothesize about how much Lawless injected her feelings about her own dead sisters (not to mention her own disastrous and early departed father), and to wonder about her acquaintance with Aran women on the basis not only of this novel but also of the several poems addressed to Honor and to an "old friend" in her volume *With the Wild Geese* (1902). Unfortunately, however, there is no biography of Lawless available to support or clarify these connections.

What remains clear is that the woman-to-woman relationship remains more important and more rewarding to Grania than the marriage to Murdough that she had planned. She desires love, but as for Murdough, "He wanted to marry her it is true, but why? because she was strong, because she owned the farm, because she owned [the cow] Moonyeen, and the pigs, and the little bit of money; because she could keep him in idleness; could keep him, above all, in drink; because he could get more out of her perhaps than he could out of another!" (242). Murdough never grows beyond his original patronizing acquaintance with her as a little girl, and is unable to deal with Grania as a mature, strong woman:

> That he had liked her better in the old days when she was still
> the little Grania of the hooker, before she had shot up into this
> rather formidable woman she had so suddenly become, there is
> no denying. The little Grania had admired him without criti-
> cism; the little Grania had no sombre moods; the little Grania
> never gazed at him with those big, menacing eyes—eyes such as
> a lioness might turn upon someone whom she loves, but who
> displeases her—the little Grania was natural, was comprehen-
> sible, was just like any other little *girsha* in the place, not at all
> like this new Grania, who was quite out of his range and ken; an
> unaccountable product, one that made him feel vaguely uneasy;
> who seemed to belong to a region in which he had never trav-
> elled; who was "queer," in short; the last word summing up
> concisely the worst and most damning thing that could be said
> of anyone in Inishmaan. (289)

It is not surprising that eventually Grania finds "death on her own terms preferable to becoming his wife" (Brewer 1983, 125).

The pious Honor may be a sentimentalized, conventional por-trait of a woman, but Grania is unconventional both in her strength and in her growing unrest, which is perceived as "madness." Early on we are told that "for sheer muscular strength and endurance she

had hardly her match amongst the young men of the three islands"
(68). Pitted against the difficulties of her life, however, strength
and endurance are not enough, and the result is the depression
found by Nancy Scheper-Hughes among women in rural Ireland,
described as deepening particularly in the winter months (1979,
56). Grania asks herself, "Could she really be going crazy? . . . It
seemed to be literally like some disease that had got into her bones—
this strange unrest, this disturbance—a disease, too, of which she
had never heard; which nobody else so far as she knew had ever had;
a disease which had no name, and therefore was the more mysterious and horrible" (254).

Grania's "madness" is to try to be strong and independent in
the face of a desolate environment and patriarchal culture. The
hopelessness of life on the island, not only for Grania but for others,
is suggested from the beginning of the novel: For the islanders
"their dreams . . . clung limpet-fashion, to these naked rocks, these
melancholy dots of land set in the midst of an inhospitable sea,
which Nature does not seem to have constructed with an eye to the
convenience of so much as a goat" (29). As Lawless wrote to her
friend in the dedication, "They are melancholy places, these Aran
Islands of ours, as you and I know well, and the following pages
have caught their full share . . . of that gloom" (n.p.). The hopelessness of life on the island, particularly for a woman such as Grania,
makes her death in a seastorm seem naturalistic in both climatic
and cultural terms. She is presented as a strong woman vitally
linked to her island environment, but the poverty and bad weather
of Inis Meáin as well as the patriarchy of its culture (as embodied
in the exploitative, do-nothing Murdough) overwhelm her in the
end.

Lawless's daring entry into the mind of a female protagonist in
Grania has been followed up by her twentieth-century successors,
many of whom have been fellow Anglo-Irishwomen such as Elizabeth Bowen and Jennifer Johnston, who focus on upper-class rather
than peasant women. Edna O'Brien returns to Irish peasant girlhood and young womanhood in *The Country Girls Trilogy*, which
advances different, much franker portraits: O'Brien's County Clare
protagonists escape the confines of rural Irish marriage by leaving
their homes in favor of life in Dublin and London and extramarital
affairs. In some respects it is a long way from Lawless to contemporary Irish women writers, but in another important sense, it is
hard to imagine Edna O'Brien or Julia O'Faolain with the freedom

to speak their own fictional truths if a pioneer such as Emily Lawless had not gone before them.

⚜

Grania's moment of foreknowledge of the hardships that she will endure as a woman calls to mind a very similar epiphany in O'Flaherty's story "Spring Sowing," which I discuss below. Somewhat like Peadar O'Donnell in his Donegal novel *Islanders* (1928), O'Flaherty similarly links the lives of people and animals to their natural island environment, though feminist or ecofeminist impulses are only rarely found in his work.

The polar views of Sandra Gilbert and Susan Gubar (1988) and Declan Kiberd (1985), as cited in my introduction—with Gilbert and Gubard criticizing male modernists as misogynists and Kiberd championing their androgynous aspects—allow us to envision a spectrum running from misogyny to androgyny, against which to measure a writer such as O'Flaherty. Was he more misogynist or androgynous, more disdainful of women or sympathetic to them? The quick answer is that misogyny is by far the stronger current running fairly obviously through his letters and essays, in particular, and through some of his stories. He often viewed women in the most sexist terms, as erotic and procreative objects for men. Though they do not mention him, Gilbert and Gubar would have a much easier time fitting O'Flaherty into their critique of misogynist male modernists than Kiberd would into his celebration of androgyny. At the same time, O'Flaherty registered occasional guilt about his poor treatment of women, and he wrote several stories centering on women victimized by men and on strong female protagonists. The challenge here will be to explain such stories in light of their author's blatantly recorded misogyny.[9]

9. Gender is an issue rarely dealt with in O'Flaherty criticism. Angeline Kelly (1976) remarks briefly on the subject, but previous to my 1991 book on O'Flaherty, the only critical commentaries focused on gender were Hedda Friberg's essay (1990) about women in O'Flaherty's *The Assassin* (1928a), *The Martyr* (1933), and *I Went to Russia* (1931a), in which she notes his "tension-ridden feminine/ masculine duality" (45); and a four-page piece accessible only to readers of Irish: "Mná" (Women) in Fiachra Ó Dubhthaigh's pamphlet (1981) on *Dúil,* in which he argues that O'Flaherty's women characters tend to be simplistic and stereotypical and that Máirtín O Cadhain's fiction was superior in this regard.

O'Flaherty grew up speaking both Irish and English within a large family and a close-knit community. He was a talented school-boy whom others hoped would become a priest, and he won schol-arships that took him to Rockwell College in County Tipperary in 1908 and University College, Dublin, in 1914–15. O'Flaherty later claimed that he decided to leave the university after reading Karl Marx for a week in the National Library in Dublin. He subse-quently attacked O'Casey's play *The Plough and the Stars* (1926) for its irreverence about the Easter Rising rebels, but in 1916 O'Flaherty was out of the country, serving in the British army. He fought in World War I from 1915 until he was injured in 1917, often later complaining about remaining shell-shocked, a theme also reflected in his fiction. The "two years" of his first autobiographical book were spent wandering and working in London, South America, Turkey, Canada, and the United States, between 1918 and 1921. After a return visit to Inis Mór, O'Flaherty led a brief workers' occupation of the government Rotunda building in early 1922. Soon thereafter he left for London, determined to become a writer.

A key turning point was meeting the London editor Edward Garnett, who became a key mentor to O'Flaherty, much as Garnett was also for Joseph Conrad, D. H. Lawrence, and several other key modernists (see Cahalan 1991a). Garnett's advice was always to keep it short and tell the truth. He sent O'Flaherty back to Inis Mór to write about what he knew most intimately: the animals and people there. In 1923 O'Flaherty began writing the short stories that made his reputation, often translating himself from Irish to English and vice versa. As reflected in his many letters to Garnett during the 1920s, however, he also maintained an ambition to write the great Irish novel—which is what he thought *The Black Soul* (1924a) would be. O'Flaherty married the writer Margaret Barrington in 1926, but they separated in 1932. He lived in a variety of locations in Ireland and England during the 1920s, spent several years in Connecticut beginning in the early 1930s, and then returned to Dublin in 1946, soon settling there for the rest of his life.

In his autobiographical book *Shame the Devil* (1934), O'Flaherty advances a portrait of the artist that suggests androgyny—or her-maphroditism—at first but then quickly explodes with misogynist, highly stereotyped versions of gender:

> A creative artist is half man and half woman. The woman in him is always craving for luxury and public esteem, holding up her

child for admiration, longing for the position of honour at a
public banquet. But the man in him, the possessor of the seed,
becomes corrupt and impotent under the influence of wealth and
flattery. And for that reason he must always hold the woman on
the flat of her back. (103)

O'Flaherty meant this as a confession of his own predilection for
popular success and praise, for good reviews and sales, but his
presentation of it as a feminine trait deserving of repression and
abuse (rather than as a clear function of the male ego) is twisted and
offensive. On more than one occasion he expressed his male ideal of
creative passion and violence—art as contained in "the seed," and
fiction as "a relentless picture of life, as lashing in its cruelty as the
whip of Christ when there are moneychangers to be beaten from
the Temple" (1925, 827).

   Yet O'Flaherty was also his mother's son, and he knew it. He
inherited her storytelling abilities, and he enlisted in the British
Army under her maiden name, Ganly. In *Two Years* he recounted
visiting her grave, feeling "as if a knife were thrust into my bosom"
(1930, 16) and realizing that "her life was a tale of hardship and
misery, an endless struggle to find food for her many children. And
yet how gay she was in spite of all her sufferings!" (17–18).
O'Flaherty's memory of his mother is very similar to Joyce's recol-
lection of his mother's oppression, as cited in my next chapter,
though Joyce presents his mother as grim rather than "gay." In May
1923 O'Flaherty indicated to Garnett his opinion that "women
hand down the characteristics of genius, the waywardness of the
mind."[10] In a comment that underscores his deep ambivalence about
gender, he referred to "the cliff-bound shores of Aran" in *Two Years*
as "the school in which we, as boys, were taught our manhood; and
it was the school also, where I especially was taught by my mother
to appreciate the beauty of nature" (75). Elsewhere he noted that
"she used to knit and teach me to listen to the singing of larks and
to the warbling of blackbirds, and to understand the movements of
insects in the grass. She told me that everything that moved or
sang was beautiful and had been created by God" (1928b, 756).

   10. Original manuscript letter of O'Flaherty to Garnett in the O'Flaherty
Collection at the Harry Ransom Humanities Research Center of the University
of Texas at Austin. All subsequently quoted letters (dated parenthetically in the
text) are from this collection.

A rough, tough code of "manhood," but also a deep and feminine-influenced appreciation of "the beauty of nature": these were two sides of O'Flaherty's personality, and they are also two central aspects of his fiction. His recognition that life on Aran was his "school" is linked to his view of himself as a peasant both "servile" (stereotyped as a female behavioral trait) and "insolent" (typecast as male): speaking of himself in *Shame the Devil*, O'Flaherty wrote: "You have the characteristics of a low-born Irish peasant. Servile when you must, insolent when you may" (1934, 45). In this respect, Gearóid Denvir's remark about the work of oral Irish-language poets today in the neighboring region of Connemara seems apt: "Much traditional literature can at times be rather anti-woman (if not downright misogynist!). . . . Their conservatism is . . . strongly to the fore in their attitudes to . . . the role of man and woman" (1989, 99, 107). The Marxist O'Flaherty was much more radical about social and political issues than these poets, but he shared their outlook on gender. Clearly sexism was a more lasting part of his rural Irish socialization process and belief system than traditional views of church, state, and class.

There are many other instances of misogyny in O'Flaherty's private letters and public essays. To Garnett he declared in April 1923 that "a woman is not necessary to my life," adding a month later that "all women I have ever lived with were a curse," that one of D. H. Lawrence's books "I have heard . . . condemned by a bitch of a woman so it must be good," and (in August 1923) that Mrs. Morris (with whom he was living at the time) "is not that kind of an intellectual woman . . . I don't think I will encourage her writing. She would be far better occupied loving." Perhaps his most flagrantly sexist essay is the otherwise forgettable "Secret Drinking" (1932a), in which he celebrates the Irish male camaraderie of drinking:

> In other countries people drink out in the open air, in full view of passing traffic, with their wives, daughters, sisters; just as if they were having a cup of tea. An Irishman has a natural antipathy for drinking in public and as for drinking with women . . . It's not done. We gave women the vote without any question but I curse the day when we give them the right to drink with us. It will ruin the country, kill all romance and put us on the same low level as the other countries. (110)

Again, O'Flaherty reveals himself here as reactionary in terms of gender roles.

The women with whom O'Flaherty lived during the 1920s were each, to some extent, his patrons (again calling Joyce to mind, as we shall see in my next chapter). Margaret Barrington, who married O'Flaherty and bore his only child, Pegeen, offered him a door into upper-crust Dublin society since she was married to the well-known Trinity College historian Edmund Curtis when O'Flaherty met her (but left Curtis for O'Flaherty). During their years together she was a careful editor of O'Flaherty's work. During 1923 his letters to Garnett changed from typescript to longhand just after he left another woman (a "Miss Casey," unknown to us)—because the typewriter was hers. In June 1923 he did feel remorseful about leaving her: "I couldn't do it. It's awful. Terrible torture to injure a *friend*. She has been a friend to me—the most sacred thing in life, a friend, a comrade. And to make her unhappy. This is awful." A few years earlier he had stayed with his sisters in Boston, "but as I am incapable of showing my feeling towards those whom I love intimately," he noted in *Two Years,* "they thought me cold" (1930, 296). In April 1924 he sent Garnett "a story by a friend of mine, a young woman, which I think is very good, because it's very true to life. She knows these damn people better than I do because I suppose she is a woman." In the same month he wrote that "women are very queer and"—he admitted in his most confessional comment on the subject—"I do not understand them very well."

The fact that O'Flaherty did not "understand them very well" is proven by his novel *The Black Soul,* a novel parallel to but drastically different from Lawless's *Grania.* If Lawless was a foreigner to the Irish-speaking world of Inis Meáin, one gains the impression from *The Black Soul* that O'Flaherty was equally foreign to the women of Inis Mór, even though he had grown up amidst them. Significantly, he calls his protagonist "the Stranger." *The Black Soul* is a highly compelling yet ultimately failed novel (a not unusual combination in the case of O'Flaherty). He struggled mightily writing it in the early 1920s. Edward Garnett's editorial attention was first caught by *Thy Neighbour's Wife* (1923), O'Flaherty's first novel and a forgettable one—except for the fact that it too shows O'Flaherty trying to make sense of gender relationships at the beginning of his career.

Like *Grania, The Black Soul* has four sections, following the seasons. *Grania* moves from "September" (1–58) to "April" (59–165), to "May to August" (166–284), and to "September Again"

(285–355); *The Black Soul,* from "Winter" (7–84) to "Spring" (85–127), to "Summer" (128–64), and to "Autumn" (165–91). Both novels are strongly attuned to the natural world, and each focuses on an island protagonist who feels alone. O'Flaherty shows very clearly how separate men and women are on "Inverara," in a passage that reads as if it could have been one of the ethnographical observations of the anthropologist Nancy Scheper-Hughes: "Men stood at their gables leaning against the wind, . . . their oilskin hats bound around their heads with strings. . . . Women with their red petticoats thrown over their heads hurried to the well for water. They stopped for a moment with their arms akimbo and their heads bent sideways close together, like birds" (1924, 9). He explains that on the island, "all women obeyed their husbands, even though they hated and despised them. It was a custom, and customs are stronger than desires" (17).

The Black Soul is certainly at least partly autobiographical, as "the Stranger," Fergus O'Connor, is a shell-shocked young man looking to find himself on the island—much as O'Flaherty himself did by returning to Inis Mór during 1921, after his years fighting in World War I and then wandering the globe for two years. Just how autobiographical the novel is we cannot easily know, in the absence of any biography of O'Flaherty, who detested the genre even though (or perhaps because) he himself published a biography of the politician Tim Healy in 1927, and he attempted to preempt any would-be biographers by publishing two volumes of autobiography himself.

In the course of this novel, O'Flaherty's protagonist reluctantly falls in love with "Little Mary (so called because she was the tallest woman in Inverara)" (1924a, 11), in whose home he is staying, and who is married to Red John. Little Mary had agreed to marry Red John, but then hit him when he tried to embrace her, "and in all the five years he had never possessed her" (13). Red John ultimately goes mad and dies, and the Stranger and Little Mary leave the island and sail for the mainland. In both the characterization of Little Mary and its plot, *The Black Soul* is similar to a later short story (discussed below), "Red Barbara."

The Black Soul makes an impression not so much for its plot, an overly melodramatic one, as for its exceptionally stereotypical presentation of gender roles. In this case, the sexist tendency to divide women into "virgins" and "whores" is not merely detected by a feminist analysis that we can apply to this novel, but rather part of the rhetoric of the novel itself. Repulsed by the idea that Little Mary must have had sex with Red John, the Stranger thinks to himself, "It was like loving a prostitute" (139). For the Stranger (and, one has to feel, for O'Flaherty himself), Little Mary is a purely sexual being, a whore, who is contrasted with Kathleen O'Daly, a virgin and "the first educated woman with whom he had come in contact for a long time. In fact he had never known the companionship of educated women. The kind who gave their love easily attracted him more" (81). A character who calls to mind Joyce's Miss Ivors in "The Dead," Kathleen is attracted to the Stranger, but he cares nothing for her, and lest we think that she is an individual rather than a type, he rebukes himself, "Fancy setting a woman like that above Little Mary," as Kathleen is "a shallow conceited woman, just like the artificial unsexed ladies who haunt the suburbs of large cities" (104). We learn that the Stranger, with unmistakable misogyny, "felt sure that all the women in the world were engaged in a conspiracy to trap him" (124).

Though initially so disdainful of Little Mary that he struggles through much of the novel to avoid her, the Stranger is ultimately drawn into a sexual relationship with her that O'Flaherty suggests is as natural as the animals that he wrote about in some of his most celebrated stories. Here the Stranger finds two mating crabs lying together in a ball. "They never moved when he touched them with a sprig of seaweed. They were in a love-swoon, careless of their lives. 'So that is love,' he said" (137). The Stranger comes to the island a lonely, alienated man, but he leaves with Little Mary as a man who has found his natural mate. In *Grania*, the island is a forlorn place where Grania's status as a woman is ultimately her downfall; in *The Black Soul*, O'Flaherty's island is a place where a man like Fergus O'Connor takes hold of a woman like Little Mary much as an Aran fisherman might catch a fish. Women are victims in both Lawless and O'Flaherty, but in this case the male versus the female point of view makes all the difference in the world.

O'Flaherty had grown up observing women who were closely confined within the rigid gender roles found in traditional rural Irish societies such as Inis Mór. Several of his stories depict these gender roles, and the best of them are more subtle and compelling than *The Black Soul*. Even well-known stories describing apparently idyllic young mating and marriage relationships, such as "Spring Sowing" and "Milking Time," contain within them suggestions of the darker side of gender differentiation from the point of view of Aran women.

"Spring Sowing" (1924b), the title story of O'Flaherty's first volume of stories, is an elegiac delineation of a young couple's pride and pleasure in "the first day of their first spring sowing as man and wife" (1973, 1). Martin and Mary Delaney exchange terms of endearment translated from Irish, such as " 'pulse of my heart, treasure of my life,' and such traditional phrases" (2). They experience their relationship, however, in different ways. Martin "looked at his wife's little round black head and felt very proud of having her as his own" (5). As Angeline Kelly points out, in the field he " 'absolutely without thought' works furiously for he, as a male, is already proving himself," whereas Mary "walks with 'furrowed' brows seized by a sudden terror as she realises the extent of her double enslavement, to the earth, and to her body" (12–13). For Mary "a momentary flash of rebellion against the slavery of being a peasant's wife crossed her mind. It passed in a moment" (7). The young couple's positive feelings at the end of the story are undercut by a grimmer prognosis: "They had done it together. They had planted seeds in the earth. The next day and the next and all their lives, when spring came they would have to bend their backs and do it until their hands and bones got twisted with rheumatism. But night would always bring sleep and forgetfulness" (8).

Similarly, at the end of "Milking Time" (1925) Michael and Kitty walk home romantically, "silently hand in hand, in the twilight" (1973, 80), but they are also characterized in sentences notable for the mix of present satisfaction with darker premonitions as well as for a syntactic complexity that runs counter to O'Flaherty's celebrated simple style:

> It was like a ceremony, this first milking together, initiating them into the mysterious glamour of mating; and both their minds were awed at the new strange knowledge that had come to their simple natures, something that belonged to them both, making their souls conscious of their present happiness with a dim realization of the great struggle that would follow it, struggling with the earth and the sea for food. And this dim realization tinged their happiness with a gentle sadness, without which happiness is ever coarse and vulgar. (79)

Another of O'Flaherty's very best stories is "Going into Exile," his unforgettable account of the "American wake" held for a family's oldest daughter and son who are forced to leave their native island to work in Boston, at a time when such a departure meant that their parents would probably never see them again. Here O'Flaherty vividly depicts the emotions of these parents and children, brilliantly distinguishing the males from the females. Father and son are unable to show their emotions. Together outside the cabin in the middle of the night, "They stood in silence fully five minutes. Each hungered to embrace the other, to cry, to beat the air, to scream with excess of sorrow. But they stood silent and sombre, like nature about them, hugging their woe" (1973, 56).

Mother and daughter remain inside, with the daughter huddled on the bed with a dozen of her female friends: "they stayed with her in that uncomfortable position just to show how much they liked her. It was a custom" (57). Like the father, the mother represses her emotions all through the story, until the end when, unlike him, she finally lets them out:

> She burst into wild tears, wailing, "My children, oh, my children, far over the sea you will be carried from me, your mother." And she began to rock herself and she threw her apron over her head.
> Immediately the cabin was full of the sound of bitter wailing. A dismal cry rose from the women gathered in the kitchen. . . .
> "Come back," she screamed; "come back to me."
> She looked wildly down the road with dilated nostrils, her bosom heaving. But there was nobody in sight. (64, 65)

With its separated, alienated men versus its communal, emotive women, "Going into Exile" powerfully illustrates the kinds of behavioral differences between men and women examined by social scientists since at least the time of Margaret Mead. In *Women in Ireland: Voices of Change* (1987), Jenny Beale notes concerning this story, "as a woman, it was acceptable for her to keen for the loss of her children, whereas her husband had to stay controlled throughout the parting" (1987, 67). Beale praises "Going into Exile" and "Spring Sowing" for their realistic portraits of women's feelings about the hardships of their lives, much as in *The Feminization of Famine: Expressions of the Inexpressible?* (1997), Margaret Kelleher commends O'Flaherty's novel *Famine* (1937a) for its rich characterizations of women, making a rare feminist link between O'Flaherty and Lawless by similarly focusing on Lawless's essay

"Famine Roads and Famine Memories" (1897) and her 1887 history of Ireland.[11]

Stories such as "Selling Pigs" and "The Reaping Race" show that the longer Aran couples endure, the more their lives are subsumed by economic and traditional forces. Michael and Mary Derrane have been married for only six months, but already the art of negotiating the sale of their pigs is central to their experience. "The Reaping Race" is a version of Aesop's "The Tortoise and the Hare" in which communal ritual is dominant. All of the participants in this customary harvest competition, for example, wear traditional garb. Out to prove that slow and steady will indeed win the race, the eventual victors are a married couple thoroughly ensconced in well-practiced roles:

> Nobody took any notice of Gill and his wife, but they had never stopped to eat and they had steadily drawn nearer to their opponents. . . . Then, when they reached the stone at half-way, Gill quietly laid down his hook and told his wife to bring the meal. She brought it from the fence, buttered oaten bread and a bottle of new milk with oatmeal in the bottom of the bottle. They ate slowly and then rested for a while. People began to jeer at them when they saw them resting, but they took no notice. After about twenty minutes they got up to go to work again. (1976, 205)

In disgust over her husband's exhaustion, Kate Considine takes over from him—"I'll carry on myself" (206)—but it is too late to stop the Gills from winning.

---

11. See Beale 1987, 38, 67. Kelleher writes, "*Famine*'s female characterizations possess dimensions rare in famine narratives: unlike the superficial depictions of female victims to be found elsewhere, O'Flaherty explores women's motivations, allows each character a voice and foregrounds the dangers and difficulties of judgement. Kitty's speech to Coburn and Mary's gradual comprehension of what Sally has done are among the most affecting representations of famine" (1997, 141). She also notes, "in Emily Lawless's essay 'Famine Roads and Famine Memories,' first published in 1897, the author testifies to the 'poor perishing memorials' to the 'great Irish Famine' which linger in the west: 'wrecks of cabins . . . the last trace of what was once a populous village' and the 'famine road' " (114); and "in her history of Ireland, first published in 1887, Emily Lawless pays tribute to the 'untiring energy and the most absolute self-devotedness' shown by men and women" (130).

Life is hard for everyone on the Aran Islands, but generally O'Flaherty shows that it is a man's world if it is anyone's. Gender roles are particularly separate and stereotyped in his stories of childhood and youth. He tends to show young boys as taking pleasure and pride in receiving affection and gifts from their parents and in moving toward manhood, in stories such as "Fishing," "Swimming," "Mother and Son," "The Test of Courage," and "The New Suit" or "An Chulaith Nua." In "Fishing," for example, a father saves himself and his son from the rough tide and declares, "You darling, you were worth getting drowned for. So you were" (1976, 187). The maternal bond is similarly strong in "Mother and Son," which appears clearly drawn from O'Flaherty's own relationship with his storytelling mother. After coming home late, the son narrates to his mother a fabulous vision of a horse running through the air, and thus gains forgiveness:

> "Sure you won't tell on me, mother?"
> "No, treasure, I won't."
> "On your soul you won't?"
> "Hush! little one. Listen to the birds. They are beginning to sing. I won't tell at all. Listen to the beautiful ones."
> . They both sat in silence, listening and dreaming, both of them. (1976, 186)

O'Flaherty almost entirely neglects girlhood in his stories. When he does focus on female adolescence in "An Scáthán" or "The Mirror" (1953), describing a girl taking pleasure in seeing herself naked for the first time, O'Flaherty can only imagine, as Kelly notes, "the male reaction" and place it "in the mind of the girl who is physically affected by the sight exactly as most men would be" (20). This story ends by assigning her to the status of "a radiant virgin wantoning naked in the sunlight on silken moss and no longer afraid in the least of love's awe-inspiring fruit, the labour of pregnancy" (1973, 233).

Passion is everything in O'Flaherty's vision of positive bonds between the sexes, as in his view of many aspects of life. His stories repeatedly suggest that women and men are best occupied making love and producing children. His essential model is drawn from Aran animal life as captured in "The Water Hen" or "An Chearc Uisce," in which the cock knows no sexual repression; after defeating his opponent in a fight over a water hen, "in a moment he was upon her and she lay down in a swoon" (1973, 157). A human version of this story is "The Caress," which O'Flaherty positioned at the end of *Shame the Devil* to demonstrate that writing it had allowed him to overcome writer's block—thus directly linking artistic creativity to sexual passion. In this story Martin Derrane and Mary Madigan make love wantonly in the grass and then prepare to escape to America, leaving behind old drunken Delaney and his would-be arranged match with Mary.

A more powerful and realistic story, however, is "Teangabháil" or "The Touch," with a plot directly opposed to that of "The Caress." Here Kate Hernon's desire for Brian O'Neill, whom she is able to embrace only briefly, is crushed by her father, who has arranged her marriage to an older neighboring farmer and utterly rejects Brian, a mere laborer on the Hernon farm.

> First she thought of her hands touching his hands and of his bosom touching her breasts and of the intoxication produced in her by that touch. Then the sorrow of eternal hell followed close upon that drunkening thought, as she realised that this first touch of love would be the last touch and that she was henceforth sold to a man whose touch would be a torture to her flesh. (1973, 150)

A few other stories portraying victimized women and evil men— "The Tyrant," "The Ditch," and "The Outcast"—similarly picture young women as victims of a patriarchal, marriage-market, priest-ridden island culture. "The Tyrant" tells the story of a woman who finally leaves her hateful attorney husband. "The Ditch" describes the victimization of a poor woman by an ignorant and fearful young farm laborer who kills her newborn baby that he fathered. "The Outcast" was assessed and summarized by O'Flaherty to Garnett in October 1924 as "another short story of which I am proud . . . a servant girl, cast out of a village by the parish priest, because she has a child, drowns herself in a mountain lake."

Some other stories fix themselves on men who make fools of themselves because of their misdirected passion. These are not among O'Flaherty's better stories, but they are worth mentioning because they further complicate his varied treatments of gender. The protagonist of "The Fall of Joseph Timmins" tries to force himself on his maid, only to be immediately witnessed by his nephew, to whom he has to agree therefore to give the money for which the nephew has been asking. In several stories, men are duped by women. "The Intellectual" concerns a schoolmaster infatuated with a young woman who flirts with him and then laughs at him behind his back with her boyfriend. Very similarly, in "The Sensualist" a hotel proprietress at whom a visiting attorney makes a pass tells him to wait for her in his room, and then goes to bed with the hotel manager instead, with both of them mocking the attorney. It is significant that each of these foolish men is a middle-class or upper-class person—an unusual type of protagonist among O'Flaherty's stories. In these cases sexism is closely tied to class conflict in a manner distinct from most of the aforementioned Aran stories, except for "The Touch," in which the farm laborer is spurned by the farm owner.

At the same time and as we have already seen, O'Flaherty was certainly capable of the most offensive chauvinism. In "The Sinner" he informs us that Julia Rogers, when possessed by her brutish husband, Buster, "shuddered in ecstasy at the realization of all the happiness which life is capable of giving a woman" (1929, 192). This from the author of "The Touch"! Stories like this were not included in O'Flaherty's best known collections, and one strongly suspects that he wrote them for the money. As he remarked in *Two Years,* "Even now when I am weaving tales, I am unhappy because I have to sell them in order to buy leisure for weaving more. I have sometimes to think of the future" (1930, 14).[12]

O'Flaherty's occasionally maudlin, sexist representations of gender in his stories cannot be dismissed entirely as a sellout to the periodical marketplace. One of his more frequently anthologized and longest stories, "The Wedding," sends the message that women are happy only if they are married. Here a forty-three-year-old woman's wedding creates sharp jealousy in her unmarried neighbor. Likewise, "The Lament" centers on the desperate emotions of an unmarried woman attracted to a young man from Dublin who hires her father's boat near Galway to go to Inis Mór. Although only twenty-six, "she had a horrid feeling that this was the turning-point in her life, that she had missed her last chance of happiness

12. The clearest example of this failing is "Indian Summer," a story that no one would ever guess was written by O'Flaherty if his byline did not appear above it. Published in *Good Housekeeping,* obviously aimed at the American housewife and motivated by profit, this lamentable story describes two Americans who fall in love while on vacation in Cuba, complete with a flowery happy ending and accompanied (thanks to the editors) by a sappy romantic picture of the business-executive hero reclining in his bathrobe. There is no indication within the story itself, which was never anthologized, that it was written by an Irish writer. Similarly, "Light" indulges lovemaking on a Caribbean beach, and "The Mermaid" was an unfortunate romance penned for *John O'London's Weekly.*

and that the future was going to be barren" (1948, 138). Such women may indeed have experienced such jealousies and despair, but O'Flaherty's continual view of women strictly in mating terms is very limiting. He also falls prey to the virgin-or-whore syndrome. The protagonist of "Josephine" cannot have the young man to whom she is attracted, so she agrees to marry a man on the mainland whom she does not love simply in order to escape Inis Mór, meanwhile planning to indulge her sexual desires in extramarital encounters. This was one of the stories that he felt would prevent good sales in Ireland of the volume in which it appeared, *Spring Sowing,* as noted to Garnett in May 1924. The story ends as follows: "After all, Ballymullan was on the mainland within easy reach of Dublin. There would be social calls, week-end trips and a liberal allowance. . . . Anything was better than Inverara in winter. And perhaps the curate in Ballymullan. . . . And Josephine smiled again" (1924b, 236). In *Two Years* O'Flaherty recorded the opinion that "the harlot is a poacher on the rights of marriage, which, in turn, is the respectable woman's chief means of livelihood. The harlot, to put it crudely, retails what the respectable woman sells wholesale for a fixed annuity, and various other emoluments, personal and social" (1930, 12). In this view a woman is either a virgin, unfulfilled because excluded from sex and procreation, or a whore, bartering sex for security whether within marriage or on the streets.

Complicating such sharp sexism, however, are not only the stories already considered in which women are presented as sympathetic victims of evil men and traditional patriarchy, but other stories whose protagonists are strong older women whom O'Flaherty clearly admired. He indicated to Garnett in July 1927 that "Red Barbara" was "a great story. . . . Yes, it's a good one—about the beautiful widow of Feeney the fisherman. She refused to conceive of a weaver." On one level, the story is a "fable" (self-described in the last sentence of the story) of pagan passion opposed to Christian repression. In contrast to "The Fairy Goose," however, in which the priest makes sure that paganism is brutally obliterated, here erotic paganism wins out over Christianity when Barbara rejects Joseph (whose name echoes the biblical Mary's celibate husband) and remarries after his death, choosing "a dark young fisherman, who had wrists like steel" (1973, 139), and bears him children. On another level, "Red Barbara" is a grim realistic tale that shows that Barbara is not at all entirely either the mythical heroine or the modern liberated woman we might otherwise expect or hope from this denouement. Her first husband before Joseph

> had treated her sometimes with cruelty, but she understood him and was happy as his wife. When he threw her down with violence and embraced her she was content. At other times he fondled her like a child. Often he was drunk and beat her. She used to wait patiently for him in the town, standing in the road outside a tavern, while he got drunk with the neighbours. That was not pleasant, but it was the custom among the people. (1973, 133)

Unhappy with and mystified by the ascetic Joseph, Barbara strongly reaffirms this peasant lifestyle by marrying the fisherman at the end. "She was a happy woman of the people once more. . . . She led him staggering from the town, singing drunkenly, to her wild bed" (139).

The later story "The Old Woman" shows a rare willingness to examine women apart from sex, procreation, or men. Like "The Wedding," which was written during the same period, "The Old Woman" is unusual in its focus on women interacting among themselves in the absence of men, and it is even more atypical because its characters are not obsessed with marriage and in fact do not talk about men at all. Old Maggie Crampton visits Julia Duggan and her daughter. "Her lips moved in prayer. Strands of white hair hung down on either side of her wrinkled yellow cheeks. The colour had almost completely faded from the pupils of her eyes. She had no teeth left" (1973, 213). By the end of the story Maggie emerges as a courageous voice countering Julia's skepticism and negativity about the ugly things in life: " 'There are only lovely things in God's world,' she kept muttering as she advanced slowly up the lane with her hands on her knees" (221). "The Old Woman" appears to represent a new departure in O'Flaherty's treatment of women as well as Christianity. Written during his last period of publication, it makes one wonder whether he might have gone on to write more stories in this vein if indeed he had chosen to continue publishing at all after the early 1950s. In any event, the appearance of "The Old Woman" fairly late in O'Flaherty's prolific but truncated career indicates a mellowing of his misogyny.

O'Flaherty's most ambitious treatment of the relation of male and female was his long tale *The Ecstasy of Angus* (1931b), published in 1931 in a fifty-eight-page edition limited to 365 signed copies.

It is singular in its length—intermediate between his generally truly short stories and his full-length novels (though much closer in length to some of his longer stories such as "The Wedding"). Even more so, it is unique as the only fabulist, nonrealist work of fiction he ever published. Unlike even "The Fairy Goose" and "Red Barbara," which incorporate folkloric and mythical elements within realist narratives, *The Ecstasy of Angus* is a philosophical tale set amidst the ancient Irish mythical world of Angus and Fand. O'Flaherty appears to have remained attached to this work. He chose, forty-seven years after its initial publication, to fill two-and-a-half sides of his 1978 double-album recording (including also "Red Barbara" and "Dúil") with his rendition of it, in the same year in which it was reprinted by Wolfhound Press. The gist of the story, following a well-known mythical motif, is that Angus enjoys sex with Fand and produces a son ("Genius," the first man in this creation myth), but at the expense of his youth, beauty, property, and life. Fand successfully tempts Angus not with an apple, but with her body:

> Here between the snowy mounds of my breasts, soft, swooning love shall overcome the memory of that foolish vow, which the jealous ignorance of your father Youth imposed on you, lest Angus, grown to Manhood through the food of wisdom, should reach a magnificence beyond the comprehension of the gods themselves. Sleep, sweet love, while I bear you to my magic tent. There you shall awaken to find my promises do not do justice to the ecstasy you shall experience. (1931b, 25)

Assisted by erotic fairies, the aggressive Fand enacts her seduction of and copulation with Angus according to her own dictates. For Angus only "submission changed the pain of laceration into ecstasy" (1931b, 33). As Kelly emphasized in her 1978 afterword, Fand "emerges as dominant, not subject to or emanating from the male as Eve did. Male and female are thus polarized. Male/female mutual dependency follows, with potential for both cooperation and antagonism" (61).

Further, "Genius" is "born victim of an inescapable duality," Kelly notes, "for which he himself is not responsible" (60). This is the tension between *agape* and *eros,* between love and lust. It is interesting and significant that O'Flaherty records this conflict between love and lust, rather than pride, as containing his original sin (or most basic flaw). Writing presumably just as he was about to separate from his wife (which he stated in his final letter to Garnett, of 3 March 1932, that he had already done), he tacitly recognizes lust as the most essential male imperfection. He celebrated passion above all else, but his aforementioned stories about foolish males misled by lust, as well as *The Ecstasy of Angus,* demonstrate that passion can involve lust as well as love and can be destructive as well as constructive. The birth of "Genius" from sin reflects his ambivalence.

This duality or conflict between love and lust, like the strain between the "servile" and "insolent" sides of O'Flaherty's peasant status, may help us to explain the apparent contradiction between the clear presence of misogyny in his writing and those stories that present women as victimized or strong and men as foolish or evil. Such tensions are in turn closely linked to perhaps the most basic cultural disparity of all in his life: his status as a native of Inis Mór (sharing many of the values of that conservative place) yet at the same time a critical outsider most of his life (living in London, New York, and mostly Dublin, and looking back at his native culture with considerable clarity if not complete objectivity). He was both an insider in that culture and at the same time an outsider, "a tourist to his native rock" as Patrick Sheeran (1976, 63) put it (paraphrasing Benedict Kiely 1949, 185). O'Flaherty the insider maintained a sexist view of women; O'Flaherty the outsider described their exploitation.

In the ways in which I have discussed, Lawless and O'Flaherty provide us with a bifurcated model for contrasting female and male views of Ireland. In *Grania* Lawless presents a sympathetic, sensitive, and detailed study of a victimized island woman's consciousness and experiences. In *The Black Soul* and many of his stories, O'Flaherty looks at women very much as alien creatures, from the point of view of a patriarchal man, as occasionally countered by his best stories, such as "Spring Sowing" and "Going into Exile." We might do well to wonder skeptically which writer was more poorly equipped to try to understand peasant women of the Aran Islands, Lawless or O'Flaherty? Here gender meets back up with class. Lawless could think like a woman, but probably not like a peasant woman, since her background as an upper-class Ascendancy woman who could not even speak the real language of Grania O'Malley inevitably kept her isolated from the real thoughts and experiences of such a woman. O'Flaherty knew the women of the Aran Islands intimately, but in another sense, his male sexism often kept him from really knowing them at all. We emerge with contrasting portraits that perhaps cannot be trusted: Lawless's genteel-minded Grania versus O'Flaherty's animalistic Little Mary and Red Barbara, in particular. Certainly their class distinctions separated the genteel Lawless and the angry O'Flaherty almost as completely as did their gender differences; in fact, it may be impossible to unravel gender from class in deciding which made a bigger difference, and safer to decide that gender and class fed off each other in both cases. To really enter the minds of rural women close to the peasantry, we do better to stay tuned for the novels of Edna O'Brien.

Nonetheless, the fictions of Lawless and O'Flaherty are not to be lightly dismissed, or I would not have included them in this book. As flawed as it might be, *Grania* is a noble effort on the part of an Ascendancy writer to transcend the boundaries of class, understand a woman of the Aran Islands, make imaginative common cause with a woman from a different background, and achieve perhaps the first modern Irish feminist novel. And at his best, no writer has written better fiction about the Aran Islands than O'Flaherty. Although at his worst he could be very bad indeed, his best stories are indispensable depictions of life on the Aran Islands; there are many other Aran stories, particularly his animal stories, that I have not discussed here because they do not fit my focus on human gender relationships, but I have studied them elsewhere (see Cahalan 1991b). The Aran Islands are among my favorite places on earth, and I would not think of going there without the writings of O'Flaherty and Lawless in my head. From these writers, we can learn much about life on these remote islands and, more generally, about the distinctions between women and men in Ireland and perhaps elsewhere as well.

3

All in the Family

*Somerville and Ross's Feminist Collaboration
vs. James Joyce's Male Sibling Rivalry*

To trace the contrasts between Somerville and Ross and James Joyce is, in some respects, to reiterate those between Lawless and O'Flaherty. There are sharp, parallel differences between the Protestant Ascendancy women and the Catholic men from humbler backgrounds— even if we allow for the variation that whereas Somerville and Ross grew up in rural, western Ireland as Lawless also partly did, Joyce was born and bred in a middle-class Dublin family on the decline, unlike the proletarian O'Flaherty and his island of Inis Mór, the most western, rural, remote place in Ireland. Again, we have the outspoken, rebellious, often obnoxious men versus the women from genteel Victorian backgrounds, just as determined to make their own way in the world but much more confined by their gender in trying to do so. Katie Donovan's emphasis (1988) on public men versus private women is particularly applicable here: whereas Joyce and O'Flaherty made many outlandish public pronouncements deliberately intended to create a stir, Somerville and Ross, like Lawless, proceeded much more indirectly, concealing their sternest words about the world around them within their own private correspondence.

I have to say that Somerville and Ross and Joyce were both more alike and more unlike each other than Lawless and O'Flaherty were. For all of their many differences, Lawless and O'Flaherty did, after all, share some similarities: as we have seen, both grew up in large families, both pursued solitary writing careers, both suffered some psychological problems or mental imbalances as partly provoked by their experiences, and both focused on the Aran Islands as beautiful but also lonely and alienating places. Somerville and Ross and Joyce, however, not only wrote very different fictions, but they went about writing them in completely opposite ways.

Somerville and Ross wrote together, handing the pen back and forth, supporting each other and collaborating more closely than any other two major writers I know of. Joyce was the classic ego-centric male, determined to immortalize himself, continually borrowing material from others but always subsuming it all into his own idiosyncratic, magnificent fictional world. The sibling rivalry between Joyce and his younger brother Stanislaus offers itself as a quirky yet also quintessential case study of male styles of interaction that are completely antithetical to the collaborative, mutually supportive, feminist lives of Somerville and Ross.

For all of the complexity of these writers' lives, their gender differences are as stark as anything that anthropologists such as Nancy Scheper-Hughes ever observed in obstensibly simpler peasant society in the west of Ireland. Where in the last chapter my emphasis was on the fiction of Lawless and O'Flaherty as reflecting these authors' different life experiences, here I am primarily interested in the lives and careers of the collaborative Somerville and Ross and the self-centered Joyce, with their fiction as part of these life stories. In my other chapters my focus is on heterosexual, male-female relationships, but here the connection is female-to-female in Somerville and Ross and male-to-male in the Joyce brothers. Although both of these relationships were platonic rather than sexual, both were laden with much emotion and significance, and they are likely to be of interest to students of homosexual relationships in the most general sense.

As with Lawless and O'Flaherty, again we might ask if Somerville and Ross are so different from Joyce, why even bother to compare them in the same pages? Half of the answer here is the same as in the other case: because we can thereby learn much about the distinctions between female and male writers. But the other half of the answer is that Somerville and Ross's and Joyce's fictions share a number of similarities. As we have seen, Lawless and O'Flaherty wrote diametrically opposite prose—Lawless's long, digressive, Victorian, English style versus O'Flaherty's blunt, compact, modernist, Gaelic manner—and they lived in distinct cultural worlds at different times, with O'Flaherty never mentioning and apparently never reading his predecessor. Although Violet Martin ("Ross") died in 1915, Edith Somerville (1858–1949) and James Joyce (1882–1941) were contemporaries. Like Joyce, Somerville and Ross steered clear of Yeats and his movement and were scorned by the Irish literary and cultural establishment for many years, because they were mis-apprehended as anti-Irish, "stage-Irish" writers, while Joyce's writing was likewise attacked as anti-Irish as well as obscene. As we shall see, these writers came into crucial contact with the suffragist movement, of which Somerville was a significant leader, and with feminism in general. As Declan Kiberd notes, Somerville "became a type of the New Woman of the Nineties" (1995, 80), and Joyce's extensive interactions with such new women have been amply documented by Bonnie Kime Scott in *Joyce and Feminism* (1984).

These writers wrote not only somber and tragic fiction, but also some of the very best comic fiction, and in this chapter I focus particularly on their serious personal plights as worked out in very funny books: Somerville and Ross's *The Irish R. M.* and Joyce's *Finnegans Wake*. Moreover, Joyce read Somerville and Ross and was influenced by their work (see Powell 1970, 102–3). Although this chapter offers the first extended comparison of Somerville and Ross with Joyce, I am by no means the first to notice their similarities; as cited below, decades ago Patrick Kavanagh connected these writers' wonderful command of Irish-English dialect and dialogue. Much of the humor in each case depends on a contrast of high and low, of educated, effete speech with demotic dialect from the streets and fields. Also, although Somerville and Ross's most well developed characters are female and Joyce's are male, each also wrote compellingly of the opposite sex; it is hard to imagine Somerville and Ross without Major Yeates and Flurry Knox, and Joyce without Molly Bloom and Anna Livia Plurabelle.

⚮

Ever since the publication of the first story in 1898—"Great Uncle McCarthy" in London's *Badminton Magazine*—Somerville and Ross's *Irish R. M.* stories have been among the most popular and successful works of comic fiction to have come out of Ireland. The three volumes of stories (subsequently collected in a single volume) deal with a cast of characters who develop in an ongoing fashion that makes these delectable short stories, when considered together, fairly similar in form to the Irish novel—episodic and filled with realistic Irish-English dialect and some rather fantastic occurrences.[1] Here,

---

1. The edition of *The Irish R.M.* that I cite is a reprint of the 1928 edition collecting the original three volumes: *Some Experiences of an Irish R.M.* (1899), *Further Experiences of an Irish R.M.* (1908), and *In Mr. Knox's Country* (1915). Regarding the episodic nature of the Irish novel, see my book *The Irish Novel: A Critical History* (1988).

however, I am interested less in the form of the R. M. stories than in how they were a product of the unique, collaborative careers of the two women who wrote them, the cousins Edith Somerville and Violet Martin, and in how they interrelate with the cultural world of their time (and our own time), as reflected in their reception history. No fewer than seven biographies and critical books on Somerville and Ross have appeared during the past four decades. Gifford Lewis's biography and edition of the letters provide a valuable feminist perspective on their overall careers.[2] Here I intend to focus more specifically on the R. M. stories, because they provide a fascinating case study of Somerville and Ross's close collaboration, and also because these stories have been often misunderstood.[3]

The *Irish R. M.* stories have enjoyed a persistent international popularity. They were first collected in three successive volumes of 1899, 1908, and 1915—and subsequently they were published all together in 1928, have always stayed in print, and became well known to many people through the British Channel 4 / UTV / RTE television series that aired more than once beginning in the early 1980s. An inexpensive, collected paperback edition sold briskly in Dublin following the 1991 rebroadcast of the television series there. Ever since the turn of the century, the popularity of the R. M. stories has extended well beyond Dublin and London. In late 1901, during the Boer War, Edith wrote to Violet, "Mrs Purdon told H that her son & his company came upon a dead Boer, & examined

2. See Cummins 1952 (*Dr. E. OE. Somerville: A Biography*); Collis 1968 (*Somerville and Ross: A Biography*); *Somerville and Ross: A Symposium* (1969); Powell 1970 (*The Irish Cousins: The Books and Background of Somerville and Ross*); Cronin 1972 (*Somerville and Ross*); Robinson 1980 (*Somerville and Ross: A Critical Appreciation*); Lewis 1985 (*Somerville and Ross: The World of the Irish R. M.*); and Somerville and Ross 1989 (*The Selected Letters of Somerville and Ross,* edited by Lewis). Also, Ann Owens Weekes's *Irish Women Writers: an Uncharted Tradition* (1990) contains a chapter (60–82) devoted to Somerville and Ross's most celebrated novel, *The Real Charlotte* (1894); Weekes does not discuss *The Irish R. M.*

3. Since they were by far Somerville and Ross's most popular works, the R. M. stories have provoked a wide range of critical responses, and thus best serve my cultural focus here, which is informed by both reception theory and new historicism. A fuller study of comedy and culture in Somerville and Ross would also consider their other, less celebrated comic works and hunting tales, such as *Through Connemara in a Governess Cart* (1893b), *In the Vine Country* (1893a), *Beggars on Horseback* (1895), *The Silver Fox* (1898), *A St. Patrick's Day Hunt* (1902), *All on the Irish Shore* (1903a), *Slipper's ABC of Fox Hunting* (1903b), and *Dan Russel the Fox* (1911).

him for despatches & etc.—They found a copy of the R. M.—'He died of laughter-' . . . They took the copy, & it became the camp bible" (Somerville and Ross 1989, 258). The stories first appeared in the *Badminton Magazine,* a kind of British *Field and Stream* of its day, and its publishers, Longmans and Green, immediately encouraged book publication of the stories and the subsequent sequels. Somerville and Ross were encouraged by the minor success of the earlier hunting stories of Robert Martin, Violet's brother (Collis 1968, 116). The closest earlier Irish analogue to *The Irish R. M.* was W. H. Maxwell's *Wild Sports of the West* (1832).

However, the R. M. stories have been repeatedly misunderstood, and Somerville and Ross had to survive considerable hostility, misogyny, and misdirected nationalism. Their protagonist, Major Sinclair Yeates—a well-educated, well-meaning chap with some Irish blood—is sent from England, in classic Irish fictional fashion, to remote southwestern rural Ireland as a resident magistrate (an archaic legal post whose closest American equivalent is the justice of the peace). There he—and subsequently his wife, Philippa—encounter many unforgettable Irish characters who really run the area, particularly Flurry Knox and his grandmother Mrs. Knox, and participate in many racy Irish pastimes, most of which center on hunting. Many of these stories' early readers were incredulous that two women could write so effectively about traditionally male sites such as the courtroom and the hunt; typical was the reader cited by Somerville in *Irish Memories:* "First I read it at full speed, because I couldn't stop, and then I read it *very* slowly, chewing every word; and then I read it a third time, dwelling on the bits I like best; and then, and *not* till then, thank Heaven! I was told it was written by two women!" (quoted in Somerville 1917, 288).

Added to such misogyny was the even more persistent Irish nationalism that misrepresented the R. M. stories as "stage-Irish" tales along the lines of Samuel Lover's novel *Handy Andy* (1842), misunderstanding and marginalizing Somerville and Ross much as Yeats and others had done with Lawless. This point of view completely misses the fact that in sharp contrast to Lover, who made fun of the peasant Andy's ignorance, Somerville and Ross adopted Major Yeates, an Anglo-Irishman, as their central comic victim as well as narrator. This was the Ascendancy laughing at itself more than at the peasantry—or more specifically, it was a case of two women making fun of an Anglo-Irish*man,* whose comedy is greatly leavened by the fact that he himself participates in it and narrates it: to some extent, he laughs at himself. (Their most foolish and most duped character is a visiting Englishman without any Irish blood at all, Leigh Kelway, especially in "Lisheen Races, Second-Hand.")

It is also very ironic that Somerville and Ross were dismissed as "anti-Irish," given that during the Great Irish Famine or Hunger of 1845–51, Violet Martin's family "worked ceaselessly to feed all who depended on them, and all who turned to them for help," despite the fact that her aunt Marian caught typhus and nearly died (Sawyer 1993, 29). Somerville and Ross followed in the tradition of enlightened Irish gentry exemplified by Maria Edgeworth, but unlike Edgeworth, who was championed by many Irish nationalists, Somerville and Ross fell victim to a harsher post-Famine nationalist mindset embittered against the landed gentry. Nor did their "stubborn choice," Kiberd adds, "to stay on and work in Ireland rather than marry and settle in England (as so many others were doing) cut any ice" (1995, 69). As Somerville declared, "My family has eaten Irish food and shared Irish life for nearly three hundred years, and if that doesn't make me Irish I might as well say I was Scottish or Mormon or Pre-Diluvian!" (quoted in Kiberd 1995, 69).

Nonetheless, partly because Somerville and Ross stayed out of the Literary Revival movement led by their protagonist's namesake, Yeats, and went their own way, nationalist critical commentators such as Ernest Boyd (author of the canon-forming book *Ireland's Literary Renaissance*) gave them at best backhanded praise, briefly praising their great 1894 novel *The Real Charlotte* but lamenting the supposed "subsequent squandering of the authors' great talent upon the trivialities of a superficial realism" (Boyd 1922, 90). In *The Lonely Voice* Frank O'Connor admitted that he enjoyed reading the R. M. stories but described them as "yarns, pure and simple" (1962, 4). Herbert Howarth omitted Somerville and Ross entirely from his 1958 study of their period; Vivian Mercier mentioned them only once in his pioneering but male-dominated study of *The Irish Comic Tradition* (1962); and in *The Comic Irishman* (1984) Maureen Waters claims that there was "a racist consciousness at work in Somerville and Ross, and they undoubtedly contributed to the stereotype of the Irish countryman as a tricky clown" (1984, 20).[4] Only recently have critics begun to understand Somerville

4. As innovative as it purports to be in its groupings of Irish writing, the three-volume *Field Day Anthology of Irish Writing,* edited by Seamus Deane (1991), is quite traditional in filing Somerville and Ross among realist practitioners of "Prose Fiction 1880–1945," a section edited by Augustine Martin (2:1021–

•

and Ross. In his brilliant postcolonial study *Inventing Ireland,* Declan
Kiberd includes a chapter on Somerville and Ross as major Irish
writers, declaring, "So far are they from stage Irishry that they
noted with dismay the willingess of Irish country people to play
Paddy or Biddy for the amusement of their social superiors" (1995,
69). I aim to show that far from being "racist" victimizers, Somerville
and Ross were victimized women who nonetheless managed to
become successful, and that intermixed in the R. M. stories with a
nostalgia for a dying way of life was a subversively gendered portrait of strong, vital women. In this sense, comedy could be—in the
words of the title of a useful book by Nancy Walker (1988) about
American women's humor—"A Very Serious Thing."

Early criticism was dominated by misogyny and nationalism,
but it also included such nuggets as the anonymous reviewer in the
London *Daily Graphic* who noted, in Somerville and Ross's 1891
novel *Naboth's Vineyard,* "their keen sense of humour—qualities which
many male critics deny to their literary sisters" (quoted in Somerville
and Ross 1989, 178). And we do well to recover and pay attention
to a little-remembered, brief, but perceptive and trailblazing 1922
article in the *Atlantic Monthly* by Elizabeth Stanley Trotter: "Humor with A Gender." Trotter argued that men tend to laugh "at"
while women tend to laugh "with," avoiding ridicule and often
aligning themselves with the victims of jokes (as Somerville and
Ross do by making Major Yeates their narrator). Suggesting that
feminist humor can, however, be practiced by men as well as women,
Trotter recounts an anecdote about Mark Twain having a joke at a
Frenchman's expense (with the anecdote usually ending, in its common male retelling, with Twain's punchline). Then (in the part that
interests Trotter), when the Frenchman complained about the in-
sult, Twain offered to reverse positions and be the butt of the joke
himself. The joke is the thing, not who wins and loses, not who is
victim and who is victor.[5] Best of all, Trotter quotes Somerville and
Ross's "ideal of a woman of humor in the larger sense: 'Inherently
romantic, but the least sentimental; the most conversational and

---

1216); it includes only a selection from *The Real Charlotte* (2:1046–59) and a
brief author's note referring to their "strange literary partnership" (2:1217). The
inclusion of four chapters from a long novel, rather than any complete story,
seems an odd decision; apparently none of the R. M. stories were deemed "serious" enough for the *Field Day Anthology.*

5. Not inconsequently, in 1885 Somerville published a *Mark Twain Birthday
Book* (London: Remington) filled with his quotations.

the most reserved; silent about the things that affect us most deeply (which is perhaps the reason we are considered good company)— light-hearted, cheerful, and quite convinced that nothing will succeed!' "(1922, 787).

This perhaps rare combination of being at the same time both "cheerful" and "quite convinced that nothing will succeed" is understandable given the two cousins' personal—which is to say family—situations. Like their admired predecessor Maria Edgeworth, who (far from having a room of her own) had to write at the corner of the table in the family room, Somerville and Ross were compelled to eke out writing time whenever they could in the midst of bustling Big Houses for which they themselves became responsible after the deaths of parents. These authors had to develop what their narrator Yeates calls, in "The Friend of Her Youth," "that strange power of doing one thing and talking about another that I have often noticed in women" (1928, 463–64). Edith complained to her brother, "It is almost impossible to work quietly here: it is not the time so much as the want of mental tranquility plus the feeling that interruptions incessantly impend. It is impossible, I think, for anyone, who has not tried, to realise how exhausting interruptions are when one is engaged in imaginative creative work" (quoted in Mitchell 1969, 21).[6] Somerville and Ross thus perfectly exemplify the "nonbounded" quality of women's work as described by Nancy Chodorow (1978, 179).

Of course, Somerville and Ross's own interests were anything but entirely "quiet": both were avid hunters, though it was much more the chase than the kill that interested them. Somerville was the first woman in Ireland to become a "Master of Fox Hounds" or "MFH," in 1903 (Cummins 1952, 12 and Collis 1968, 121). Yet

6. It might also be of interest for readers to know that whereas Somerville's Drishane House in County Cork has remained in the Somerville/Coghill family, Martin's Ross House in County Galway left the Martin family in the 1920s and fell into extreme disrepair in ensuing decades—until it was bought in 1984 by George McLaughlin from Belmont, Massachusetts, who has since restored the house and built some additions next to it. In 1992 "Ross Castle" near Moycullen was open to visitors in April, May, and September, and the big house as well as several luxury apartments (recently erected adjoining the house) were available for rental in the summer months. Mr. McLaughlin added a garden and told me that among the items included in his restoration and addition are window sills and stained-glass windows from Lady Gregory's Coole Park (destroyed in the 1950s).

even in this position she had to follow the repressive Victorian code of female decorum by riding sidesaddle, with her right leg swung across to the same side of the saddle as her left (as can be seen in photographs in Lewis's biography and edition of the letters). As a result, she developed serious "rheumatism" in her right leg that grew worse and worse as she got older. Violet Martin's 1898 riding accident—linked to the subsequent development of a brain tumor and her eventual death in 1915—has been mentioned by several biographers and critics, as a postscript to Francie Fitzgerald's fatal riding accident in *The Real Charlotte*. Yet no one has ever stopped to wonder (at least in print) whether Martin would have been thrown from her horse if she had been permitted to ride securely in the normal, male position instead of the convoluted, precarious, and painful sidesaddle posture imposed on women at the time.

With Martin based, until 1906, at Ross House near Galway, and Somerville anchored at the other end of the country, at Drishane in County Cork, these two women had to struggle to find opportunities to collaborate as closely as they did. Nonetheless, they managed to achieve the most successful close coauthorship in Irish literature—arguably, in fact, the most successful among writers in English since the Middle Ages. Addison and Steele collaborated on the eighteenth-century *Tatler,* but they did not write everything together as Somerville and Ross did. Carolyn Heilbrun's perceptive book *Writing a Woman's Life* (1988)—which rightly notes that the implications of women's friendship together, their collaboration, and their use of pseudonyms have been too little considered—would do well to include Somerville and Ross as more apt examples of such crucial collaboration than anyone in English or American literature. Similarly, Sandra Gilbert and Susan Gubar omit Somerville and Ross from their *Norton Anthology of Literature by Women* (1985) even though they would have provided a unique example of women's collaboration; that anthology, whose 148 writers are all individuals rather than coauthors, includes only four Irish ones. Ironically, the closest contemporary analogue may be the team of Gilbert and Gubar themselves; speaking together at the 1988 Summer Institute for Teachers of Literature to Undergraduates (sponsored by the National Council of Teachers of English), they described how they try to accept as many joint speaking engagements as they could since those provided them with relatively rare opportunities to get together (from Indiana and California) and write. One of the few advantages that Somerville and Ross enjoyed, relative to women in earlier generations, was that although they were unable to attend university, both did graduate from Alexandra College, founded in 1866, where "education . . . breached a succession of dams that had previously held women's potential in check" (Sawyer 1993, 53).

Collaborating without long-distance telephone calls and university budgets for air travel, Edith Somerville and Violet Martin spent the most productive twenty years of their careers, from 1886 to 1906, writing and traveling back and forth between Cork and Galway in order to get their work done. They talked out and wrote down everything together, so closely that scholars have been unable to tell who wrote what or identify separate segments of writing. Their collaboration was so close that after Martin's death in 1915, Somerville (who survived her by thirty-four years) insisted on publishing everything under their joint names; believed that she could maintain mystical communication with Martin; and took the idea for her most successful solo work of fiction, her 1925 novel *The Big House of Inver,* from a suggestion in a 1912 letter from Martin (Somerville and Ross 1989, 294).[7] Given the close nature of their collaboration, their geographical isolation from each other, and the many distractions in their lives, they had to work very hard when they could work together at all. The first R. M. stories were composed between October 1898 and September 1899, following Martin's accident when (as Somerville later recalled) "Martin hardly knew . . . what it was to be out of suffering" (quoted in Cronin 1972, 51). The bleakest R. M. story, "The Waters of Strife" (about a man who commits a murder and later commits suicide), was written just after Martin's accident. Each story, "as we finished it, seemed to be the last possible effort of exhausted nature" (quoted in Cronin, 59). These stories were very carefully planned, as Guy Fehlmann (1979) has shown. Somerville and Ross made deliberate, extensive use of their own experiences and people they knew, keeping big notebooks they called *Stock Pot Irish Memories* and making notations when they incorporated materials from the notebooks in the stories (Robinson 1980, 51).

In order to succeed, as two late Victorian women writers invading the male provinces of satire and hunting, Somerville and Ross needed each other. As Martin aptly put it to Somerville in 1889, thinking about the impediments facing women writers, "I am not

---

7. See also Bi-ling Chen, "De-mystifying the Family Romance: A Feminist Reading of Somerville and Ross's *The Big House of Inver*" (1998).

man enough for a story by myself" (1989, 153). They shared an inherited family code language of sorts, the vocabulary of the "Buddhs" (or descendants of Lord Chief Justice of Ireland Charles Kendal Bushe), which they collected in the form of a glossary (Somerville and Ross 1989, 297–302) and used in their letters for comic effects and sometimes for self-protective purposes. Their first novel, with the fitting title of *An Irish Cousin* (1889), was published under the pseudonyms of "Giles Herring" and "Martin Ross," but thereafter Somerville insisted on signing all her books with her own habitually initialed name; as for Martin, all her friends (including Somerville, in her letters) addressed her as "Martin" rather than "Violet" and she was proud to carry the family Big House name of "Ross." Thus, at first many readers assumed that "Somerville and Ross" were men, but their true status was generally known by the turn of the century.

Their close relationship later misled one of their biographers, Maurice Collis, into the impression that they were lesbians (1968, 36–38), but Gifford Lewis refuted this inaccuracy (1985, 233–38).[8] Somerville and Ross's friendship and collaboration were emotionally close and nonsexual in a Victorian way of thinking that saw sex as undignified and animalistic. Their protagonist Charlotte Mullen speaks for them when she thinks to herself, "A human soul, when it has broken away from its diviner part and is left to the anarchy of the lower passions, is a poor and humiliating spectacle, and it is unfortunate that in its animal want of self-control it is seldom without a ludicrous aspect" (1894, 267). Neither ever got closer to a man than they were to each other, but Somerville and Ross kept their relationship mental, emotional, and spiritual rather than sexual. They were hostile to the earlier lesbians Eleanor Butler and Sarah Ponsonby, the celebrated or infamous "Ladies of Llangollen," who eloped together; Somerville and Ross described the Ladies' lifestyle as a "grotesque romance" (quoted in Sawyer 1993, 54). Later, in 1919, four years after Violet Martin's death, when the lesbian Ethel Smith proposed a sexual relationship to Somerville, she declined, somewhat shocked (Lewis 1985, 205–6).

The Real Charlotte was the book that made Somerville and Ross's reputation, appearing before any of the R. M. stories, and it is important to understand this somber, tragic book before turning to

---

8. Shawn R. Mooney (1992) usefully critiques "Heterosexism in Biographical Representations of Somerville and Ross."

the comic stories. Unlike the other major "Somerville and Ross" novel, *The Big House of Inver,* this one was written completely collaboratively, not by Edith alone on an idea from Violet, and it is one of the best two or three Irish novels of the nineteenth century. Its opening chapters are set in Dublin, where Violet Martin lived for awhile, retaining an ear for the cadences of the city's speech that, as reflected in these chapters, connects this writing to Joyce's. Most of *The Real Charlotte* is set in Somerville's native Big House world of rural County Cork ("west Cork," as it is called).

As in Lawless's *Grania* where the most enduring relationship is one between two sisters, *The Real Charlotte* depends on a double structure, to be continued in such twentieth-century novels as Kate O'Brien's *The Land of Spices* and Edna O'Brien's *The Country Girls Trilogy* (both discussed in my next chapter), and focused on not one, but two protagonists. The link between *The Real Charlotte* and *The Land of Spices* is particularly close, as each novel interrelates the life of an older woman with that of a closely related younger one, though *The Land of Spices* shows how two women help each other, whereas *The Real Charlotte* sets them in conflict, illustrating a tension between the two women similar to the male rivalry found in Joyce. Whereas *The Real Charlotte*—the closest approach in the Irish novel to English "novels of manners" by Jane Austen and others—develops a rich and varied range of characters, the other characters all rotate around Charlotte Mullen and her niece, Francie Fitzgerald.

Based on women well known to Somerville and Ross, Charlotte Mullen is tragic and Francie Fitzgerald, pathetic. Caught midway between the Big House aristocrats embodied in the Dysart family and the peasants with whom she is able to speak Irish, the crafty Charlotte plots for many years to marry Roderick Lambert, the Dysarts' land agent. Subverting gender stereotypes, Charlotte has a keen acumen about money, as did Somerville and Ross themselves. Having led Charlotte on in order to borrow money from her, Lambert marries the beautiful young Francie instead. Charlotte tries to revenge herself on Lambert by calling in her debt, but when Francie falls from her horse and dies, Lambert is left alone and penniless, no longer any fit object for the embittered and forlorn Charlotte's revenge.

The presentation of gender roles in this novel is very bleak indeed. When Charlotte arrives at the Dysarts' party, she receives the following greeting from the sharp-tongued Lady Dysart: "Have you ever seen so few men in your life? And there are five and forty women! I cannot imagine where they have all come from, but I know where I wish they would take themselves to, and that is to the bottom of the lake!" (1894, 11). Misogyny, in a world in which women are expendable commodities, is so deeply ingrained that often women are its mouthpieces. Charlotte herself thinks nothing of describing Lambert's first wife, Lucy, as "the turkey-hen" (178, 202, 206), and Charlotte's perhaps largest act of hubris is to hasten the weak-hearted Lucy's death by making sure that she has an opportunity to read Francie's letters to Lambert. As for Francie, when Lambert buys her a bangle and snaps it "quickly on to her wrist," she remarks, "It's like a policeman putting on a handcuff" (105). Another novel that critiqued the Darwinian mating game of the late nineteenth century was George Moore's *A Drama in Muslin* (1886), which was equally scathing though not nearly so well written. Donovan notes that "Moore takes on the role of the impersonal historian, while Somerville and Ross are the domestic biographers" (1988, 12). Somerville and Ross were able to be much more personal about the plight of a "spinster" such as Charlotte Mullen for the simple reason that they, too, remained unmarried, though for somewhat different reasons; Somerville, in particular, rejected at least one marriage proposal because she wanted to maintain her independence.

The many dark sides evident in *The Real Charlotte* already suggest that the common and persistent view of Somerville and Ross as two wealthy Ascendancy "ladies" writing comic tales for a lark could not be further from the truth. With rents withheld during the Land War era, and given the general decline of the fortunes of Ascendancy families such as the Somervilles and the Martins, they wrote the R. M. stories in order to survive—to avoid the depression and total dependency on the family of unmarried women such as Martin's own pathetic sister, Selina. As Martin wrote to Somerville in 1890, "I *must* make money—so must you" (1989, 164); Somerville replied, "I also am very poor, only for the *Art Journal*—as yet unpaid—I should be bankrupt" (165). They always considered their somber, tragic novel *The Real Charlotte* to be their greatest work, but the *Irish R. M.* stories sold much better, and when they saw that those stories were a hit, they continued to write more of them. J. B. Pinker—their agent and also agent to Henry James, Joseph Conrad, and D. H. Lawrence—was amazed at how well these stories sold. Martin's letters in particular are very hardheaded about sales and display a craftiness about making sure of the right reviews. In 1906 Martin complained to Somerville about a man who was working on a biography of her own brother Robert (author of some lesser-known hunting stories) and asked her to contribute to it, to " 'write all you like, and we can select what is wanted.' I at once said I was too busy to write stuff that might not be wanted and he seemed quite surprised—I don't think that he realises at all the position, or that I am a *professional writer*" (1989, xxiii, my emphasis). Male critics such as Boyd (describing their work as "trivial") perpetuated this kind of sexist attitude.

It should be noted that Somerville and Ross felt quite removed from the Irish Literary Revival, despite the fact that Violet Martin was Lady Gregory's cousin, visited her at Coole Park, and was invited in 1905 to write a play for the Abbey Theatre. Martin wrote to Somerville that Lady Gregory told her, "A week at Coole would do it. We could give you all the hints necessary for stage effects etc—even write a scenario for you" (1989, 274). It is clear that Martin was no more persuaded by this proposal than by the biographer's assurance that "we can select what is wanted." In response to Lady Gregory's invitation, Martin wrote Somerville, "I gave no further encouragement of any sort—and said we were full up" (274). Like Katharine Tynan and Georgie Hyde-Lees, Gregory had willingly subsumed her own career into Yeats's, but Somerville and Ross kept to a different female path, sticking close together yet steering clear of Yeats's movement.

Martin had also met W. B. Yeats at Coole, and there remains the slight, teasing possibility that their Major Yeates might have been named partly as a private joke at the poet's expense. Years ago Thomas Flanagan noted that "one can only hope that he was not given the name in malice" (1966, 65). Martin met Yeats in 1896, two years before the first R. M. story appeared, and was bemused by him: "He is a *little* affected and knows it—He has a sense of humour and is a gentleman" (Somerville and Ross 1989, 240). Five years later, in 1901, Martin encountered him again at Coole, reporting, "I liked him. . . . He is not at all without a sense of humour, which surprised me. . . . But he doesn't approve of humour for humour's sake—(here Miss Martin said beautiful things about humour being a higher art) I will tell you more when we meet" (1989, 252). One can only wonder about what "more" Martin told Somerville later, in private conversation. Gifford Lewis believes that Major Yeates was "a tribute to [their earlier benefactor] Edmund

Yates, and not to the poet W. B. Yeats" (Somerville and Ross 1989, 138), further noting in a letter to me of 30 October 1991 that "Yeates" was the same spelling as the well-known Grafton Street opticians of the day—thus perhaps ironically reinforcing the Major's English inability to see what is in front of his nose when trying to make sense of the deceptive Irish scene.

It seems clear that Major Yeates is no simple copy of a single Yates, Yeats, or Yeates, and that as protagonist and narrator he is as much a dupe as a tribute. But the possibility of a link to the poet may continue to beguile us. Somerville and Ross, avowed realists, had little patience for his shadowy romanticism; like the poet, Major Yeates is often quite abstracted. It would not have been out of character for Somerville and Ross to have a private little joke—rather along the lines of their use (noted earlier) of the language of the "Buddhs" as a confidential comic code—protecting themselves by keeping quiet about it and by spelling their Major's name "Yeates" rather than "Yeats." Slipper (Flurry's comic, peasant sidekick) was the only character in the R. M. stories whose real-life source they openly admitted, even though it is clear that several of their characters were similarly based on actual persons they knew. In 1915 Lady Gregory wrote to Martin concerning *The Irish R. M.* that she "was reading the book slowly . . . because she was reading it aloud to W. B. Yeats. 'He at first mention of Major Yeates asked anxiously if it was spelt with a second "e," and hearing it was, gave himself up to uninterrupted enjoyment" (quoted in Powell 1970, 166). A notoriously bad speller, Yeats did not meet Somerville until 1931, when he addressed an invitation to the inaugural meeting of the Irish Academy of Letters to "Miss Summerville." Edith "was so incensed . . . that she threatened to address her reply to 'Major Yeates' " (Powell 1970, 119).

Criticism on the Irish R. M. stories generally focuses on Major Yeates and Flurry Knox, though as I noted earlier, there has been a failure to fully appreciate the extent to which Yeates embodies the Anglo-Irish Ascendancy (an Ascendancy on the descent) having some fun at its own expense. Flurry Knox is a "half-sir," a Protestant who outfoxes Yeates and nearly everyone else and who is in fact as much a part of Somerville and Ross's own social stratum as Yeates. Flurry is Master of Fox Hounds, as was Somerville's brother Aylmer (on whom Flurry was based), and then Yeates becomes the MFH when Flurry leaves for the Boer War, just as Edith did when Aylmer left to fight in that war. However, here I want to attend to the stories' major female characters, who have been largely ne-glected, yet are very important. Somerville and Ross's depiction of Yeates—and even Flurry—as outmatched by the *women* who really control the Big House is parallel to their portrayal of the Ascen-dancy, in the person of Yeates, as rather hopelessly powerless in the face of the lower classes. Thus, in terms of gender as well as class, the R. M. stories are subtly and deliciously subversive.

The first story, "Great Uncle McCarthy," describes the arrival of Yeates (still a bachelor at this point) to Skebawn, where he takes up residence in the windswept, rain-drenched house of Shreelane. Yeates may be the R. M., but his house is controlled by his inimitable cook, Mrs. Cadogan. We learn just how total her control is when it comes out that she has permitted a whole group of friends and relatives to continue to operate their fox-poaching operation in Yeates's attic, drinking his whiskey and producing noise and clatter that Yeates thinks is a ghost. Mrs. Cadogan's dialogue is marvelous; as Patrick Kavanagh recognized, Somerville and Ross "had a better ear for Irish dialogue than anybody except James Joyce" (quoted in Cronin 1982, 82), and their writing definitely influenced Joyce (see Powell 1970, 102–3). Much as in the "Cyclops" chapter of Joyce's *Ulysses*—where the narrative alternates between mock-heroic, pseudo-classical language and the folksy language of a barroom wag—a good deal of the comedy of the R. M. stories has to do with reg-isters of language shifting between Yeates's impeccably standard Oxford English and the racy dialogue of characters such as Mrs. Cadogan. Furthermore, Major Yeates is not unlike Joyce's Leopold Bloom, as a well-meaning man often laughed at by others and played for a fool by his wife.

The Irish R. M.'s dialogue provides a veritable glossary of Irish English usage: "Indeed it came into my mind on the way here," remarks Farmer Flynn to Yeates in "A Conspiracy of Silence," "to try could I coax you to come over and give us a day's hunting. We're destroyed with foxes" (1928, 304). In this respect Somerville and Ross were influenced by Maria Edgeworth, who liked to write down Irish-English dialect "verbatim" and whose letters to her close friend Nancy Crampton, their great-grandmother, had been inherited by Martin (Lewis 1985, 8–9); as with Lawless, Edgeworth's literary and cultural legacy was very important to Somerville and Ross. Somerville and Ross's realistic style could not be further from stereotypes about women's reputedly florid, romantic, "feminine" writing. A common stylistic feature in the R. M. stories is the deflating simile, as in the description in "The Friend of Her Youth" of "the small, rat-like head of Bill's kitchen-maid, Jimmy" (1928, 464).

Somerville and Ross's women tend to be strong and their men weak. In one of the very first references to Major Yeates's wife, Philippa, Yeates reports, "Philippa has since explained to me . . . a mere male fallacy" (1928, 21), and right through to the end of the stories, he notes, "I followed her, uttering the impotent growls of a husband" (1928, 476). When she first actually appears, in "Philippa's Fox-Hunt," she gives him a fierce piece of her mind for keeping her waiting at the train station, and she then proceeds to earn her spurs at the foxhunt. She gets on much more easily with Mrs. Cadogan and other female servants than Yeates does, and unlike her husband, she makes an effort to learn Irish. As Maurice Collis noted, Philippa "is the stronger character of the two, a marriage relationship which Edith approved of" (1968, 126). Yeates is often ordered about while women cook, clean, and socialize, as in "A Royal Command," where he complains that his cigarettes, "in common with every other thing that I wanted, had been tidied into oblivion. From earliest dawn I had heard the thumping of feet, and the swish of petticoats, and the plying of brooms" (1928, 200–201). In the celebrated story "Poisson d'Avril," Yeates is under Philippa's orders to buy a salmon for an upcoming relative's visit, and is overcharged at the market by fish-hawker Eliza Coffey: " 'How would the gentleman be a match for her!' shouted the woman on the floor. . . . 'Sure a Turk itself wouldn't be a match for her! That one has a tongue that'd clip a hedge!' " (1928, 66). The character closest to Edith Somerville herself is Bobby Bennett, who (Lewis tells us) "shares many characteristics with Edith herself" (1985, 136); in "The Bosom of the McRorys," Somerville and Ross write of Bobby Bennett that "her dancing is a serious matter, with a Cromwellian quality to it, suggestive of jack boots and the march of great events" (1928, 533).

In these ways, Somerville and Ross show how the Big Houses were really run by women. At a time when the economic power of the Ascendancy was fading rapidly,[9] the chief arena for Ascendancy activity was no longer the marketplace, but rather the theatre, the dinner party, and the hunt—a social world regulated very often by

9. See Wayne E. Hall, *Shadowy Heroes: Irish Literature in the 1890s* (1980), for a thorough study of the effects of the Ascendancy's decline on the literature of the period, including Somerville and Ross's novel *The Real Charlotte* (1894). In his book Hall is much more interested in issues of class than of gender.

women. The character who most interests me, and the most dominant in all of the R. M. stories, is Flurry's grandmother, Mrs. Knox,
the impressive materfamilias of the Big House of Aussolas. Even
the usually fearless Flurry Knox is awed by her, and Flurry's wife
is always referred to only as "Mrs. Flurry," never "Mrs. Knox"—for
only his grandmother can hold that title. And even Maurice Collis,
who had trouble correctly understanding other gender issues in
Somerville and Ross's lives, recognizes that Mrs. Knox is "much
cleverer than any man. . . . What she stands for is Edith's feminine
ideal, a matriarch. . . . Mrs. Cadogan is the same type in the world
below stairs" (1968, 154).

Mrs. Knox was closely based on Anna Selina Martin, Violet's
mother—always called "Mama" in their letters, which recount anec-
dotes about her that are just as hilarious as anything in the stories.
Somerville and Ross wrote much more about their mothers than
about their typically aloof Victorian fathers. Martin remarked in 1910,
"In her outdoor life, she was what, in those decorous days, was called
a 'Tomboy,' and the physical courage of her youth remained her
distinguishing characteristic through life" (Somerville and Ross 1989,
222). Lewis notes that Mrs. Martin "never had any idea of housekeeping. She used to have a special hiding place at Ross to avoid the
servants when there was nothing to be cooked for dinner" (Somerville
and Ross 1989, 69). "Mama" was the antithesis of Virginia Woolf's
"Angel in the House" in her essay "Professions for Women" (1942),
whose contemporary American analogue is the woman in the old
Lemon Pledge commercial—dusting the table until it shines while
wearing high heels, a spotless dress, and a cheerful smile. In contrast,
Martin's mother was an uninhibited woman interested, not in house-
cleaning, but in the hunt. Somerville and Ross admired Mrs. Martin
(much more than Somerville's apparently overbearing and repressed
mother). Unlike many of their other relatives, Mrs. Martin delighted
in their work, even the unflattering novel *The Real Charlotte,* and
perhaps partly as a result their own "self-supporting literary
lives . . . pre-figure," as Lewis notes, "the description given by Virginia Woolf in *A Room of One's Own* of the sort of life that intelligent
women should work towards" (1985, 10).

Mrs. Martin could also be an outrageous character in her own
right, provoking in her daughter a remarkably loud laugh that her
collaborator, Somerville, often described as penetrating and nonstop.
As for *The Irish R. M.* itself, recalled Somerville in 1944, "One
reviewer described it as a book no self-respecting person could read

in a railway-carriage with any regard to decorum" (1944, vii). There is a riotous series of 1888 letters (Somerville and Ross 1989, 79–80, 87) from Martin to Somerville recounting an ongoing feud between Mrs. Martin and the local R. M. and his wife over the occupancy of a church pew that had traditionally been the Martins'; Mrs. Martin wins the day by smiling pleasantly at her foes, moving to another pew, and allowing the R. M. and his wife to encounter a resultant virtual boycott by the rest of the congregation before they agree to restore the pew to its rightful occupants. Around the same time, when visiting tenants began dancing in the hallway of Ross House, "Mama who was attired in a flowing pink dressing-gown and a black hat trimmed with lilac," recorded her daughter, "became suddenly emulous, and with her spade under arm joined in the jig. . . . Mama is indeed a wonderful woman" (Somerville and Ross 1989, 81). Throwing feminine stereotypes and conventions to the winds, "Mama" was completely unself-conscious and eccentric about her clothing. In 1892 her daughter described at length how at one point "Mama" was wearing, on top of everything else, a red kettle holder that she had been unable to find around the house, and at another point a woman came up to her in the street and alerted her to the fact that "her sponge *and* her sponge bag were hanging from her waist at the back" (Somerville and Ross 1989, 181).

The unforgettable fictional Mrs. Knox is a close copy of the unforgettable Mrs. Martin. Figuring impressively in several of the earlier R. M. stories, Mrs. Knox takes over completely in the third volume of 1915. This suggests that following Mrs. Martin's death in 1906 (after which her daughter moved to Drishane, the Somerville estate, where she lived until her own death in 1915), Somerville and Ross were determined to memorialize her properly. Mrs. Knox is introduced in the first volume in "Trinket's Colt," where we learn that she danced with Yeates's grandfather and she discovers (and appreciates) Flurry's ruse of hiding her colt in a bush. "The Aussolas Martin Cat" and "The Finger of Mrs. Knox," the first two stories of the final volume, are my own favorites—in contrast to some critics who see this volume as a weaker one, perhaps because the central men, Yeates and Flurry, are less substantial in it. Mrs. Knox was already eighty-four when first encountered in an earlier volume, and thus is presumably several years older in the final volume. Here Mrs. Knox is seen "swathed in hundreds of shawls, in the act of hurling . . . tongs and some unseen object" (1928, 434), and she is described by "her kinswoman, Lady Knox" as "a rag bag held together by diamond brooches" (437). Mrs. Knox governs all at Aussolas; as Yeates notes, "She pervaded all spheres" (436), "her personality was the only thing that counted" (437), and "I hope it may be given to me to live until my mood also is as a dark tower full of armed men" (425). Her admiring grandson Flurry, who is quite an operator himself, adds: "There's no pie but my grandmother has a finger in it" (436). Mrs. Knox's voice is so commanding, Yeates feels, that it "would have made me clean forty pig-sties had she desired me to do so" (63).

In "The Finger of Mrs. Knox," a tenant comes to her complaining about his neighbor Goggin, who has seized his livestock because he owes him five pounds. Mrs. Knox's ominous statement (in this period following the Wyndham Land Act of 1903, which legislated a peasant proprietorship) and the tenant's reply are both memorable:

> "I have no tenants," replied Mrs. Knox tartly; "the Government is your landlord now, and I wish you joy of each other!"
> "Then I wish to God it was yourself we had in it again!" lamented Stephen Casey; "it was better for us when the gentry was managing their own business." (1928, 440)

Despite her remonstrations, the next morning Mrs. Knox has Yeates take her to Killoge Wood to lay Goggin low. The story ends when, believe it or not, she convinces Goggin to lend the five pounds to himself, in effect, and leave the offended tenant alone. This is no romantic heroine, though. Somerville and Ross describe her impressively but unflinchingly; Yeates observes how Mrs. Knox "blinked her eyes like an old rat. . . . I felt as if I were being regarded through a telescope, from the standpoint of a distant century" (507). She even speaks Latin (539). Mrs. Knox is the old, dying Ascendancy at its best, in the view of Somerville and Ross: a powerful woman who lords it over her house and lands—and they do seem to be *hers,* despite Victorian convention—and takes joy in life.

These are funny stories with a serious point behind them. As Langston Hughes wrote in *The Book of Negro Humor,* "Humor is laughing at what you haven't got when you ought to have it. Of course, you laugh by proxy. . . . Humor is your own unconscious therapy" (quoted in Walker 1988, 101). Laughing "by proxy" seems a particularly appropriate notion when applied to Somerville and Ross, who were active in the women's suffrage movement. Somerville was president of the Munster Women's Franchise League in the period surrounding World War I. As early as 1889, Martin angrily wrote to Somerville, "I certainly think it is absurd that the people Mama employs should have a vote, and that she herself should not have one. After all most women who have to stand alone and manage their houses or places themselves are competent" (1989, 141). In 1910, Edith Somerville became president and Violet Martin vice-president of the Munster Women's Franchise League. After Martin's death in 1915, Somerville continued this work; as Kiberd notes, "the ways in which the police abused and manhandled working-class suffragists convinced her that it was the duty of aristocratic women to put their bodies on the line at demonstrations" (1995, 81). Whereas Martin had been an avowed supporter of the Union with Britain, Somerville later moved closer to the nationalism shared by many of her fellow suffragists. Much as moderate, Redmondite nationalists waited out World War I in hopes that the British would deliver on the promise of Irish home rule in exchange for their support for the war effort, Somerville and other suffragists patiently waited for the vote. In 1918, the Representation of the People Act finally granted the vote to women over thirty.

As Nancy Walker notes, the long tradition in African-American humor of "laughing at the man" takes on a new relevance when applied to women's humor (1988, 109). In another of the relatively few considerations of women and comedy, Regina Barreca writes: "Comedy is a way women writers can reflect the absurdity of the dominant ideology while undermining the very basis for its discourse. They can point to the emperor's new clothes" (1988, 19)—or the R. M.'s, permit me to add. Of course, Somerville and Ross *forgive* the R. M.; they even allow him to narrate these stories, following the pattern of identification and role-reversal with the comic victim, as outlined in that now obscure but insightful essay by Trotter, "Humor With A Gender." If Major Yeates is made a fool of, we are nonetheless permitted to emerge from the R. M. stories liking him. As Maria Edgeworth wrote to Somerville and Ross's great-grandmother, Mrs. Bushe, in 1832, "It is good to laugh as long as we can . . . and whenever we can" (quoted in Lewis 1985, 220).

As different as his background, career, and writings were, James Joyce shared some important experiences with Somerville and Ross.

For our purposes, it is especially significant that the cultural movements that affected each of these writers perhaps most crucially and most in common—the suffragist struggle and feminism in general—were focused on gender issues. Somerville and Ross were Ascendancy Protestants who wrote Victorian fiction, and Joyce was a Dublin Catholic who became the high priest of modernism, yet each of these writers was decisively influenced by feminism and most likely would not have succeeded as writers at all without feminism and the "New Women" who surrounded them.

James and Nora Joyce left Ireland in 1904 largely because they felt too constricted by its rigid moral codes, especially in terms of gender; in violation of Catholic dictates, they lived together and had two children without getting married until July 4, 1931 (in a private civil ceremony carried out only for legal purposes of inheritance). Nora remained her husband's chief inspiration and female guiding light, "my angel," as he wrote to her. "*Everything* that is noble and exalted and deep and true and moving in what I write comes, I believe from you" (quoted in Henke 1983, 129). Joyce's memories of his mother, Declan Kiberd notes, were "fired by an almost feminist sense of outrage against her predicament," with Joyce cursing "the system which had made her a victim" (quoted in Kiberd 1985, 173).

Joyce's very first Irish publication, his 1901 essay "The Day of the Rabblement," which criticized Yeats's Celtic Revival movement, was published as a pamphlet together with a feminist essay by Francis Skeffington, Joyce's Royal University (later University College, Dublin) classmate and friend. Thus, at the outset of his career, "Joyce in effect collaborated in a feminist publication" (Scott 1984, 31). When he married Hannah Sheehy, Francis Skeffington changed his last name to Sheehy-Skeffington—another unheard-of practice for an Irish man during that period. He was the source for McCann in Joyce's *A Portrait of the Artist as a Young Man*—the activist whose petition Stephen Dedalus refuses to sign, but whom Stephen tells, "You are right to go your way" (1916, 173). As a feminist, pacifist, and socialist, Sheehy-Skeffington bravely went against the grain of Irish society—and met his doom in 1916, the same year that the *Portrait* appeared, when he was murdered by a deranged British officer during the Easter Rising and buried in quicklime, after he had been captured while walking through the streets of Dublin in order to urge people to lay down their arms and stop looting the shops. Joyce's friendship with the Sheehy-

Skeffingtons was certainly an important one for this writer whose own socialist and pacifist views (voiced most famously by Bloom late in *Ulysses*) have been traced by Dominic Manganiello in *Joyce's Politics* (1980), and whose interrelations with feminism have been increasingly examined and appreciated by a number of scholars.

In her comprehensive study of the subject, *Joyce and Feminism* (1984), Bonnie Kime Scott notes that "most of James Joyce's early education on feminism came from men: Sheehy-Skeffington, [George] Moore, Shaw, Hauptmann, and Ibsen. This is more a comment on Joyce's era than on Joyce" (53). Even before "The Day of the Rabblement," an eighteen-year-old Joyce published, in the London *Fortnightly Review* in 1900, a review of Ibsen's play *When We Dead Awaken,* emphasizing about Ibsen, "that he knows women is an uncontrovertible fact" (quoted in Scott 1984, 53). With time, he would meet a second set of feminist women who were more approachable because of his increased maturity and their greater interest in literary, rather than political action" (53). Like O'Flaherty, Joyce came to depend on women for their patronage. Those women included Harriet Shaw Weaver, Dora Marsden, Sylvia Beach, Maria Jolas, Djuna Barnes, and others. They became Joyce's most important literary allies and funding sources, without whom he could not have published either *Ulysses* or *Finnegans Wake;* Beach, for example, paid for the publication of *Ulysses* when no established publisher would touch the book.

Scott argues that "the mature and capable women who lived through *Finnegans Wake* with Joyce repeatedly suggest that this was a man who had grown beyond the limits of Stephen Dedalus" (1984, 115), Joyce's autobiographical protagonist who was guilty of sexist attitudes toward women but who was meant to be seen as an immature adolescent, a would-be artist *as a Young Man.* Joyce was never a joiner; unlike Edith Somerville or Francis Sheehy-Skeffington, he did not work for women's rights. In male and mixed company Joyce sometimes made sexist remarks as part of a pose that he abandoned in his serious works. Perhaps the single most revealing anecdote in this regard is one recounted by Mary Colum, who sought in conversation to get Joyce to admit his debts to Freud and Jung. "Joyce squirmed and retorted, 'I hate women who knew anything,' to which Colum replied, 'No, Joyce, you don't. . . . You like them,' and recalls: 'After a few seconds of silent annoyance, a whimsical smile came over his face, and the rest of the afternoon was pleasant for all three of us'" (Scott 1984, 117).

Joyce's interactions with women and with feminism is a large subject that has already been much discussed; I myself have examined it in a more general way elsewhere.[10] I outline this topic here as a link to Somerville and Ross and as background to my particular subject, which is not Joyce's relationships with women, but rather his longest and perhaps closest male relationship, with his brother Stanislaus. Like most aspects of Joyce, this relationship has also been much studied already, within a voluminous Joyce industry limping toward exhaustion at the end of the millenium. However, I want to put a new spin on Joyce's sibling conflict by contrasting it with Somerville and Ross's female collaboration, and also by placing in chronological context his series of writings about Stanislaus in *Finnegans Wake,* the only book in which he directly addressed his brother. Somerville and Ross do not directly address each other in the more conventional stories of *The Irish R.M.,* but these cousins and their female relatives lurk behind many of these stories' characters, as we saw in the case of Violet Martin's actual "Mama" and the Mrs. Knox of the stories.

Stanislaus Joyce (1884–1955) was nearly as crucial to James Joyce (1882–1941) as Violet Martin was to Edith Somerville. Much as Somerville took an idea from Martin in order to create *The Big House of Inver,* Joyce frequently borrowed from Stanislaus, in each of his books, some of whose very titles (*Chamber Music* and *A Portrait of the Artist* as well as its earlier draft, *Stephen Hero*) had been suggested by Stanislaus. However, whereas Somerville insisted on giving her cousin full, even exaggerated credit by continuing to list her name on all of her books that she wrote solo after the other's death, Joyce's behavior was just the opposite: he continually stole his brother's ideas and even words and phrases, representing them as his own, without giving any public credit at all to Stanislaus.

These two family relationships involve a contrast between feminist collaboration and mutual support, in Somerville and Ross's case, and male sibling rivalry, competition, and creative plagiarism, in the instance of James Joyce's treatment of Stanislaus. Much as I focused on *The Irish R. M.* in tracing Somerville and Ross's collaboration, here I am particularly interested in *Finnegans Wake* as Joyce's forum for addressing his sibling conflict with his brother. The fact

10. See Cahalan 1988, 169–74 (a section subtitled "Feminist Criticism," within my comprehensive chapter on Joyce's novels and critical approaches to them).

that both of these books are comic works is significant. Much as older siblings and close cousins often carry on their relationships through jokes, jibes, and good humor, rather than through more serious communication, Somerville and Ross and Joyce worked out their own associations most memorably in comic form. In his introduction to *Blood Brothers: Siblings as Writers* (1983), Norman Kiell notes that sibling relations, especially in maturity, have been relatively little studied by psychologists, let alone literary critics (8). Given that feminist theorists have often depended on the findings of social scientists' examinations of gender roles in family relationships—as in the writings of Miller, Chodorow, and Gilligan, as outlined in the introduction to this book—it makes particular sense that we examine the family dynamics of the Somerville and Ross cousins and the Joyce brothers. Gilligan even mentions Stephen Dedalus in passing as an example of an adolescent version of male notions of "the separate self and of moral principles uncompromised by the constraints of reality" (1982, 98).

Stanislaus Joyce's career in regard to (and as dominated by) James has been amply recorded by Richard Ellmann, by Stanislaus himself in his *Dublin Diary* and *My Brother's Keeper* (1958), and by others. James's father and friends derided young Stanislaus as merely James's "jackal." Stanislaus's 1903–5 *Dublin Diary* (a source for "A Painful Case" and the *Portrait*) described how "It is terrible to have a cleverer elder brother" (1971, 50). Significantly, the very first anecdote in the *Dublin Diary* describes a very young Stanislaus playing Adam, and James the devil, in a nursery skit (1971, 3): James the tempter and Stanislaus his victim. During the decade of 1905–15, Stanislaus lived with James and Nora in Trieste, turning over his pay as an English teacher to his brother and trying to keep him out of the pubs; as Ellmann put it, "James spent the ten years getting into scrapes and . . . Stanislaus spent the ten years getting him out of them" (1958, xi). Later Stanislaus was disappointed that *Dubliners* was not dedicated to him, as James had earlier promised, and that his character (Maurice), so prominent in *Stephen Hero,* was mostly deleted from the *Portrait*. Following his period of internment during World War I, Stanislaus became estranged from James, and subsequently he dismissed the *Wake,* in the form of "Work in Progress," as "drivelling rigmarole about half a ball hat and ladies' modern toilet chambers (practically the only things I understand in this nightmare production)," adding, "It is unspeakably wearisome. . . . I for one would not read more than a paragraph of it, if

I did not know you." He concluded that the *Wake* "suggested "soft-ening of the brain" and "the witless wandering of literature before its final extinction" (quoted in Ellmann 1982, 577).

James Joyce shamelessly exploited Stanislaus from early in their lives. As Stanislaus put it in his *Dublin Diary* (writing in 1904, even before the more blatant Trieste years), "He has used me, I fancy, as a butcher uses his steel to sharpen his knife" (1971, 20). James plagiarized his writing and even tore up some of his essays during their boyhood. Although James certainly held the upper hand during his lifetime and in terms of his use of Stanislaus in his books, Stanislaus outlived James and was able to have, if not the last, at least the later word on their relationship, not only in his own book *My Brother's Keeper,* but also in Ellmann's biography, also first published in 1958. Ellmann edited and introduced *My Brother's Keeper* and relied on Stanislaus in his biography, which frequently contrasts a responsible, reliable Stanislaus with his dependent, un-reliable brother, and which Ira B. Nadel (1991) argues was overly dependent on Stanislaus. The two fullest scholarly assessments of the Joyce brothers' relationship can be found in Hélène Cixous's *The Exile of James Joyce* (1976) and Jean Kimball's "James and Stanislaus Joyce: A Jungian Speculation" (1983). Cixous and Kimball present an interesting contrast, with both of them turning to non-Western, tribal relationships in order to understand this Western author, much as Margaret Mead examined both non-Western and Western cultures in order to make sense of gender relationships, in her classic study *Male and Female* (1949).

Cixous sees James as a "cannibal" and argues that "the victim who suffered most from the cannibal was certainly Stanislaus" (1976, 120). In contrast, Kimball views the Joyce brothers' relationship as resembling interdependent tribal brothers who (in the words of ethnopsychologist Lucien Lévy-Bruhl) "make but one person: One does not steal from oneself" (quoted in Kimball 1983, 76). Noting that Stanislaus inherited James's teaching job at the University of Trieste and lived a longer and healthier life, Kimball concludes that "the extraordinarily close and complementary relationship between the Joyce brothers can be seen as a significant means of survival and indeed success for both" (77). Both Cixous and Kimball agree that Stanislaus was very sensitive about what others thought of him, whereas James was more rebellious and determined to satisfy him-self. Stanislaus was an "extravert" and James an "introvert," in the Jungian terms adopted by Kimball (rather than in the American

popular usage of these terms); the "extravert" focuses on what others think about him, whereas the "introvert" cares more about what
he thinks about himself. Agreeing with Ellmann, Kimball explains
that while their conflicts in Trieste made Stanislaus 'miserable,' as
might be expected of an extravert with his sensitivity to relationships, 'they made James comfortable,' providing the opposition which
was essential to his well-being" (1983, 104).

Both brothers also invoked the relevant biblical pairings of
Cain-Abel and Jacob-Esau. Concerning the title of his memoir, *My
Brother's Keeper,* Stanislaus remarked to Ellmann, "smiling wryly,
'You know . . . Cain" (Ellmann 1958, x). Cixous argues that "Stannie
was really a false Cain; he began as Jim's Abel, and only after ten
years of being the real keeper and undergoing great troubles did he
become Cain" (1976, 129), and explains that "when he tells Ellmann,
'You know . . . Cain,' Stanislaus becomes doubled and speaks for
Jim (hence against himself)" (131). She also notes, "In *Finnegans
Wake,* Mercius, one of the types of Shem . . . boasts to his brother
Justius of being a 'pariah, cannibal Cain' (p. 193). This was what
Joyce had been, fully and selfishly, his whole life long, making use
of others to feed his work" (119). Similarly, J. Mitchell Morse
(1954–55) pointed out many years ago that Shaun is identified
several times as Esau, who was tricked out of his inheritance by his
brother Jacob.

Stephen Hero includes a scrupulously autobiographical description of just how important Stanislaus (fictionalized as "Maurice")
was to his older brother and just how close the two of them were
when studying together in Dublin in their youth:

> Every evening after tea Stephen left his house and set out for the
> city, Maurice at his side. The elder smoked cigarettes and the
> younger ate lemon drops and, aided by these animal comforts,
> they beguiled the long journey with philosophic discourse. Maurice
> was a very attentive person and one evening he told Stephen that
> he was keeping a diary of their conversations. Stephen asked to
> see the diary but Maurice said it would be time enough for that
> at the end of the first year. (1944, 36)

Joyce goes on both to stress their similarity and to claim his own
superiority: "Both looked upon life with frank curious eyes (Maurice
naturally serving himself with Stephen's vision when his own was
deficient). . . . On their way in every evening the heights of argument were traversed and the younger boy aided the elder bravely

in the building of an entire science of esthetic. They spoke to each other very decisively and Stephen found Maurice very useful for raising objections" (36). This account concludes as follows:

> When they came to the gate of the Library they used to stand to finish some branch of their subject and often the discussion was so protracted that Stephen would decide that it was too late to go in to read and so they would set their faces for Clontarf and return in the same manner. Stephen, after certain hesitations, showed Maurice the first-fruits of his verse and Maurice asked who the woman was. Stephen looked a little vaguely before him before answering and in the end had to answer that he didn't know who she was. (36)

A dozen pages later, however, Joyce abruptly puts an end to brotherly intimacy with the explanation that "the evening walks with Maurice had been prohibited for it had become evident that Stephen was corrupting his brother to idle habits" (48). "Maurice accepted this prohibition with a bad grace and had to be restrained by his brother from overt disobedience" (49).

Joyce wrote his brother almost entirely out of *A Portrait of the Artist as a Young Man,* as part of his extensive revision process that generally increased the spotlight on Stephen while pushing several other characters (including also his young female friend Emma Clery, for example) to the margins of the novel (see Reynolds 1988). Here "Maurice" is seen only amidst his several other, similarly unnamed siblings as they wait outside Christmas dinner "in the nursery . . . till the pudding came" (1916, 39), while Stephen sits amidst the adults in his "Eton jacket" (39). The unnamed "brother" similarly waits amidst the lesser cousins outside the Bank of Ireland while Stephen goes in to collect his award for winning an essay contest (92).

Significantly, the only time that "Maurice"/Stanislaus is named and described in the *Portrait* is when their father treats him as a second-class sibling in contrast to Stephen, who has been sent to the best boarding school and always gets his hands first on the family food:

> —O, Holy Paul, I forgot about Maurice, said Mr Dedalus. Here, Maurice! Come here, you thickheaded ruffian! Do you know I'm going to send you to a college where they'll teach you to spell c.a.t.: cat. And I'll buy you a nice little penny handkerchief to keep your nose dry. Won't that be grand fun.

> Maurice grinned at his father and then at his brother. Mr
> Dedalus screwed his glass into his eye and stared hard at both his
> sons. Stephen mumbled his bread without answering his father's
> gaze. (72)

Subsequently, Stephen's mother washes her favored son even when
he is a university student, which provokes his father to call him a
"lazy bitch," to which Stephen replies, "He has a curious idea of
genders if he thinks a bitch is masculine" (154).

Stephen later shows a brief glimmer of guilt about his own
privileged status as the white-headed boy of the family, at the
expense of his disenfranchised siblings, when we read of "a sudden
instinct of remorse in Stephen's heart. All that had been denied
them had been freely given to him, the eldest; but the quiet glow
of evening showed him in their faces no sign of rancour" (145). But
he does nothing about it. Lest the reader wonder if Stanilaus's
importance and Joyce's generally callous indifference to his siblings
were matters of fact rather than just fiction, listen to his telling
remark in a letter to Nora in August 1904: "My brothers and
sisters are nothing to me. . . . One brother alone is capable of understanding me" (quoted in Kimball 1983, 74). In February 1905,
he wrote Stanislaus about the *Portrait*, "Your criticism of my novel
is always interesting" (Joyce 1966, 52).

Before he wrote his brother mostly out of the *Portrait*, Joyce
had already made important use of him in *Dubliners*. After reading
Stanislaus's report of their father's remark when going to a religious
retreat with his friends, "I bar the candles," Joyce inserted the line
in "Grace." Similarly, Stanislaus's sarcastic account in a letter of
serving with their father on an election committee helped inspire
Joyce's favorite story in the collection, "Ivy Day in the Committee
Room" (Ellmann 1982, 133). Even more telling was Joyce's use and
plagiarism of Stanislaus in "A Painful Case," which was based partly
on Stanislaus's description of meeting a married woman at a con-
cert. Joyce also included in this story two specific lines from
Stanislaus's journal, among his aphorisms which James derided to
him as "Bile Beans": "Every bond is a bond to sorrow," and "Love
between man and man is impossible because there must not be
sexual intercourse and friendship between man and woman is impossible because there must be sexual intercourse" (quoted in
Ellmann 1982, 133). The portrayal of Mr. Duffy as a despicable and
heartless prig, who turns his heart against the pathetic Mrs. Sinico,

surely must have offended Stanislaus to the extent that he saw that it was a caricature of him.

Also relevant in this context is Cixous's fascinating argument that in fact Joyce did not so much delete Stanislaus/"Maurice" from the *Portrait* as subsume him into the character of Stephen (1976, 146), who becomes very much a pedantic prig himself, as many critics have noted. She notes that Stanislaus's *Dublin Diary* and the *Portrait* are closely comparable in many cases (147–48). It was Joyce's habit to plagiarize Stanislaus not only in his writings, but in his everyday life; Stanislaus noticed, for example, how James dismissed a clever quip of his when Stanislaus made it to him, but then repeated it to a friend the following day as if it were his own (Ellmann 1982, 134). This habit of plagiarism began very early. After a librarian warned their father that adolescent James was "reading dangerous books," Joyce sent his unwitting brother to check out *Jude the Obscure* for him. "Stanislaus, confused by what he had heard of Hardy, started out to ask the librarian for *Jude the Obscene*. Joyce liked this slip so well that in later life he told the story as if it had happened to him and not to Stanislaus" (Ellmann 1982, 53–54).

The simultaneous removal and absorption of Stanislaus are even more complete in *Ulysses*. On the one hand, we can note that he does not appear at all there; in "Wandering Rocks," Stephen encounters only his sisters, feeling particular and brief guilt about one of them, Dilly. On the other hand, Stanislaus may be a shadow figure who is actually almost everywhere in *Ulysses*. Kimball (1988) argues that the character of Leopold Bloom was based partly on Stanislaus, and that the encounter of Bloom and Stephen, in which a cautious Bloom tries to take care of a drunken and reckless Stephen, is a version of the Joyce brothers' relationship, especially during their Trieste years. Neither Stanislaus nor Bloom liked Joyce's flippant friend Oliver Gogarty (Buck Mulligan), for example. Given that Bloom is Joyce's hero, whereas Stephen is revealed as a failed artist in *Ulysses* and a parody of Joyce himself, then if Stanislaus is Bloom's shadow, we can discover a concealed softening of Joyce's attitude toward Stanislaus in this novel, a process continued in *Finnegans Wake*. Norman Kiell notes the common pattern whereby siblings mellow to each other as they grow older and live farther apart (1983, 43). Much as Joyce (by then a nostalgic expatriate who had not lived in Ireland for many years) portrayed Ireland much more positively in *Finnegans Wake* than he had in the *Portrait*, similarly he addressed Stanislaus sympathetically and plaintively in the *Wake* after having treated him more poorly in the *Portrait*.

Stanislaus's view that "Love between man and man is impossible because there must not be sexual intercourse and friendship between man and woman is impossible because there must be sexual intercourse" can be read as a revealing comment on his relationship with his brother and Nora. He was always very devoted to his brother, to the point that he was jealous of Nora. When James fell in love with Nora, in 1904, Stanislaus even tried to convince Nora to drop him (Ellmann 1982, 160), and when James returned to Trieste from a period away in Dublin, in 1909, and he and Nora "encountered each other . . . like bride and bridegroom," it was "to the secret disgust of Stanislaus" (300). Ellmann adds that Stanislaus "felt some jealousy too, at his brother's hold over Nora, whom he also found very attractive, and he was sensitive to her indifference to him" (312).

Moreover, Stanislaus's service to his brother, especially during the Trieste years, followed a stereotypical female (more than male) pattern: he fished him out of bars, for example; he stayed at his house; he turned over his income; and in general he was there as much to serve James and Nora as to live his own independent life. Whereas Nora was James's wife, it can be argued that symbolically (rather than literally), Stanislaus was his "whore." I advance this idea in line with the thinking of Sandra Gilbert and Susan Gubar, who write that for Joyce in the "Circe" episode of *Ulysses*, "to become a female or to be like a female is not only figuratively but literally to be de-graded, to lose one's place in the preordained hierarchy that patriarchal culture associates with gender. If this is so, however, Joyce is also hinting that to be a woman is inevitably to be degraded, to be 'a thing under the yoke'" (1988, 333).

According to such an interpretation, as the figure of the exploited, nonsexual "woman," Stanislaus could be (and was) later replaced by literal women who gave James Joyce financial and other support, such as Harriet Shaw Weaver, Sylvia Beach, and the other female patrons who replaced Stanislaus after World War I when Joyce moved to Paris. Stanislaus was jealous of these women, too. He turned increasingly against his brother's writing after World War I, believing that it took a turn for the worse and lost all discipline after he moved to Paris. Having earlier sung the praises of *Dubliners* and the *Portrait*, Stanislaus was mixed about *Ulysses*, writing to James, "Dublin is spread out before the reader," but adding, according to

Ellmann, "that parts of it were merely technical monstrosities, and that the whole of it lacked serenity and warmth. He disliked the *Circe* episode," the chapter closest to the subsequent style of the *Wake,* "and was bored and repelled by *Penelope.* He also insistently laid claim to some of the ideas in the book, but got no confirmation from his brother" (1982, 531). As we have already seen, he scorned the *Wake,* viewing it as "a waste" (Ellmann 1958, x).

Even previous to his years in Trieste, Stanislaus himself referred to "whoring," in his diary in September 1903, as a term by which to distinguish himself from his brother:

> It is terrible to have a cleverer older brother. I get small credit for originality. . . . Jim, I think, has even taken a few opinions from me. In some things, however, I have never followed him. In drinking, for instance, in whoring, in speaking broadly, in being frank without reserve with others, . . . in mannner, in ambition, and not always in friendships. I perceive that he regards me as quite commonplace and uninteresting—he makes no attempt at disguise—and though I follow him fully in this matter of opinion I cannot be expected to like it. It is a matter beyond the power of either of us to help. (1971, 134)

Stanislaus's diary entries reflect his love/hate attitude to James, shifting among the following series of reactions: "I do not like Jim" (1971, 50); "I am wrong . . . in saying I dislike Jim. I have no liking for him but I see that his life is interesting" (75); "I wrote once that I dislike Jim, but I see now how I was led to believe a lie" (143); and "I think I understand Jim, however, and like him in the way of admiration" (144).

Their blood-brother relationship clearly remained important to both brothers after their estrangement. In James's case, he spent seventeen years trying to sort it out in *Finnegans Wake.* He offered a copy of the *Wake* to his brother in 1939, but Stanislaus refused it. Raleigh described James's address to "Stainusless" in the *Wake* as a delicious instance of "the guilty forgiving the innocent," concluding that "the moral would seem to be this: that it is infinitely easier for the guilty to forgive the innocent for the presumption of proffered guidance than it is for the innocent to forgive the guilty for not taking that guidance" (1953, 110).

How *did* James Joyce treat Stanislaus in *Finnegans Wake*? In his *Dublin Diary,* Stanislaus reported that their old family friend John Kelly (the Mr. Casey of the *Portrait*) had a song for each member of the Joyce family; his song for Stanislaus was "Finnegan's Wake."

And there is certainly much of Stanislaus in the *Wake*. For example, Shaun "insinuates that all the ideas are his (as did Stanislaus Joyce): 'robbing leaves out of my taletold book' (453.18) . . . The stories he does tell to humiliate Shem—the Mookse and the Gripes, Burrus and Caseous, and the Ondt and the Gracehoper—all backfire and make him look ridiculous" (Begnal and Eckley 1975, 54). Similarly, William York Tindall paraphrased pages 422–24 of the *Wake* as follows: "The letter, says Shaun, is his in part. Indeed, Shem stole the entire document from Shaun; for, at this point, he is clearly Stanislaus Joyce" (1959, 289). Elsewhere, Tindall claimed, Shaun blames his brother "for not having taken a job in Guinness's brewery or for not having become a priest (190.13–28)" (137), whereas Shem calls Shaun "a plain clothes priest" (1959, 88).

In these ways, James Joyce's use of Stanislaus in the *Wake* has been cited often, but not systematically traced. After reviewing what we already know about Stanislaus's most obvious appearances in the *Wake,* I want to analyze the chronology, point of view, and placement of five key chapters and what they show us about Joyce's changing attitudes to Stanislaus. At least since John Henry Raleigh's 1953 article on the subject, it has been recognized and noted frequently that Stanislaus was a leading source for the character of Shaun (in his various manifestations) and that the Shem-Shaun relationship is largely a working out of Joyce's closest sibling relationship.[11] Shem and Shaun are twins; Kiell calls them Doppelgängers, "striking examples of the difficulties twins have with the problem of individuation" (1983, 40). Raleigh cited the single most direct address to Stanislaus, in book 2, chapter 1 (called "The Children's Hour" by Campbell and Robinson [1961, 19, 142]), in which Joyce appears to invite his brother to get back in touch with him and come see him:[12]

> —Enchainted, dear sweet Stainusless, young confessor, dearer dearest, . . . our barnaboy, . . . send us, your adorables, . . . a wise

11. I recognize that there were other sources for the character of Shaun (such as Gogarty), but I do not agree with Ellsworth Mason, who claimed in his dissenting "Mr. Stanislaus Joyce and John Henry Raleigh" that "What Raleigh considers Joyce's letter to the world about his brother's 'purity' is actually a multi-level phallic worship and is not about Stanislaus Joyce" (1955, 191). Stanislaus is clearly addressed on page 237 of *Finnegans Wake* and was the leading source for Shaun.

12. Like the other chapter "titles" listed below in my chart, this one is borrowed from the *Skeleton Key* for convenience's sake. As in *Ulysses,* Joyce listed no chapter titles in *Finnegans Wake.*

and letters play of all you can ceive, chief celtech chappy, from
your holy post now you hast ascertained ceremonially our names.
Unclean you art not. Outcaste thou are not. . . . You are pure. You
are pure. You are in your puerity. You have not brought stinking
members into the house of Amanti. . . . Your head has been touched
by the god Enel-Rah and your face has been brightened by the
goddess Aruc-Ituc. Return, sainted youngling, and walk once more
among us! (237.11–30)

Cixous argues that "here Stanislaus is in chains, a confessor, pure,
puerile, stainless, useless . . . everything Joyce detested" (1976, 159).
At the same time, there is a positive, even imploring quality to his
invitation to his brother to return to him. The complex quality of his
attitude toward Stanislaus is reflected in his very name in the passage
above, "Stainusless," which could be read variously as positive (stainless), negative (useless), or ambivalently beseeching ("stain us less," or
"don't condemn myself and Nora for how we treated you").

Was James Joyce out to deride Stanislaus or to heal the rift
between them? We can advance our understanding of James's treatment of Stanislaus in the *Wake* a step further by looking specifically
at the key chapters in which the Stanislaus/Shaun character figures
and in which James addresses or alludes to his brother. Several
scholars have cited allusions to Stanislaus in the *Wake,* but no one
has closely considered the most relevant chapters in terms of the
chronology of their composition and revision, in order to discover
the pattern of Joyce's developing presentations of and attitudes
toward his brother. I list below the five chapters in which Stanislaus/
Shaun is most central or addressed most directly, in the order in
which these chapters were composed and revised (rather than in the
order in which they appear in the *Wake*):

Book Chapter	Pages	Chapter "Title"	Composition/ Revision Dates
III.1	403–28	"Shaun before the People"	1924–29[13]
III.2	429–73	"Jaun before St. Bride's"	1924–28
III.3	474–554	"Yawn under Inquest"	1924–30
I.7	169–93	"Shem the Penman"	1924–27, 1936–38
II.1	219–58	"The Children's Hour"	1930–34, 1937–38

13. My dates are taken from Hayman's "Draft Catalogue" in *A First-Draft
Version of "Finnegans Wake"* (Joyce 1963), 319–21 (for III.1); 319–20, 321–22 (for
III.2); 322–24 (for III.3); 300–2 (for I.7); and 305 (for II.1).

We know that Joyce wrote the *Wake* in a "circular" fashion, continually working on sections scattered throughout the whole book and adding more and more allusions, puns, and other details all the way through—rather than composing the book in the traditional linear way, from the beginning to the end. Thus, it is no surprise that the three chapters in book 3 on "Shaun," "Jaun," and "Yawn" were completed earlier, but placed later in the *Wake,* than "Shem the Penman" and "The Children's Hour." But it is worth reexamining these five chapters, in the order in which Joyce wrote and completed them, to see what we can learn about Stanislaus/Shaun.

The sharpest chronological distinction reflected in my chart is that Joyce worked on "The Children's Hour," in which the celebrated "Stainusless" passage occurs, entirely during the 1930s, after he had completed all work on the "Shaun," "Jaun," and "Yawn" chapters during the 1920s. We can therefore compare his 1920s and 1930s presentations of Stanislaus. When we do so, a contrast quickly emerges. The 1920s "Shaun," "Jaun," and "Yawn" chapters are dominated by satiric parodies of Stanislaus. However, in the 1930s "Children's Hour," Joyce mocks himself at least as much as he makes fun of Stanislaus, confessionally deriding himself and openly addressing "Stainusless." Even more self-critical is "Shem the Penman," which Joyce began in 1924 but then added to and revised in his last period of work on the book during 1936–1938. In these instances, we see Joyce laughing both "at" and "with," in Elizabeth Stanley Trotter's terminology about male versus female humor, or moving from laughing more "at" Stanislaus, earlier on, to laughing more "with" him and "at" himself later.

The "Shaun"-"Jaun"-"Yawn" chapters were examined by Larry Smith in order to try to answer the question, "Why would Joyce, so rigorous a taskmaster . . . expend so much time, space, and energy in exploring . . . Shaun-Jaun-Yawn . . . his most despised character?" (1986, 561). Smith's answer is that Shaun-Jaun-Yawn is a reincarnation of HCE, and that these three chapters are therefore an important bridge between the HCE chapters that precede and follow them, for "Clearly the historical cycle will regenerate" (566–67). If Smith is correct and Shaun (rather than Shem) is HCE's true successor, then these chapters are truly very much James's revenge on Stanislaus: the revenge of the guilty on the innocent. Stanislaus detested John Joyce, their father and a main source for HCE, much more thoroughly than did James. Father and son shared the same exact name, John Stanislaus Joyce, but Stanislaus abandoned his father's first name and renounced his father. So James brings him back as his father's clone: Shaun (Seán, the Gaelic of "John"). Aptly, this section begins with HCE dreaming of Shaun (403.18–22).

The very names "Shaun," "Jaun," and "Yawn" reflect Joyce's successive versions of Stanislaus in these three chapters as a copy of HCE, a ludicrous Lothario, and finally a bore who induces sleep. Shaun attacks Shem but seems ridiculous in doing so; his authorial interlocutor replies to these attacks by asking "How?" (422.22, 424.25) and "Why?" (424.16) and by wondering why, if Shaun is so upset with Shem's writing, he has not accomplished any writing himself. Stanislaus reported that James once baited him in the same way, suggesting to him in Trieste, "You ought to start writing yourself, now that I've 'gone on the beer,' " to which he replied, "I have no talent" (1971, 248). In the *Wake* Shaun can only pathetically respond that he will do so "one of these fine days, man dear, when the mood is on me" (425.24–25). Stanislaus's two main complaints about James—that his later writing was too obscure and that he drank too much—are succinctly summarized and lampooned when Jaun tells us that Shem, or "Dave the Dancekerl" (whom he subsequently calls an "Illstarred punster" [467.29]), "would be the unicorn of his kind" (462.20) "could he quit doubling and stop tippling" (462.19–20).

In "Shem the Penman" and "The Children's Hour," Joyce's parody and humor are turned much more onto himself (in the form of Shem, "short for Shemus" [169.1] or Séamus, the Gaelic of "James"). Self-mockery and self-criticism dominate "Shem the Penman." The tone is set at the beginning: "Shem was a sham and a low sham" (170.25). The theme of exile that seemed so elevated in the *Portrait* is now laid low: "He even ran away with hunself . . . saying he would far sooner muddle through the hash on lentils in Europe than meddle with Irrland's split little pea" (171.4–6). The *Portrait* was written "to kill time" (173.11), whereas *Ulysses* was "his usylessly unreadable Blue Book of Eccles" in which he was "telling himself delightedly . . . that every splurge on the vellum he blundered over was an aisling vision more gorgeous than the one before" (179.26–27, 179.29–32). He freely accepts any and all of Shaun's accusations; appropriately, Shem openly calls himself "an Irish emigrant the wrong way out" (190.36) who would "sing us a song of alibi" (190.29). None of these quoted sections are found in the version of "Shem the Penman" in Hayman's edition of the *First-Draft Version of "Finnegans Wake"* (Joyce 1963); presumably Joyce added many of his most pointed passages of self-ridicule during his later work on this chapter.

Shem's thoroughgoing attacks on himself set him up to invite his old adversary, Stanislaus/Shaun, to "walk once more among us!" (237.30). His direct address to "Stainusless" in "The Children's Hour"—what Raleigh calls "the guilty forgiving the innocent"—comes in a chapter that Joyce began and completed entirely in the 1930s, during a period when he and Stanislaus were almost completely out of touch with each other. Ellmann includes no reference to direct contact between the two brothers from 1929 until 1936, following Stanislaus's attacks on "Work in Progress" in 1924 and 1926 and his marriage in 1927. It appears that late in his life, Joyce missed Stanislaus and their difficult but rich yin/yang relationship, and felt moved in his masterpiece to address him directly (as directly as he invokes anyone in the *Wake*). In contrast to the earlier-composed "Shaun"-"Jaun"-"Yawn" chapters so devoted to lampooning Stanislaus/Shaun, "The Children's Hour" is a fairly balanced account of the two brothers in their manifestations as "Glugg" (James/Shem, "the bold bad bleak boy of the story books" [219.24]) and "Chuff" (Stanislaus/Shaun, "the fine frank fairhaired fellow of the fairytales, who wrestles for tophole with . . . Glugg" [220.12–13]). Of course, Joyce has it both ways, since his more negative "Shaun"-"Jaun"-"Yawn" chapters may have been written earlier, but they were placed later in the *Wake*. Joyce intended that his book be "circular," but most readers move in a linear way from Joyce's self-mockery in "Shem the Penman" and "The Children's Hour," in books 1 and 2, to the dismissal of Stanislaus/"Shaun"/ "Jaun"/"Yawn" in book 3.

Stanislaus refused the proffered copy of *Finnegans Wake* in 1939, but James's invitation to "Stainusless" to "walk once more among us!" was accepted after James's death in 1941. On the one hand, Stanislaus held to his view that "If I had been at his elbow, *Finnegans Wake* would never have been written in its present form," as noted in his 1949 article in *The Listener,* which would develop into *My Brother's Keeper* (897; quoted in Kiell 1983, 20). But he did read the *Wake,* finding there not only his brother's address to "Stainusless," but also such passages as this one in the tale of the "Ondt" (another version of Stanislaus/Shaun) and the "Gracehoper" (James/Shem): "I forgive you, grondt Ondt, said the Gracehoper, weeping" (418.12). This was positively "the guilty forgiving the innocent." Ellmann explains that James had depended upon Stanislaus's savings especially during the summer months, when their students would leave Trieste but there were still pints to be drunk: "When he revamped in *Finnegans Wake* the fable of the dancing grasshopper and the saving ant, who had a seasonal problem too, he drew upon his experience with his brother by letting the improvident grasshopper carry the day" (1958, xvi). Stanislaus wrote in "James Joyce: A Memoir" (1941), "When *Finnegans Wake* was published . . . my brother wrote to me offering a copy in homage. I refused it. . . . There is little need to tell how much regret this refusal has since cost me—even less need when the uselessness of regret is considered" (497; quoted in Benstock 1965, 220–21).

It undoubtedly made an impression on Stanislaus that his brother's last letter, five days before his death in 1941, was a note to him in Italian in which James offered Stanislaus the names and addresses of several contacts who might prove helpful to him, and concluded, "Saluti da tutti" or (as translated by Ellmann) "Greetings from all of us" (Joyce 1966, 409; letter of 4 January 1941). One might note with peculiar irony the fact that Stanislaus himself died in 1955 on Bloomsday, June 16, the date commemorating his brother's first meeting in 1904 with Stanislaus's rival for his brother's affections, Nora. As is well known, after James Joyce's death Stanislaus championed his work and was a key, supportive source for Ellmann's biography. The only books Stanislaus ever published were about his brother, and the later *My Brother's Keeper* (1958) was much more positive about him than the earlier *Dublin Diary* of 1903–5. He named his only son James in 1943. Thus, once more James prevailed on Stanislaus; the pleas in the *Wake* of "the guilty forgiving the innocent" were heard and answered.

❦

In his classic book *The Irish Comic Tradition* (1962), Vivian Mercier quoted examples from both *The Irish R. M.* ("Lisheen Races, Second-Hand," 67) and *Finnegans Wake* (58–59) of what he described, according to the title of the chapter in which he cites both of them, as "Macabre and Grotesque Humour in the Irish Tradition," arguing that these writers and many other Irish writers in English followed comic conventions of the old Gaelic tradition even "without being fully aware of it" (236). Except for Somerville and Ross, the writers Mercier examined were virtually all male. *The Comic Tradition in Irish Women Writers* (O'Connor 1996b), a collection of essays edited by Theresa O'Connor, corrects Mercier's oversight, arguing that Irish women writers' humor can best be understood not only within the Irish tradition, but also in comparison with the comedy of other oppressed groups, such as African Americans.[14] What neither book does, however, is compare and contrast the comedy of Irish men and women; Mercier's book concentrates on men and O'Connor's on women.

My own study of *The Irish R. M.* and *Finnegans Wake* suggests significant parallels as well as key differences between these marvelous female and male books. On the one hand, both works can be read in a feminist light; like Somerville and Ross, in Trotter's terminology, Joyce laughs both "at" and "with." He may make fun of Stanislaus in the form of Shaun, but a great deal of his sharpest and wildest humor is aimed at himself in the shape of Shem—much as Somerville and Ross poke fun at peasants but generally play their biggest jokes on the R. M. himself, the representative of their own Ascendancy class. Moreover, in *Ulysses* as well as the *Wake,* we see Joyce moving away from an egocentric focus on a single male— Stephen in the *Portrait*—into a much more diverse set of characters. Bloom may dominate *Ulysses,* but he comes in sympathetic contact with many others; he is the kind of man (to cite just one small but significant example) who worries about women not being able to find a bathroom in the city center of Dublin (1922, 175). Then in the *Wake,* "here comes everybody"; it is perhaps the most democratic novel ever published in terms of its range of characters. The *Wake* and *The Irish R. M.* are similar in their episodic, encyclopedic styles: in both cases the comedy depends not on coming fairly concisely to the point, as in O. Henry or James Thurber, but on always rambling on, piling joke upon joke.

On the other hand, as we have seen in some detail, these two books—and these authors' other works discussed in this chapter— were written in virtually opposite ways: Somerville and Ross depended on mutual support and constant collaboration, whereas Joyce's method was self-centered and avaricious, cannibalizing not only his own brother's ideas and words but those of many others for his own

14. A version of my essay " 'Humor with a Gender': Somerville and Ross and *The Irish R. M.*"—the original version of which appeared in *Éire-Ireland* in 1993 (as listed on my acknowledgments page)—appeared in Theresa O'Connor's collection (1996b, 58–72) and provided the basis for my discussion of *The Irish R. M.* in the present chapter.

fictional stew. If Joyce were not one of the most brilliant and funny writers in history, we would probably not forgive him for being also among the most egotistical and greedy. This was a writer who told Yeats—in 1902, when Joyce was twenty and Yeats thirty-seven, in the middle of his career with his greatest poems still to come—that he had met the poet too late, as Yeats himself later recounted (Ellmann 1982, 103). Joyce fully believed that he would become the greatest novelist ever to walk the face of the earth. And he backed up his arrogance with superlative writing.

The contrast between the collaborative, feminist duo of Somerville and Ross and the monolithic, male personage of Joyce may be the most compelling example that I have to offer in this book, because these behaviors dominated these writers' very lives, not just their writings. The contrast between male separation and female cooperation that social scientists such as Gilligan and Chodorow have observed in human behavior is very evident in Joyce and in Somerville and Ross. These patterns are perpetuated in the fictional characters of other Irish women and men who all wrote solo. Central female pairs are also repeatedly found not only in the fiction of Somerville and Ross (Charlotte Mullen and Francie Fitzgerald in *The Real Charlotte*), but likewise in Lawless (the sisters Grania and Honor in *Grania*), as we have already seen, as well as in the works of the women to whom we turn next: Kate O'Brien's Helen Archer and Anna Murphy in *The Land of Spices,* and Edna O'Brien's Kate Brady and Baba Brennan in *The Country Girls Trilogy*. Similarly, we find many male conflicts and the traces of Joyce's solitary Stephen in the autobiographical protagonists of the men studied next: John McGahern's unnamed protagonist in *The Dark,* and Brian Moore's Gavin Burke in *The Emperor of Ice-Cream*.

4

Female and Male Perspectives on Growing Up Irish

Edna O'Brien, John McGahern, and Brian Moore

The bildungsroman—a novel describing its protagonist's coming of age—more closely examines a character's early, formative life experiences than any other type of fiction. The contrasting cases of Somerville and Ross versus Joyce offered striking examples of male-female differences, because of the ways in which these patterns were reflected in these authors' very lives. Bildungsromans such as Joyce's *Portrait* are among the closest fictional analogues to such real lives, since they describe young, autobiographical protagonists who come of age. This coming of age is all tied up with gender, as Nancy Chodorow reminds us when she makes the crucial distinction that separation is the key of the adolescent growth process for boys, whereas for girls separation is less important and relationships more central (1978, 93). In my last chapter I stressed how Joyce revised *A Portrait of the Artist as a Young Man* so as to maximize the spotlight on the boyhood and adolescence of his egocentric, autobiographical protagonist, Stephen Dedalus, while marginalizing other characters such as women and Stephen's brother Maurice, his version of Stanislaus Joyce. It is thus no surprise that Stephen Dedalus is the fictional character named by Carol Gilligan as epitomizing the "separate self" of the adolescent male (1982, 98). When Stephen prepares at novel's end to leave Ireland alone—not in the company of Nora, as Joyce actually did in that year of 1904—and declares, "I go to encounter for the millionth time the reality of experience and to forge in the smithy of my soul the uncreated conscience of my race" (1916, 218), his is only a particularly grandiose statement of the late-adolescent male's need to feel separate. No doubt part of why the *Portrait* appealed to so many readers (including the influential, male-dominated first generation of Joyce critics) was

that Stephen's assertions reinforced their own glorification of separation and individuality—ideals which are peculiarly Western and
male, but which were taken to be normative and universal.

Stephen's male separation anxiety was increased by the alien-
ation of modernism and his Irish rebelliousness. In contrast to
Goethe's *Wilhelm Meister* and nineteenth-century bildungsromans,
modern and contemporary bildungsromans have required critics to
revise their traditional definitions. Noting that bildungsromans no
longer conclude consistently with the protagonist's success in the
big city, Jeffrey Sammons (1991), for example, argues that it is the
process (the *Bildung*)—not the protagonist's success or failure—that
matters, and that makes a bildungsroman. Gregory Castle (1989)
notes that in his *Portrait,* Joyce substitutes exile for the traditional
bildungsroman's journey to the city, and that rather than take his
place in society like Wilhelm Meister, Stephen Dedalus rejects
society, both British and Irish.

The *Portrait* is of course the most influential modern bildungsroman for Irish as well as for many other novelists. But especially
in a book addressing gender differences, I want to add a second
important model and precursor: the 1941 novel *The Land of Spices*
by Kate O'Brien (1897–1974), the upper-middle-class County Lim-
erick woman who became one of the best Irish novelists. This work
has gained increasing critical appreciation in recent years as an
important mid-century feminist model for contemporary Irish
women writers. Ludicrously banned because of a single sentence
referring obliquely to Helen Archer's father's homosexual relationship, *The Land of Spices* examines the friendship that develops between Helen, the English mother superior of an Irish convent, and
Anna Murphy, a young student in her convent school. Helen ends
up making it possible for Anna to go to University College, Dublin
on a scholarship—despite the opposition of Anna's domineering
grandmother, who identifies for Helen the crucial difference why
Anna must be denied the same scholarship that her older brother
Harry was allowed to accept: "Harry is, after all, a man" (1941,
259). This novel employs a very realistic style, an often epistolary
framework, and an ending in which young Anna goes off to Dublin
to find her way in the world. In general this novel compellingly
explores the parallel growth of Helen and Anna, with each learning
from and supporting the other. Both Helen and Anna have lost the
most important person in their lives—Helen's father, Anna's brother
Charlie—and they take solace in their own positive, nurturing

relationship. Though Helen and Anna are more than thirty years apart in age, the platonic, mutually supportive nature of their relationship makes it possible for each to survive in a man's world, as was the case in Somerville and Ross's actual lives.

The Land of Spices is closer to the classic form of the traditional bildungsroman than the *Portrait* is, as Anna goes to the big city at the end to make her way in the world. It was clearly influenced by the *Portrait,* with a setting dominated by a Catholic boarding school (and eventually University College, Dublin) and with an ending in which Anna's "wings were grown and she was for the world" (281). *The Land of Spices* even opens in 1904, Joyce's epiphanic year in both the *Portrait* and *Ulysses*. Like Stephen, Anna feels that she must be "cunning" (1941, 157)—a survival skill perhaps even more necessary for a young woman than a young man. Declan Kiberd reminds us that Stephen's celebrated strategies in the *Portrait* of "silence, exile, and cunning" are traditional feminine survival tactics (1985, 173). If Anna echoes Stephen Dedalus, Helen is her Bloom—foreign in origin, older, unsettled yet directed, gradually becoming a surrogate parent and guide for the younger character.

However, *The Land of Spices* departs from Joyce's focus on Stephen as an isolated male protagonist—one feature of *Portrait* that is quite traditional. Instead, Kate O'Brien creates a double-female bildungsroman: she interrelates the growth of *two* protagonists, showing us how each depends on the other, much as Somerville and Ross did in their actual lives and as Grania and Honor did in Lawless's novel *Grania*. Indeed, Mitzi Myers (1988) has indentifed a "double-voiced narrative" tradition in Irish women's bildungsromans running all the way back to Maria Edgeworth.

Kate O'Brien shows us how these protagonists are able to succeed partly because of the female institution in which they live and work: the convent, which is as positive an overall force here as it is negative in Julia O'Faolain's *No Country for Young Men*. As we shall see in my next chapter, a convent is merely Judith Clancy's prison in O'Faolain's novel, closer to the *Portrait,* where the convent is glimpsed only second-hand in the form of a mad, screeching nun. For Edna O'Brien's young girls Caithleen Brady and Baba Brennan, the convent is also a bad place, a restrictive institution in which they deliberately get in trouble so that they can be expelled from it. C. L. Innes notes that Irish convents have been both conservative and progressive, institutionalizing women in an inferior place yet also providing a career outlet for women to be teachers and leaders

(1993, 120–21). The religious life offers Helen Archer a career ladder that she can climb and that is unavailable to her in secular Irish life, and for Anna Murphy the convent is a refuge from her family, which is useless to her after her brother's death. Among this novel's best scenes are those in which Helen is able to use the power of her position to tell off oppressive characters such as the condescending Father Conroy, the cruel Mother Mary Andrew, and Anna's conservative and domineering grandmother.

In its attention to how Anna and Helen depend on each other for their mutual growth, however, *The Land of Spices* is much closer to contemporary women's bildungsromans such as Alice Walker's *The Color Purple* than it is to Joyce's *Portrait*. Stephen Dedalus develops by arrogantly separating himself from everyone else—a characteristic for which feminists and others have faulted him. Anna Murphy and Helen Archer grow together. The *Portrait* and *The Land of Spices* thus provide bipolar models for coming of age: male versus female.

These polar opposites continue to dominate the bildungsromans of contemporary Irish writers. What was it like growing up in Ireland in the 1940s, when *The Land of Spices* was published, according to contemporary Irish novelists who have sought to recapture the experience? Part of the answer may be found by examining Edna O'Brien's *The Country Girls* (1960) and its sequels, *The Lonely Girl* (1962) and *Girls in Their Married Bliss* (1964); John McGahern's *The Dark* (1965); and Brian Moore's *The Emperor of Ice-Cream* (1965). These novels were among the most popular Irish novels and the most celebrated bildungsromans of the early 1960s. All published within a single five-year period, they went a long way toward setting the tone of contemporary Irish fiction in general, especially since they were early novels by writers with long, ongoing, prodigious, and influential careers. Here I am interested in reassessing these novels as part of the subgenre of the Irish bildungsroman and in terms of their sharp gender differences. Falling prey to the pattern criticized in my introduction, previous critics have tended to treat McGahern and Moore in superficially neutral terms as simply "novelists" or "Irish novelists," while more readily foregrounding O'Brien's status as a "woman novelist." I want to examine gender issues in all three of these novelists, both female and male. After the following introduction situating all three of them in critical and historical contexts, in the body of this chapter I then discuss O'Brien, McGahern, and

Moore in sequence, pursuing a number of comparisons and contrasts in each section as well as in my conclusion.

Although each of these three novelists has attracted a number of insightful articles, each has had to suffer critical neglect not only in the broader literary canon (in which most Irish writers beyond Yeats and Joyce are neglected), but even in the standard surveys of Irish literature itself.[1] This is true even though each of these three writers has been described as among the most successful contemporary Irish novelists, with either Moore or McGahern often evaluated as the best. Cóilín Owens's claim for McGahern is not unusual among critical pronouncements about these writers: "McGahern's reputation as the leading Irish novelist is sure" (1980, 400). Yet these three leading Irish novelists have attracted a total of only five critical books to date.[2]

These novels also lend themselves to close comparison and contrast because they all dealt largely with the same historical period in Ireland, the repressive 1940s, as examined by three authors born within a dozen or so years of each other. Moore was born in 1921, O'Brien in 1930, and McGahern in 1934. This was a time when such innocent classics as Kate O'Brien's *The Land of Spices* (1941) and Eric Cross's *The Tailor and Ansty* (1942) were banned, when

---

1. Neither Seamus Deane in his *Short History of Irish Literature* (1986) nor A. Norman Jeffares in *Anglo-Irish Literature* (1982) even mention Edna O'Brien, with Jeffares also omitting McGahern altogether and Deane failing to refer to Moore's *The Emperor of Ice-Cream*. In their *Short History of Anglo-Irish Literature* (1982), Roger McHugh and Maurice Harmon did mention each of these three novelists, but they do not discuss any of O'Brien's novels, nor do they cite *The Emperor of Ice-Cream*. Neither the limitations of space nor the date of publication provide an adequate excuse, since in a survey published earlier than any of these others, and less than a quarter of the length of any of them, *Anglo-Irish Literature* (1980), Augustine Martin managed to include astute if brief comments on each of the novels under consideration here. See my own book *The Irish Novel: A Critical History* (1988) for overviews of O'Brien (286–89), McGahern (271–75), and Moore (266–71).

2. McGahern and O'Brien have each attracted only one critical book. Grace Eckley's short monograph on O'Brien (1974) is dated. The first critical book on McGahern, Denis Sampson's, appeared only in 1993. If one counts Jeanne Flood's short 1974 survey in the same Bucknell series as Eckley's, there are three critical books on Moore. Hallvard Dahlie (1969 and 1981) published two editions of his book on Moore, as listed. Jo O'Donoghue's (1990) is the most recent book on Moore. Part of Kerry McSweeney's book (1983) is devoted to Moore, and David Rees's bibliography (1991) includes McGahern and Moore.

reading the Senate debate over Cross's delightful book was, Frank O'Connor, recalled, "like a long, slow swim through a sewage bed."[3] Mervyn Wall satirized this period accurately and mercilessly in *The Return of Fursey* (1948). He included an Irish Censor with two independently moving eyes—one to focus on the "dirty" words and one to read everything else—who rules that the Old Testament is, in the Censorship Board's infamous and recurrent phrase, "in general tendency indecent."

Irish censorship seemed to ease up after the 1940s. The early 1960s were marked by increasing liberalization of many aspects of an unusually backward Irish social life, with taoiseach Seán Lemass's administration (1959–66) often regarded as pivotal. Terence Brown asserts that "Irishmen and women believe now, as they believed then, that those five years [between 1958 and 1963] represented a major turning point in Irish fortunes" (1981, 241). Such new attitudes helped encourage O'Brien, McGahern, and Moore to write their bold new novels. But then the hoary hand of Irish censorship, a conservative force with impressive staying power, reached out to O'Brien and McGahern. O'Brien and McGahern endured their own bannings in the 1960s, and *The Dark* cost McGahern his teaching job. Both O'Brien and McGahern left Dublin during the same period and went into Joycean exile in England—McGahern after losing his job, though he eventually returned to live in County Leitrim. Brian Moore had safely removed himself to Canada in 1948.

O'Brien's *The Country Girls* and McGahern's *The Dark* offer female and male versions of strikingly similar upbringings at the hands of alcoholic, abusive fathers in rural and small-town Ireland—O'Brien's County Clare and McGahern's County Roscommon. As a novel about a middle-class youth in Belfast in the midst of World War II, *The Emperor of Ice-Cream* offers a different perspective, yet is quite similar to *The Dark* in its male preoccupations. It should also be noted that each of these novels follows a fairly traditionally realistic form, though *The Dark,* with its shifting narrative point of view, includes a somewhat ironic undercurrent. Each of these novelists went on to write more experimental kinds of novels: for example, O'Brien's *Night* (1972), McGahern's *The Pornographer* (1979), and Moore's *The Great Victorian Collection* (1975).

3. See my article "Tailor Tim Buckley: Folklore, Literature, and *Seanchas an Táilliúra*," in which O'Connor's quotation is cited from the 1942 Senate proceedings (1979, 116 n. 3).

In their autobiographical bildungsromans, however, they sought to recount their coming of age as realistically as possible. Of course, the bildungsroman, devoted to tracing its protagonist's development and coming of age, has traditionally been a subgenre dependent on a realistic mode. Weldon Thornton has argued that "this genre is inherently conducive to an antimodernist perspective" (1994, 65), and he even makes the more unusual claim that Joyce's *Portrait,* the most celebrated and influential Irish bildungsroman, is itself antimodernist. O'Brien, McGahern, and Moore are only three examples among many who disprove Thornton's unfounded assertion that "in more recent decades, since World War II, interest in the *Bildungsroman* has waned" (69). The genre of the bildungsroman is certainly alive and well in Ireland and elsewhere.[4]

McGahern's *The Dark* and Moore's *The Emperor of Ice-Cream* both expose male protagonists who are unable to relate meaningfully to women, and both culminate in their reconciliation with their fathers. In contrast, Edna O'Brien's entire *Country Girls Trilogy* is devoted to Caithleen/Kate Brady and Baba Brennan, best friends and double protagonists. These novelists refer to Joyce as a key influence, but their novels, like *The Land of Spices,* are more realistic than the *Portrait* in form and style, and end in the traditional setting of the big city. Whereas Stephen Dedalus leaves Dublin for the Continent, the protagonists of Kate O'Brien, Edna O'Brien, and John McGahern all go to Dublin—and then on to London, in *The Country Girls Trilogy*—to make their way in the world, while Brian Moore's Gavin Burke is determined to stay in Belfast even (or especially) in the midst of the German bombing.

Joyce's *Portrait* does remain the quintessential bildungsroman as well as *Künstlerroman* (artist-novel). As an account of Stephen's attempt to grow up as well as develop as an artist, it is truly *A Portrait of the Artist as a Young Man.* The novels I consider here are

---

4. Denis Cotter's unpublished dissertation, "Irish Novels of the Developing Self, 1760–1960" (1982), demonstrates the staying power of the bildungsroman in Ireland. Elsewhere, the great success of Alice Walker's *The Color Purple* (1982) is just one example of how popular and adaptable the bildungsroman is in contemporary fiction. In fact, the bildungsroman has experienced a recent rebirth of vitality as women, people of color, and others discover that it lends an effective form in which to tell their stories. See Laura Sue Fuderer's *The Female Bildungsroman in English: An Annotated Bibliography of Criticism* (1990). Although bildungsromans tend to be realistic works, Philip Roth's *The Ghost Writer* (1979), for example, is a somewhat postmodernist bildungsroman about a young novelist trying to write a bildungsroman.

bildungsromans, but not *Künstlerroman*s. Their protagonists read literature, but they are not depicted as trying to write themselves. The formative encounters of O'Brien's Caithleen Brady and Moore's Gavin Burke with literature are simply part of their education rather than part of an attempt to develop as artists. These bildungs-romans thus belong more to the subgenre of the *Erziehungsroman* (or novel of education) rather than the *Künstlerroman*.[5] Of course, avoiding the *Künstlerroman* may very well have been part of these novelists' determination not to be subsumed by Joyce's overwhelming influence. Moore has remarked: "As Seán O'Faoláin once said, at the end of an Irish novel the hero gets on a boat and goes to England. So I didn't want my character to do that" (quoted in Sale 1969, 72).

Denis Cotter (1982) argues that the Irish bildungsroman has not created a true tradition, because most of its practitioners have lacked self-consciousness about it; to some extent, each of them has composed his or her bildungsroman as if no predecessor had ever written this kind of novel before. However, Kate O'Brien, John McGahern, and Brian Moore were *very* self-conscious about Joyce. O'Brien reports that T. S. Eliot's *Introducing James Joyce* was "the first book I ever *bought*" (Guppy 1984, 29), while Moore admits that *Ulysses* "was the only book I ever stole—my cousin never got it back" (Sale 1969, 71). Joyce prompted O'Brien to "realize that I wanted literature for the rest of my life" (O'Brien 1984a, 29); moreover, "reading bits of Joyce was the first time in my whole life that I happened on something in a book that was exactly like my own life" (quoted in Eckley 1974, 25–26). She told fellow novelist and bildungsroman author Philip Roth, "In the constellation of geniuses, he is a blinding light and the father of us all" (quoted in O'Brien 1984b, 39). It is therefore not surprising to find many Joycean traces in her fiction. Fritz Senn (1966) notes the clear echoes of the final passage of Joyce's "The Dead" in this one in *The Country Girls:*

> We drove along the Limerick road and while we were driving it began to snow. Softly the flakes fell. Softly and obliquely against the windscreen. It fell on the hedges and on the trees behind the

---

5. For an informative, clarifying discussion of these terms, see James Hardin's (1991) collection of essays, especially his introduction.

hedges, and on the treeless fields in the distance, and slowly and quietly it changed the colour and shape of things, until everything outside the motor car had a mantle of white soft down. (1986a, 90)

Joyce's influence is not limited to this first novel. O'Brien's novel *A Pagan Place* (1970) has been described by Lotus Snow as a female *Portrait*, though "an unstructured, diluted" one (79), much as *Night* (1972) imitates the "Penelope" chapter of *Ulysses*. *A Pagan Place* shows Joyce's influence more obviously than *The Country Girls Trilogy* and remains more focused on childhood than the later parts of the trilogy.

Interestingly, both McGahern and Moore are on record as embracing the realist rather than the experimental side of Joyce. In an essay on *Dubliners*, McGahern quotes extensively from a debate between George Sand and Gustave Flaubert, siding with Flaubert and his insistence on being a realist, tied to the ground. Moore has similarly stated that "I agree with Joyce; he said, 'All my work is the celebration of the commonplace' " (quoted in Sale 1969, 72). Moore has indicated that for him Joyce was a "tremendous influence" and that the *Portrait* "seems to me, as it does to almost every Irish writer, even today, almost the story of one's early life. It's our generation's *Catcher in the Rye:* our *Huck Finn*—all those things. The retreats, the hellfire, the feeling of hopelessness with girls" (quoted in McSweeney 1976, 55). Interestingly, as early as 1962, before he had written *The Emperor of Ice Cream,* Brian Moore was assessed by at least one critic as "probably, at this stage of things literary, the writer best fit to be Joyce's heir" (Ludwig 1962, 5). In 1982, Moore reiterated that "Joyce remains our mentor: he who helped us fly past those nets of home, fatherland and church, who taught us the rebel cry of *non serviam*" (quoted in O'Donoghue 1990, 28).

My sense of the male versus female aspects of the novels considered here is complicated by the fact that Moore and McGahern are both cognizant of and interested in women's problems, whereas Edna O'Brien is not easily labeled in feminist terms. Moore and McGahern both began their careers with powerful, sympathetic novels about women as victims—Moore's *The Lonely Passion of Judith Hearne* (1955) and McGahern's *The Barracks* (1963)—and they have often returned to this preoccupation, as in Moore's *I Am Mary Dunne* (1968) and *The Temptation of Eileen Hughes* (1981), for example, and McGahern's *Amongst Women* (1990). Writing sympathetically about women does

not, of course, necessarily and simply make a man a feminist; as
Laura Claridge and Elizabeth Langland note, "A male writer may
simply need the space of what he or his culture terms the feminine
in which to express himself more fully because he experiences the
patriarchal construction of his masculinity as a constriction. He
may . . . appropriate the feminine to enlarge himself" and still
"sidestep . . . the issue of gender equality" (1990, 4). Yet McGahern
writes in a fairly recent essay that "I think that women fared worst
of all within this paternalistic mishmash" (1991a, 27).

Edna O'Brien is arguably the pioneer of the current generation
of women writing about Irish women's struggles. But she has commented in an interview, "A lot of things have been said by feminists
about equality, about liberation, but not all of these things are gospel
truth. . . . I am not the darling of the feminists. They think I am too
preoccupied with old-fashioned themes like love and longing" (quoted
in O'Brien 1984a, 33). As O'Brien herself notes here, some feminists
have steered clear of her work because her women characters constantly seek to resolve their problems and find happiness in romantic
relationships with men, despite the bad relationships they themselves
and their mothers have with men. Yet many feminists are themselves
critical of essentialist notions that all women's experiences are the
same, or that "women" and "men" are clear categories, so it is unfortunate if O'Brien is left outside the feminist circle—especially since
the critique that one finds in her fiction of women's victimization by
men is a valuable feminist lesson. Particularly as she makes it in an
essay on "A Portrait of the Artist as a Maturing Woman," it is worth
reiterating the remark by Hélène Cixous that I cited in my introduction: "I reproach myself for using the words *men* and *women*. We have
difficulties nowadays with these words. . . . Maybe a man would have
had something to say about female or 'feminine' writing, or vice
versa. . . . Please use as many quotation marks as you need to avoid
taking these terms too literally" (1987, 1). Nonetheless, "male" and
"female" constantly impress themselves upon us in the novels examined here. We can read them in the spirit of Cixous: "what I am
interested in is the libidinal education of the artist" as "determined
particularly by sexual difference" (2).

Popular and critical responses to Edna O'Brien's work have not
taken us very far toward understanding her central artistic vision.

As Raymonde Popot notes, Edna O'Brien's frequent bannings "invited some doubtful curiosity fostered now by the paperback edition[s] and [their] advertising, which [are] more likely to allure the reader on the look-out for 'shimmering sensual stories' than the watcher of sombre anguished experiences" (1976, 255). Critics have noted O'Brien's sharp country insights, evident in such descriptions in *The Country Girls* as one of how "the pinkness of his skin reminded me of young pigs at home" (1986a, 191). As an Irish novel published in 1960, *The Country Girls* broke new ground in terms of depicting female sexuality, from its very first pages describing the elm grove: "Baba and I sat there and shared secrets, and once we took off our knickers in there and tickled one another. The greatest secret of all" (1986a, 8). Darcy O'Brien notes that she was "the first country girl to write of this experience and to make her own kind of poetry of it, and the bravery of the accomplishment ought not to be slighted" (1982, 183). He adds: "Even in her mature years she continues to see herself as the country girl, equal to the challenge of the city but much abused by it" (185). Such statements, however, only the skim the surface of O'Brien's work.

Edna O'Brien has been openly obsessed with childhood—"that trenchant childhood route," she calls it at the end of her significantly entitled memoir *Mother Ireland,* where she concludes that she still wants to make "the leap that would restore one to one's original place and state of consciousness, to the radical innocence of the moment just before birth" (1976b, 144). "It's amazing," she has indicated, that "childhood really occupies at most twelve years of our early life . . . and the bulk of the rest of our lives is shadowed or coloured by that time" (quoted in Darcy O'Brien 1982, 179). To Philip Roth, she said: "The time when you are most alive and most aware is in childhood and one is trying to recapture that heightened awareness" (O'Brien 1984b, 39). She was much marked by Joyce and his own portraits of childhood, as emphasized earlier, but actually the young Edna O'Brien, the country girl from Clare, was much more like Nora Barnacle Joyce, the country girl from Galway. Early during her time in Dublin, O'Brien tells us in *Mother Ireland,* while still a young girl herself, "I went down the quays, to Finn's Hotel—where Nora Barnacle had been a chambermaid" (1976b, 137–38). At the equivalent point in *The Country Girls,* Caithleen Brady is reading James Stephens's *The Charwoman's Daughter* and Chekhov as well as Joyce (1986a, 195–96).

The final three chapter titles in O'Brien's *Mother Ireland* could just as well be the titles of the three parts of *The Country Girls Trilogy:* "A Convent," "Dublin's Fair City," and "Escape to England." When she leaves the semi-Gaelic, rural Irish world of County Clare for Dublin (and then London), O'Brien's Caithleen Brady significantly becomes "Kate" (the clipped, more thoroughly Anglicized version of her name). *The Country Girls* (which we might call the "bildungsroman proper," given its spotlight on Caithleen's adolescence) and its sequels take us from the early 1940s through the end of the 1950s. *The Country Girls* follows Caithleen and her best friend, Baba, from their homes to a convent boarding school, from which they get expelled, and then to Dublin, where they go to work. If the story ended here, we would be left much as we are in Kate O'Brien's *The Land of Spices,* with Kate in Dublin, looking hopefully to the future: "I'm finding my feet, and when I'm able to talk I imagine that I won't be so alone" (1986a, 377). But this is not the end of the story, which Edna O'Brien continued more bleakly in the sequels. In *The Lonely Girl,* both of O'Brien's main characters end up in London, with Caithleen/Kate moving into and out of a relationship with Eugene Gaillard. She marries him in *Girls in Their Married Bliss,* they have a son, and then she loses both of them—while Baba marries a contractor for his money. The movement in these three novels is toward increasing exile, loneliness, and loss.

Irish fathers' alcoholism and physical and sexual abuse are central problems in both *The Country Girls Trilogy* and *The Dark* that need to be exposed in order to understand these novels (and others that confront such lamentably common realities). It is striking how many bildungsromans—not only Irish ones, but others such as the Australian Miles Franklin's *My Brilliant Career* and, of course, Lawrence's *Sons and Lovers*—have alcoholic, abusive fathers at their cores. Caithleen Brady's life is forever marked by her nightmarish father and by her victimized mother, who drowns early in *The Country Girls*. The entire *Country Girls Trilogy* begins and ends with her father; in the 1986 epilogue, her lifelong friend Baba Brennan, contemplating Kate's probable suicide, declares: "Father—the crux of her dilemma" (1986a, 531). *The Country Girls* begins this way: "I wakened quickly and sat up in bed abruptly. It is only when I am anxious that I waken easily and for a minute I did not know why my heart was beating faster than usual. Then I remembered. The old reason. He had not come home" (1986a, 3). When her father does come home, "His face was red and fierce and angry. I knew that he would have to strike someone" (27). Later, as he is about to strike Caithleen, "I hate you," she tells him "suddenly and vehemently" (107).[6]

O'Brien has commented that her own father "was what you might call the 'archetypal' Irishman—a gambler, drinker, a man totally unequipped to be a husband or a father" (O'Brien 1984a, 38). As Baba puts it in the sardonically entitled *Girls in Their Married Bliss,* "An Irishman: good at battles, sieges, and massacres. Bad in bed" (1986a, 384). One calls to mind the bad joke about how one can identify a true Irishman: he would step across the bodies of ten naked women to get to a pint of Guinness. In *The Lonely Girl,* the crude, pathetic marriage proposal of Caithleen's significantly nicknamed acquaintance "the Ferret" is at least as ludicrous: "I've a pump in the yard, a bull, and a brother a priest. What more could a woman want?" (1986a, 282).

Indeed, Caithleen's father is only the first in a series of men—including also Mr. Gentleman, Jack Holland, and Eugene Gaillard—who abuse her. She marries Eugene over her father's protestations, but Eugene ends up striking her (1986a, 406) and taking their son away from her, out of the country, where she cannot find them. As Lotus Snow notes, after the trilogy "O'Brien's heroines will not look for fulfillment in marriage" (1979, 76). They are separated from their husbands in such novels as *Casualties of Peace* (1966), in which the estranged husband is significantly named Herod, and *August Is a Wicked Month* (1976a), which can be taken as an alternate version of the end of *The Country Girls Trilogy:* in this case Caithleen's son is killed and she is left hungering hopelessly for love.

For Caithleen, her mother was "everything to her" (1986a, 6), and she could never get over the "commonplace sacrifice of her life" (203). Her two greatest early fears are that she will lose her mother and Hickey, their farmhand and the closest thing to a substitute father-figure for her (29). She loses both of them. Concerning her own mother, O'Brien told Roth, "I loved her, over-loved her, yet she visited a different legacy on me [than her father], an all-embracing guilt. I still have a sense of her over my shoulder, judging" (O'Brien

---

6. Peggy O'Brien's claim that Caithleen's father is a man "from whom escape would be easy" (1987, 486) is misdirected. He pursues Caithleen to Dublin, and even physical escape from him is no guarantee against the patriarchal world that he has done much to create for Caithleen.

1984b, 39). Kate Brady ends up deciding that her mother was "a self-appointed martyr" (1986a, 476–77). We need not look far for an external, psychoanalytic critique that can allow us to understand such relationships, for O'Brien advanced her own to Roth: "If you want to know what I regard as the principal crux of female despair, it is this: in the Greek myth of Oedipus and in Freud's exploration of it, the son's desire for his mother is admitted; the infant daughter also desires its mother but it is unthinkable, either in myth, in fantasy or in fact, that that desire can be consummated" (O'Brien 1984b, 39–40). James Haule speaks of O'Brien's "desire to be her own mother" (1987, 217).

Psychoanalytic and feminist social theorists can help us understand O'Brien and her protagonists. Colette Dowling writes in *The Cinderella Complex:* "Personal, psychological dependency—the deep wish to be taken care of by others—is the chief force holding women down today. . . . Like Cinderella, women today," typically obsessed with their fathers and husbands, "are still waiting for something external to transform their lives" (1981, 21). As Tamsin Hargreaves argues, "O'Brien's early writing painfully articulates this fundamental problem of loss of self. . . . Because this psychological umbilical cord between mother and child leaves Caithleen weak and dependent, she is, upon her mother's death, stranded at an infantile emotional level and condemned to carry a painful sense of loss and need throughout her life" (1988, 291). Hargreaves aptly describes O'Brien's novels as "finely written psychodramas in which the protagonists desperately attempt to replace the safety and wholeness, the sense of identity and meaning found with the mother" (291–92). Cixous notes that whereas Stephen Dedalus can appropriate his early guilt and externalize it as part of his male artistic vision, for a woman (such as the Brazilian Clarice Lispector, Cixous's example), guilt too often becomes internalized and destructive: "If what I think is good is bad, then I am the bad one. And that's the way women usually act" (1987, 12). This pattern is very evident in *The Country Girls Trilogy.* As O'Brien herself told Roth, "Men and women are radically different" (O'Brien 1984b, 40). As one compares her novels with McGahern's and Moore's, one can only agree with her.

Although some feminists have criticized Edna O'Brien for not being a sufficiently liberated feminist because she writes about women obsessed with and victimized by their relationships with men, her trilogy nonetheless can be certainly be read as a strongly feminist text, especially in its thoroughgoing attention to women's internalization of victimization, as critiqued by Cixous. We also find moments of publicly stated feminism in the trilogy. Just one example among many is the episode in *Girls in Their Married Bliss* in which Kate learns that Eugene has taken her son out of the country without telling her, and is informed by the authorities that "a mother's signature was not necessary" (1986a, 504) on her son's passport. " 'You call that just', she said" (504). Throughout her fiction, O'Brien consistently deals with women on their own terms, powerfully portraying a female world. As O'Brien herself has indicated, "One woman in *Ms.* magazine pointed out that I send bulletins from battle fronts where other women do not go. I think I do" (O'Brien 1984a, 34).

O'Brien became increasingly critical of Kate's plight, choosing in *Girls in Their Married Bliss* and the epilogue to switch the narrator to Baba, who is a much tougher feminist alternative to Caithleen/Kate throughout the trilogy. She added Kate's self-sterilization in the 1967 revised edition of the 1964 *Girls in Their Married Bliss,* and then killed off Kate altogether in the 1986 epilogue, though Kate had contemplated suicide earlier (1986a, 447). O'Brien has called Baba "my alter-ego," noting that "I did have school friends who were the opposite of myself, and they were extrovert and mischievous, more mischievous. I was drawn toward them as I always am toward opposites" (quoted in Eckley 1974, 67). In her essay "Why Irish Heroines Don't Have to Be Good Anymore" (1986b), published in the same year as the epilogue and the completed trilogy, she explained: "I decided to have two, one who would conform to both my own and my country's view of what an Irish woman should be and one who would undermine every piece of protocol and religion and hypocrisy that there was. . . . Coming back to them I knew that Baba's asperity had to prevail." Baba criticizes Kate in *Girls in Their Married Bliss:* "Her life was like a chapter of the inquisition" (1986a, 387). Kate herself realizes later in *Girls in Their Married Bliss* that her mother's status as "a self-appointed martyr" (1986a, 476–77) was like her own. Baba feels about Kate that "she was so damn servile I could have killed her" (421). So O'Brien does exactly that in her epilogue: Baba informs the reader that Kate has committed suicide.

As a double-female bildungsroman, *The Country Girls Trilogy* is comparable to but different from Kate O'Brien's *The Land of Spices.* Both books concern the interdependent lives of two female protagonists, yet otherwise they contrast quite sharply at both superficial and deeper levels. Kate O'Brien's Anna Murphy uses her scholarship to go forth positively into the world, in a happy ending; Edna O'Brien's Caithleen Brady abandons her scholarship (like the protagonist of McGahern's *The Dark*)—dropping out of school, following a dissolute life in Dublin and London, and experiencing eventual failure and death. There is no nice mother superior to rescue Caithleen from her cruel convent teacher, as in *The Land of Spices*. Helen Archer and Anna Murphy are separated by a generational age difference and by the formal nature of their relationship, yet they come to affect each other increasingly profoundly and positively. Caithleen Brady and Baba Brennan are always intimately attached as exact contemporaries and best friends, but they eventually grow apart, and the closing theme of the trilogy's epilogue is that Baba could never finally reach the despairing Kate. Whereas the convent provides a feminist oasis in which Helen and Anna can escape and overcome obstacles to their development as women, Caithleen/Kate and Baba must live and die in the large, impersonal, male-dominated worlds of Dublin and London.

The Dark and its author are similar in several respects to *The Country Girls* and Edna O'Brien. Its setting in rural and small-town County Roscommon is not too far afield from O'Brien's rural Clare.[7] Quickly attracting much notoriety, *The Dark* was published in 1965, the year after *Girls in Their Married Bliss,* and like *The Country Girls,* it centers on a repressed Irish adolescence of the 1940s. Both novels begin in medias res, with the horrible spectre of the protagonist's father. Like Joyce and also Kate O'Brien, whose decision to leave Ireland to work on the Continent and in England was reconfirmed by the banning of *The Land of Spices,* both McGahern and Edna O'Brien remained attached to Ireland. Edna O'Brien published *Mother Ireland* (1976b) more than a decade after her departure for London and has continued to write about her native country. Moreover, both writers were much influenced by Joyce and his *Portrait,* as I noted earlier. Like Moore, McGahern has celebrated what he sees as the determined realism of Joyce rather than his experimentalism. He has also emphasized the realism of an

---

7. Roscommon (like the protagonist) is never actually named in the novel, but it seems a sure bet based on McGahern's own origins and the novel's extensively autobiographical features.

otherwise very different writer: Tomás Ó Criomhthain, author of the Gaelic autobiographical masterpiece *An tOileánach* (*The Islandman*) (1929), who was usually described in a nostalgic, sentimental mode by Gaelic revivalists. McGahern emphasizes instead Ó Criomhthain's ability to strip his story down to the bare essentials, his hard-bitten realism so strong that donkeys are mentioned only twice in the whole book. McGahern notes as a parallel that "Borges argues that a proof of the authenticity of the Koran is that you can find no camels in its pages. They were so taken for granted that there was no need for them to be mentioned" (1987, 8). The terse form of *The Dark* (fewer than 142 pages long in a popular British/Irish paperback edition) illustrates this principle, even though McGahern's material is drastically different than Ó Criomhthain's. *The Dark*'s short, episodic chapters are closer in form to *An tOileánach* than to the classical, embryonic five books of *A Portrait of the Artist as a Young Man*.[8]

As in *The Country Girls Trilogy,* abuse and loss are central themes in *The Dark*. Like Caithleen Brady, McGahern's young boy must try to overcome not only his abusive father, but also the loss of his mother. O'Brien had invented such a loss, as her own mother was very much alive when she wrote *The Country Girls,* but McGahern wrote out of his own experience, since his mother died in 1945, when he was eleven, just like his protagonist at the beginning of *The Dark:* "His mother had gone away . . . and left him to this" (1965, 9). This young boy is obsessed enough with the loss of his mother to make his earliest conscious ambition the priesthood, so he can say a Mass for her. He learns, however, that he must quickly rule such out a vocation because he feels unworthy and has other obsessions—particulary masturbation.

McGahern has been perhaps even more recurrently obsessed with his father-figure than O'Brien has been: in his first novel, *The*

8. Paul Devine outlines a sequence of four "sections" in *The Dark* that he argues "helps the novel overcome its tendency to be episodic" (1979, 51), but since this outline is imposed from the outside by Devine rather than clarified internally by McGahern (as in the case of Joyce's five clearly labeled books in *Portrait*), Devine's thesis is unconvincing. *The Dark* really is an episodic novel in much the same way that *The Country Girls Trilogy* and *The Emperor of Ice-Cream* (and for that matter, most Irish novels) are. For an extensive discussion of the loose, episodic narrative structure of Irish novels, see Cahalan, *The Irish Novel* (1988) (in which my treatments of this issue are indexed on p. 355). As a "classical," five-part novel, Joyce's *Portrait* is the exception rather than the rule among Irish novels.

Barracks (1963), Reegan is a somewhat younger version of the same policeman father; and in his most recent one, *Amongst Women* (1990), Moran is an older version, a paterfamilias whose raging, forbidding nature (but also decline and impending death) absolutely dominate the novel. Unlike O'Brien and Caithleen Brady, who try their best to leave the father behind, McGahern's protagonist eventually seeks reconciliation with the father, much as Gavin Burke does too by the end of *The Emperor of Ice-Cream.* Reconciliation with the father appears to be mostly a male obsession. Nearly opposite are the experiences of women such as Edna O'Brien and her major characters, who are more often haunted by the difficulty of reconciling with their mothers.

One would never predict father-son reconciliation, however, from the opening scene in *The Dark,* which is even more startlingly riveted on the violent, drunk father than is *The Country Girls.* The boy's father is referred to as "Mahoney," though the boy calls him "Daddy."

> "Say what you said because I know."
> "I didn't say anything."
> "Out with it I tell you."
> "I don't know I said anything."
> "F-U-C-K is what you said, isn't it? That profane and ugly word. Now do you think you can bluff your way out of it?"
> "I didn't mean it, it just came out."
> He took the heavy leather strap he used for sharpening his razor from its nail on the side of the press. . . .
> "I'll teach you a lesson this house won't forget in a hurry."
> "I didn't mean it, Daddy. I didn't mean it, it just slipped out."
> "Up the stairs. March. I'm telling you. Up the stairs."
> By the shoulder Mahoney pushed him out the door into the hallway towards the stairs. (1965, 7)

Naked, below a picture of the Ascension, the boy "had to lie in the chair, lie there and wait as a broken animal. Something in him snapped. He couldn't control his water and it flowed from him over the leather of the seat" (8). And perhaps even worse, the boy must endure "the old horror" of sexual as well as physical abuse: his father rubs him, makes him kiss him, makes him say he loves him (16). The boy tries to distance himself from his father by hiding his feelings and calling him only "Mahoney." It should be noted that "mahone" (*mo thóin* in Irish) means literally "my ass."[9] McGahern never mentions the first name of either the father or the son.

With "F-U-C-K" and McGahern's extensive attention to masturbation, we are indeed a step or two beyond the likes of *Portrait;* Stephen may visit a prostitute, but even that scene is presented in very decorous, indirect language. Though he limits his sexual activities to his magazines and his sock, McGahern's boy gives up on purity more quickly than Stephen does: "Bless me, father, for I have sinned. It's a month since my last confession. I committed one hundred and forty impure actions with myself" (1965, 25).[10] This boy masturbates five times a day over an *Irish Independent* ad for women's underwear (24)—lest we miss McGahern's irreverent use of Irish journalism and popular culture. McGahern confirms in an interview that he "deliberately picked" the *Independent* as "then the most staid newspaper in Ireland. . . . No convent was without the *Independent*" (McGahern 1984). His protagonist masturbates and studies his way to academic success in school—on scholarship at, significantly, just the kind of "Brothers' College" scorned by James Joyce and his father, the type to which Maurice is sent in the *Portrait* to learn to spell "c.a.t.: cat." McGahern's boy addresses his newspapers and his sock as "My love" (104). He is conditioned by his culture to be able to enjoy eroticism only if his object is defiled, exploited, and confined to his imagination; he admires and is enamored of young Mary Moran, but (now examining himself in detached second-person pronouns), "The only way you could have her . . . was as an old whore of your mind" (43).

As for "Mahoney" in the book's early chapters, the boy and his sisters "close their life against him and . . . leave him to himself" (10). They mimic him: "God, O God, O God" (22). And when his

9. One of my father's teachers at Fordham University in the early 1930s was a Father Mahoney, who introduced himself to his class with the intent of correcting the typical American mispronunciation of the name, with the stress on the second syllable and with a long vowel there—rather than with the stress on the first syllable, with a short vowel in the unstressed second syllable, as it is pronounced in Ireland. This aim he would unforgettably address by saying, "Don't call me 'Father Ma-HONE-y.' 'Mahone' means 'my ass'!"

10. F. C. Molloy notes that "Young Mahoney's development . . . is somewhat akin to Stephen's. He must masturbate rather than go to a brothel" (1977, 14). But Molloy complains of "the inappropriateness of the confessional form for McGahern's pessimistic vision" (16).

father swings his daughter by the hair, the boy warns him, "Hit and I'll kill you" (28), adding:

> "You wouldn't swing a pig like that."
> "I'd swing anyone. . . . The whole lot of you are pigs." (29)

McGahern exposes sexual harrassment and the general abuse of girls and women by Irish males even more directly in the episodes describing the harassment of the boy's sister, Joan, by the draper to whom she's been sent to work for; the adolescent protagonist confronts him and brings Joan home. This runs parallel to the protagonist's own escape from the latent-homosexual clutches of his uncle, Father Gerald, after which he makes a definite decision not to join the priesthood.[11]

The boy's therapy and attempt at escape from these problems are found in "the grind": he devotes his mind mindlessly to preparing for his Leaving Certificate exam, since his academic success is virtually the only positive aspect of his life. His hours of study also force his father to leave him alone a bit more, and the boy has already begun to soften on him as he increases his emotional distance. He thinks to himself, "You had no right to hate him, he was there to be loved too" (33). Later the boy moves to self-accusation: "You wanted to say to him you were sorry but you weren't able" (97). When he does apologize, his father can reply only with angry words (98), but "what was strange to notice was that Mahoney was growing old" and "was far the more cautious" (110).

When the protagonist gets his "first" and wins a scholarship to University College, Galway, he fantasizes about university life, but has no real clarity about what he wants to do there or with his life in general. His father brags about his son's success throughout the town and takes him out to a fancy, unusually expensive dinner, winning his son over: "You are marvellous, my father" (119), the boy now thinks. But then UCG turns out to be abruptly disappointing: too many of his professors are cruel and cynical, and he is too bashful to throw himself into social life. He feels unable to go to a dance even though "this was the dream you'd left the stern and certain road of the priesthood to follow after" (132). After his

---

11. Exaggerating a bit yet not too far off the mark, Shaun O'Connell notes that "the whole male, adult population of *The Dark* is composed of child-molesters" (1984, 260).

physics professor sends him out of the room for smiling at the wrong time, he telegrams his father that he wants to leave UCG and accept instead a clerkship at the Electrical Service Board in Dublin, opting for safe, dull, civil-service work rather than continue in academia. Rather passive conversations with his father (who flies immediately to his side) and the dean of students confirm his decision.

In an ending that could not be more diametrically opposed to Stephen's flighty, imminent departure to the European Continent to "forge in the smithy of my soul the uncreated conscience of my race," McGahern's antihero lies in the same bed as his father (just as he did early in the novel) in a Galway rooming house on the night before his departure for Dublin. We are left with this decidedly nonmythological closing dialogue:

> "Good night so, Daddy."
> "Good night, my son. God bless you." (142)

As Eileen Kennedy notes, "Stephen Dedalus is an urban hero who can leave Ireland boldly; but young Mahoney is a farmboy whose sights are set no higher than the city" (1983, 121). McGahern's ending, which has generally left readers unhappy and critics dissatisfied, seems slyly ironic.[12] The irony is silent rather than stated.

The alternative interpretation, especially in light of the artifices and experiments evident throughout McGahern's subsequent works, seems impossible: One has to doubt that true coming of age, artistic or otherwise, will be found by dropping out of school in order to join the civil service. McGahern's novel seems much more a warning than a prophecy: Stephen Dedalus prophesizes (albeit with some irony mixed in there too, and subsequent deflation and explosion in *Ulysses*); McGahern's protagonist simply makes a questionable career choice. There's a moral to McGahern's story, even though the author doesn't state it. Particularly in the cultural context of 1965, he seems to be saying to his (particularly young Irish male) readers, "Watch out, or this will happen to you." As Shaun O'Connell

---

12. John Cronin typifies critical responses when he writes that *The Dark* is so determinedly bleak that the novel "runs the risk of finding it impossible to bring it to any kind of convincing conclusion" (1969a, 428), and he criticizes McGahern's ending as thin and unconvincing (429).

predicts, McGahern's protagonist will be "paralyzed in the civil service, an Irish purgatory" (1984, 261).[13] Although many early reviewers[14] and subsequent critics compared *The Dark* to *Portrait,* actually the closer Joycean analogy is the story "A Little Cloud," in which Little Chandler, hopelessly lost at the end of the story, seems a version of what Joyce might have been if he had lacked artistic inspiration and courage. As noted earlier, the *Portrait* is of course not only a bildungsroman, an account of a young man's attempt to come of age, but also a *Künstlerroman,* the quintessential account of the making of an artist, as its title emphasizes. McGahern's future civil service clerk is no artist.

Even though his father was initially even more scary than Caithleen Brady's, by the end McGahern's protagonist is tied to him, even virtually subsumed by him. The father-son pair is the crucial one here, just as it is by the end of Moore's *The Emperor of Ice-Cream,* whereas in O'Brien's bildungsroman(s) the crucial pair is a young woman and her best female friend. The contrast here is one between inheriting the patriarchy in McGahern—however pathetic that patriarchy may be—versus nurturing sisterhood in O'Brien, even if that sisterhood is eventually depicted as futile by the end of her trilogy.

✻

Like *The Dark,* Brian Moore's *The Emperor of Ice-Cream,* which was published in that same year of 1965, gives the reader the impression that Irish male adolescence in this period was dominated largely by masturbation and by the exam grind, and that reconciliation

13. Richard Lloyd similarly writes that at the end "McGahern's protagonist finally feels the darkness lifting. McGahern, however, does not leave the reader with the same impression. Mahoney . . . has not fulfilled his dreams: he has not said Mass for his mother, nor has he escaped the 'landscape of inhibition' " (1989, 40).

14. See Sampson 1993, 61 on early reviewers of *The Dark.* Sampson himself records his agreement (61–62 n. 2) with my own earlier-stated position in *The Irish Novel* that "the ending of *The Dark* could not more deliberately invert, subvert, and deflate the *dénouement* of *Portrait*" (274); Sampson adds the claim that "*The Dark* registers an intimate reflection on the aesthetic theories of Stephen. . . . There are marked differences of background, context, and character between the two young protagonists. While McGahern's novel shows indebtedness to Joyce, his vision in the novel reflects his need to define his own stance as an artist" (1993, 61–62 n. 2).

with the father was central to a young man's coming of age. This is the novel that Moore, painfully aware of the huge shadow of James Joyce, had tried—and succeeded in four earlier novels—to avoid writing. "I always felt maybe I should write that some day," he has remarked. "I suppose it's my bildungsroman" (quoted in Dahlie 1969, 85).

Nonetheless, *The Emperor of Ice-Cream* shows the extent to which Moore had already been writing himself through such earlier protagonists as Judith Hearne and also Diarmaid Devine in *The Feast of Lupercal* (1958), for like young Gavin Burke, these older protagonists are repressed Belfast characters who depend heavily on psychological fetishes such as Judith's picture of the Sacred Heart (see Toolan 1980, 100). *The Emperor of Ice-Cream* opens with Gavin's conversation with his eleven-inch-tall statue of the Divine Infant of Prague. The statue tells Gavin, "You are my business" (1965, 7). This morality-play leitmotif continues via intermittent, conflicting advice from Gavin's "White Angel" and his "Black Angel." But Moore does not trace his protagonist's childhood and early adolescence according to the more typical developmental model found in the *Portrait, The Country Girls,* and *The Dark.* Instead he begins with Gavin at seventeen, and centers his novel on the single, major experience that moves Gavin away from adolescence toward manhood: the German bombing of Belfast and Gavin's work with its victims as an enlisted member of the "A.R.P." (Air Raid Precautions). Only occasionally does he include a flashback to childhood such as Gavin's memory of "the washroom of the school gymnasium (the same washroom where, aged thirteen, he had been held immobile by two older boys while a third squirted urine from a water pistol into his face)" (120).

Gavin Burke has ludicrous masturbational fantasies rivaling those found in McGahern's exactly contemporaneous novel: "He saw himself, wearing his steel helmet, dashing into the house across the way to carry the typist downstairs, she half-naked and hysterical in her relief" (10–11). As in both the *Portrait* and *The Dark,* we encounter a young male protagonist who is unable to experience girls and women—whether Stephen's shadowy "E.C.," Gavin's girlfriend Sally Shannon, or McGahern's women in the underwear ads in the *Irish Independent*—as anything other than objects. But unlike McGahern's protagonist, and more like Caithleen Brady in this respect, Gavin does at least have friends and a social life. McGahern's young boy stays at home and grinds away toward an academic success that will ultimately lead him no further than the civil service; but as was the case with Moore himself (see O'Donoghue 1990, xi–xii), Gavin Burke cannot pass the "London Matric" exam because he has problems with math, yet his enlistment in the A.R.P. gets him out of his house and into instructive human relationships, both good ones and bad ones. Moore subsequently mentioned that *"Emperor* was written at a crucial time in my life. . . . I started a new life halfway through the writing of it, I fell in love, remarried and so on." Bruce Stovel's impression is that "Gavin's story is as much Moore's nostalgic *Goodbye to All That* as his bildungsroman" (189).

In the midst of the otherwise mostly seedy older males who work at the A.R.P. station, Freddy Hargreaves is a socialist and older-brother figure who introduces Gavin to the poetry of Eliot and Auden. On the one hand, much of Moore's episodic A.R.P. material—demonic chief officer Craig, older yet ambitious Soldier MacBride, alcoholic Captain Lambert—seems to take the novel a bit too far at times from Gavin's development into a rather picaresque roman à clef drawn from Moore's own wartime experiences; as John Wilson Foster notes, it is as if "Moore, with two American-based novels behind him . . . were retracing his steps to pick up anything important he may have overlooked on his post-haste trek out of Northern Ireland en route to New York City" (1974, 123). On the other hand, *The Emperor of Ice-Cream* does provide an urban counterpart to the different rural worlds of *The Dark* and *The Country Girls,* and Gavin Burke does come to grips with history in a way that the even more self-centered Stephen Dedalus does not do in the *Portrait.* "He walked, caught in a cold excitement, feeling himself witness to history, to the destruction of the city he had lived in all his life" (1965, 166). Gavin rejects both sides of the sectarian divide in Belfast, reflecting Moore's own conviction that "both Protestantism and Catholicism in Northern Ireland are the most desperate tragedies that can happen to people. . . . I feel there should be a pox on both their houses" (quoted in Foster 1974, 129). Only the "horrors of war" allowed people in Belfast at midcentury to temporarily forget the sectarian divide.[15]

Unlike Stephen, Gavin is not shown trying to write himself, but he does like reading literature, and is capable of insights about

15. See Cronin 1969b, 32. O'Connell similarly writes that "it takes a horrific external threat, a German Armageddon, to make Belfast tolerable to a Moore hero" (1988, 542).

what he reads: he decides that "Hitler was Yeats' 'Second Coming' "
(10), and that in the case of Ireland since 1916, "the terrible beauty
was born aborted" (105). Some of these insights seem to be more
the older author's rather than his younger protagonist's, and do
occasionally appear to be "unnecessary 'literary' allusions to some of
the apocalyptic literature of the age" (Hirschberg 1975, 14). Of
course, like his compatriots Moore was also well aware of the conventions of the bildungsroman. As Foster reminds us, the bildungsroman typically contains "three great forms of adolescent
'awakening' . . . : the initiation into sexuality, the questioning of
religious faith, and the discovery of literature and art" (1974, 117).
Irish adolescence at mid-century, however, as described by our three
novelists, included an "initiation into sexuality" limited to masturbation and flirtation, whereas faith could be questioned and literature could be appreciated more completely.

Gavin Burke's development appears to be more successful than
that of either O'Brien's Caithleen/Kate, who fails and dies, or
McGahern's protagonist, whose decision to join the civil service
seems like very pale success. By the end of *The Emperor of Ice-Cream*,
Gavin has shown his courage by volunteering to help prepare the
corpses of Belfast bombing victims for burial, he has stood up to
his father, and he has decided that he must strike out on his own
rather than pursue the kind of conventional life that his father,
Sally Shannon, and others have mapped out for him. Gavin's father
was typical of many people in Belfast in believing that Hitler would
not bomb their city, and that England's difficulty would be Ireland's
opportunity, with Hitler working to Irish nationalist advantage.
The German bombing of Belfast was thus a harsh dose of reality;
as Mr. Burke later admits, "The German jackboot is a far crueler
burden than the heel of old John Bull" (163). Yet at this point,
"Within Gavin there started an extraordinary elation. . . . The world
and the war had come to him at last" (151). His initial reaction is
immature, self-centered, and rather ridiculous: "Why was he filled
with excitement, with a feeling that, tonight, nothing could kill
him, that, like the knight in some ancient romance, he carried a
shield which stood between him and all harm?" (159).

Gavin's all-night work with the victims' corpses is a pivotal
experience for him. The first body that he encounters in the makeshift morgue is that of a young mill worker in her twenties, "the
first naked body of an adult woman he had ever really looked at in
his life" (177). She is no titillating sex-object, but part of the horror

of war. Later he sees "the bare, callused feet of an old woman, sticking out from the bottom of a pile of bodies" (176), and he feels that he understands for the first time the Wallace Stevens lines whose sound had earlier enchanted him:

> If her horny feet protrude, they come
> To show how cold she is, and dumb.
> Let the lamp affix its beam.
> The only emperor is the emperor of ice-cream.
>
> (McGahern 1965, 176)

Now Gavin feels that he has come of age: "he felt that, in volunteering for this job, he had done the first really grown-up thing in his life," though Moore also shows that self-centered adolescence cannot be overcome completely or quickly: "Wait'll Sally heard what he was doing. She'd be sorry she sounded off like that last night. Big baby, indeed" (178).

Like *The Dark, The Emperor of Ice-Cream* culminates in reconciliation between father and son. This reconciliation, however, does not appear to include the ironic possibilities that McGahern seemed to have in mind. Kerry McSweeney notes that "Ellmann has remarked that Joyce was more interested in paternal love than in sexual love: similarly, in Brian Moore's novels parental relationships are at least as important as sexual relationships" (1976, 56). Gavin meets his father, who has temporarily removed his family from bombed-out Belfast to Dublin, back at their house at the end:

> In the candlelight, he saw that his father was crying. He had never seen his father cry before. Did his father know that the house was condemned, did his father know that everything had changed, that things would never be the same again? A new voice, a cold grown-up voice within him said: 'No.' His father was the child now; his father's world was dead. . . . From now on, he would know these things.
>
> His father seemed aware of this change. He leaned his untidy, gray head on Gavin's shoulder, nodding, weeping, confirming. 'Oh, Gavin,' his father said. 'I've been a fool. Such a fool.'
>
> The new voice counseled silence. He took his father's hand. (189–90)

At the end, Gavin sympathizes with his father "just as Brian Moore sympathizes with all his disheartened characters" (Prosky 1971, 118).

Moore has indicated that this was the first novel he wrote in which he knew the ending in advance. Frankly, it shows: this ending seems too pat. Bruce Cook complains that at the end Gavin's father and Moore's other characters "cave in, rather than change" (1974, 458), and Jo O'Donogohue is convinced that "the crisis of the blitz has caused the suspension of normal family activity and hostility, but these will be only too ready to reassert themselves in peace-time" (1990, 74). One has to agree that at novel's end, Gavin Burke seems naïve and self-congratulatory. He has chosen to stay in Belfast; Moore himself had to leave in order to gain his freedom. Moore may have intended Gavin as an inspiration, but we respond to him as a warning of what will come to those who stay behind.

If Gavin is more successful than O'Brien's and McGahern's protagonists, it is partly because he enjoys advantages over the others: his father is a successful lawyer, neither an alcoholic nor an abuser, and Gavin's parents have provided him with a relatively comfortable home complete with even a maid (67). O'Donogohue goes so far as to call *The Emperor of Ice-Cream* "comic" because Gavin "has no reason to be depressed" and "thinks that people like him will change the world" (1990, 71–72). His father's greatest crimes apparently are that he holds overly simplistic views of Irish nationalism and the world crisis, and that, like Moore's actual father, who once called James Joyce a "sewer" (quoted in Green 1982, 170), he disapproves of the writers that his son admires. Moore commented in 1967 concerning his father, "He believed totally in the things he believed in; he was very uncompromising. . . . I thought my father was wrong. I thought all my uncles and my relatives were wrong because . . . they were idealists of their generation—narrow, parochial idealists" (quoted in Dahlie 1969, 3–4). Such political and literary disagreements seem relatively minor beside the physical and alcoholic abuses practiced by the fathers in *The Country Girls* and *The Dark*. As Foster complains, "in his ending Moore confuses Gavin's entrance into manhood with a spurious corollary—the defeat of psychological and social attitudes around him" (1974, 130).

Gender issues need to be confronted as squarely in McGahern and Moore as they have been in O'Brien, even though the critical tendency has been to foreground O'Brien's female status while nearly completely ignoring the importance of explaining the experiences of McGahern's and Moore's protagonists, beyond their masturbation, in light of their maleness. If Edna O'Brien is a woman writer, then it is equally true that McGahern and Moore are "male writers"; they are not simply "writers," within a reputedly sexless, but in fact clearly sexist canon of a male-constructed "Tradition and the Individual Talent." Is it just a coincidence that McGahern and Moore give us boys whose experiences culminate in reconciliation with their fathers, whereas O'Brien's country girl flees her father as swiftly as she can, leaving him further and further behind as she moves from Clare to Dublin, London, and her ultimate demise? The male protagonists may spend much of these novels asserting their separation according to the male pattern outlined by Chodorow, but adulthood for each of them comes when they join the patriarchy; their *fathers,* not their mothers, represent the point of reconciliation and reputed manhood. Kate Brady may appear to separate herself from her father, and her mother has died, but she can never really escape either of them, a fact that eventually destroys her.

As we have seen, these bildungsromans include franker, more graphic depictions of sex than the earlier ones by James Joyce and Kate O'Brien, in which sexual intercourse is mentioned only very briefly and obliquely. Joyce's young Stephen visits a prostitute, "surrenduring himself to her, body and mind, conscious of nothing in the world but the dark pressure of her softly parting lips" (1916, 96). The sole sentence in *The Land of Spices* concerning sex, for which the novel was absurdly banned, reads as follows, from Helen Archer's point of view: "She saw *Etienne* and her father, in the embrace of love" (1941, 157). No mention is made of any sexual experience on the part of the the novel's protagonists, Helen and Anna.

Although different from the *Portrait* and *The Land of Spices* in terms of their descriptions of sexuality, the later novels continue much the same gender distinctions that were evident in the earlier ones: Edna O'Brien's two young girls and women depend largely on their friendship with each other, whereas McGahern's and Moore's boys grow in fairly solitary fashion (despite their rather unconvincing reconciliations with their fathers at the end). Like others treated in my previous chapters, these novels confirm the findings of psychologists John Hill and Mary Ellen Lynch about female versus male adolescence: that "girls become more self-conscious and experience more disruptions in self-image than boys," and that "girls become more invested in and more competent at forming intimate friendships" (quoted in Steinberg 1993, 280).

In O'Brien's *Girls in Their Married Bliss,* Kate and Baba's friendship outlasts their marriages; their loyalty to each other is only increased by divorce, as is often the case for women. Their friendship is defeated by Kate's suicide in the epilogue to the trilogy, but this is a failure of adulthood in the sequels and epilogue, not in the bildungsroman of youth. One might imagine similar sequels to McGahern's and Moore's bildungsromans in which their boys become adults and encounter disappointment, and in fact some of their other autobiographical novels could be read as those kinds of narratives, as sequels with only the names and a few other details changed. For example, McGahern's *The Leavetaking* (1974) is a version of how he lost his job in Dublin, and in *The Luck of Ginger Coffey* (1960), Moore had already published a rather picaresque account of his life in Canada after leaving Belfast.

In their bildungsromans McGahern and Moore present us with patriarchal worlds in which either Father Knows Best—albeit partly ironically in *The Dark*—or Boy Wonder Knows Even Better than Father, in *The Emperor of Ice-Cream.* In *The Country Girls Trilogy,* O'Brien exposes a patriarchal world in which Kate Brady is almost necessarily cast aside. The Irish adult world is equally patriarchal in *The Dark,* and critiqued as such by McGahern, though his protagonist nonetheless joins this world at the end. Our three novelists suggest that the sexes scarcely met, in any constructive or meaningful way, in midcentury Irish adolescence: Kate Brady is consistently a victim of her father, Mr. Gentleman, and Eugene; McGahern's protagonist makes love only to the models in the *Irish Independent;* and Gavin Burke relates superficially to his mere shadow of a girlfriend, Sally Shannon, whose superficiality is more Moore's fault than her own. Is it the Irish male's preferred fate to take a civil service job and join the patriarchy, whereas the Irish woman can expect to leave and die? One might come to such a conclusion from these novels. Such a dichotomy, however, is complicated by the biographical facts that Moore, like O'Brien, left Ireland too, and that McGahern lost his job and went to England before eventually returning.

There are other recurrent patterns in these bildungsromans that suggest the difficult nature of trying to come of age in Ireland in the

1940s, and perhaps still today, for both women and men.[16] O'Connell notes that "it has been argued that McGahern is too much a child of his generation, locked into the problems which faced young men in the 1950s, his decade of coming-of-age. Anthony Cronin, Irish man of letters, has suggested that McGahern, like Edna O'Brien, persists in misrepresenting Ireland—which Cronin sees as urban, open and secular—by portraying characters who are dominated by rural values, taboos and religious repressions" (1984, 261). But it remains clear that the problems exposed by McGahern and O'Brien were quite real: they cost McGahern his job, and they pushed O'Brien into divorce and into exile in London. Moreover, the loss of a job, the need to leave Ireland, and the difficulty of male-female relationships continue to be typical rather than unusual problems for Irish people, unfortunately, especially in a church-dominated state that maintains severe limits on divorce. Political and social repression, both North and South, continue to create big problems for the protagonists of the more recent "Troubles" novels examined in my next chapter.

But it is also true that Moore's *The Emperor of Ice-Cream* provides a kind of antidote to the syndrome that Anthony Cronin laments in McGahern and O'Brien. As we have seen, Moore writes from an urban and international perspective, presenting us in Gavin Burke with a Belfast boy who, despite all his shortcomings, overcomes religious taboos and cultural repressions and prepares himself, as Moore himself did, to grow up, leave Ireland, and meaningfully confront more diverse human relationships and problems. Gavin appears to succeed, whereas O'Brien's Kate Brady eventually fails and dies, and McGahern's protagonist drops out and departs for the Irish civil service, seen by many Irish people as secure but also a form of death-in-life. Yet somehow O'Brien's and McGahern's protagonists seem more compelling in their disappointments and failures than Gavin Burke does in his apparent success.

---

16. Similar patterns can be found in a great many Irish novels, including male ones whose gender issues have been neglected by critics. Occasionally, Irish bildungsromans follow different, less predictable patterns, as in Desmond Hogan's novels *The Ikon Maker* (1976) and *The Leaves on Grey* ([1980] 1981), in which gay characters and postmodernist writing scramble the traditionally heavily bipolar gender roles in Irish fiction.

5

Gender and History in Trouble(s)

Jennifer Johnston, Bernard MacLaverty, Julia O'Faolain,
and William Trevor

While sectarian politics understandably have been much discussed in studies of Irish fiction concerned with the "Troubles," the question of how gender functions in such works has been little addressed, let alone answered. In this chapter, my main focus is on two pairs of Troubles novels: first Jennifer Johnston's *Shadows on Our Skin* (1977) and Bernard MacLaverty's *Cal* (1983), which deal with the effects of the conflicts of the late 1970s and early 1980s in County Derry on adolescent, male protagonists; and then Julia O'Faolain's *No Country for Young Men* (1980) and William Trevor's *Fools of Fortune* (1983), which show how the earlier Irish Troubles of the Anglo-Irish War and Civil War period of 1919–23 continue to dominate the lives of people in the Republic of Ireland, circa 1980, with a double focus in each case on both female and male protagonists. *No Country for Young Men* and *Fools of Fortune* are considerably more complex novels than *Shadows on Our Skin* and *Cal,* so I have chosen to move from the simpler novels to the more complex ones, and to devote more space to the latter.

These four novelists have coalesced in my mind for several reasons. William Trevor (b. 1928), Jennifer Johnston (b. 1930), Julia O'Faolain (b. 1932), and Bernard MacLaverty (b. 1942) are highly successful contemporary writers of roughly the same generation. Each of their four novels considered here is quite current in its concerns, at the same time that each of these authors is freighted with a strong sense of literary inheritance. Both Johnston and O'Faolain are daughters of famous literary fathers, while Bernard MacLaverty writes within a tradition of northern realist fiction that includes Michael McLaverty (no relation), and Trevor is imbued with the tradition of the Big House and all of the Anglo-Irish baggage that comes with it. I deliberately balance the two women and the two men, as well as the Protestant Johnston and Trevor with the Catholic MacLaverty and O'Faolain; the gender distinctions mean a lot everywhere in the world, and the sectarian ones signify much in Ireland.

All four novelists show how sexual (and all human) relationships have been difficult, to say the least, in the midst of the Troubles. More than one of these novels slides from Troubles fiction into the bildungsroman tradition examined in my previous chapter, with Joyce's *Portrait* (and, even more specifically, Stephen's childhood poem about "Ireland is my nation . . . heaven's my destination") a repeated point of textual reference. Three of the four novels (all but Johnston's) conjure up Italy as a kind of Irish Caribbean and refuge from the Troubles. Johnston and MacLaverty structure their short novels with untitled chapters or sections, whereas O'Faolain and Trevor build their more complex books around chapters that are labeled according to the names (and perspectives) of their main characters, carefully gender-balanced. The differences among these novels, however, finally interest me more than their similarities, for these differences are highly instructive about the distinctions not only between these particular novelists and their works, but more generally the ones separating women and men in Ireland. As we shall see, violence tends to be internalized in the men's novels, implicating the male protagonists, but externalized in the women's novels, viewed by women (and by Johnston's young male) as committed by men.

Published within six years of each other, Jennifer Johnston's *Shadows on Our Skin* and Bernard MacLaverty's *Cal* are two novels that are strikingly similar, at least on the surface. In each of these two short novels, an adolescent, working-class, Catholic, County Derry boy with an abysmal home life—Johnston's Joe Logan, MacLaverty's Cal McCrystal—is drawn to an older woman who seems to offer a positive alternative to the male-dominated Troubles. The boy's guilty contact with the Troubles, however, inevitably intercedes to end their relationship. The sensitive nature of both Joe and Cal is measured against rougher, tougher males surrounding them: Joe's brother Brendan and his friend Peter, and Cal's cruel IRA contacts Crilly and Skeffington. Both novels contain the usual Troubles clichés: in general, violence that devastates everyone's lives; and more specifically, a gun that each protagonist hides from the authorities to save someone in his family. The similarities extend beyond plot to these two novels' almost equal lengths, their focused-third-person points of view, even the "anorak" windbreakers worn by both protagonists, the name of each protagonist's older brother (Brendan), and both works' links to popular music: Cal sings American blues songs, whereas *Shadows on Our Skin* is a phrase borrowed from a song by the 1970s Irish folk-rock group Horslips that keeps playing on the radio throughout the novel.[1] Here I will provide an overview of Johnston's novel, then MacLaverty's, and then go on to focus on the gender differences between the two, which strike me as more revealing than their similarities.

Jennifer Johnston has described herself as "nominally Protestant" but "mostly Irish" (quoted in Weekes 1990, 192). Like Julia O'Faolain, Johnston came from very distinguished parentage. Her mother was the Abbey Theatre actress Shelah Richards; her father, the playwright Denis Johnston, whose best known play, *The Old Lady Says No!* (1929), an absurdist work in which Robert Emmet returns to modern Dublin, injected a boldly experimental note into Irish drama at a time when it was stagnating. However, unlike O'Faolain's books, which have focused largely on women and gender issues, most of Jennifer Johnston's books have dealt in one way or another with war and the Troubles, and she has examined both female and male protagonists. Interestingly, like Julia O'Faolain, as we shall see, Johnston told Ann Owens Weekes that she found feminism too limiting, as just another form of separation, the worst variety of which is class (Weekes 1990, 30–31). Johnston has made admirable efforts in her numerous short novels, which began to appear in 1972, to represent many diverse sides and periods of Irish society.

It has to be noted that *Shadows on Our Skin* is not by any means Johnston's strongest or one of her best novels, or even her best contemporary Troubles novel; *The Railway Station Man* (1984) and *Fool's Sanctuary* (1987) are better in this vein. In these later novels, Johnston returned closer to her own experience, focusing on female

---

1. Lauren Onkey argues that *Cal* uses African-American music in a more muted and successful way than Roddy Doyle's *The Commitments*, and notes, "It seems that an alliance with a group *outside* Ireland, like African Americans, is one of the few ways Cal can find a place for himself in Northern Ireland" (1993, 157).

protagonists in each case. In *The Railway Station Man,* middle-aged, widowed Helen Cuffe loses both her son and her lover in an IRA bombing, and similarly, in *Fool's Sanctuary,* Miranda Martin's lover falls victim to IRA gunmen after he tips off Miranda's brother about a plot to kill him. Moreover, the prolific Johnston has also published perhaps even more compelling novels about the Troubles of an earlier generation, concentrating both on young males (more convincingly than in *Shadows on Our Skin*) in *How Many Miles to Babylon?* (1974) and on an adolescent girl in *The Old Jest* (1979). Here I can only mention these few instances of Johnston's rich explorations of the Troubles and of gender in her ongoing career, which I have surveyed elsewhere.[2] Some of her novels drawing more on her own upper-class background, such as her first book *The Captains and the Kings* (1972) and her more recent one *The Invisible Worm* (1991), are stronger works.

I choose *Shadows on Our Skin* for close analysis here because of how closely parallel it is to *Cal* in its focus on an adolescent male trapped in the Troubles in County Derry. It is a reflection of the high quality of Johnston's writing that even *Shadows on Our Skin* was nominated for the Booker Prize. *Shadows on Our Skin* is one of the many Irish novels that follow the formula of the unhappy Irish childhood memorably outlined by Frank McCourt at the beginning of his memoir *Angela's Ashes:* "the poverty; the shiftless loquacious alcoholic father; the pious defeated mother moaning by the fire; . . . bullying schoolmasters; the English and the terrible things they did to us for eight hundred long years" (1996, 11). Joe Logan is an adolescent boy of unspecified age, perhaps about thirteen, who wants to write poetry, but instead finds himself oppressed by a narrow-minded teacher at school in Derry City, and by a disabled father at home whom Mrs. Logan sardonically calls a "retired hero" (1977, 54). Somehow once wounded in the Civil War, Mr. Logan, like Frank McCourt's father, is convinced that the government has deprived him of a well-deserved pension, and he is fond of Guinness and rebel songs. When Joe comes home from school, his father invariably whines for his tea and sends him out into the Trouble-torn streets to buy him cigarettes and bottles of stout, later assuring Mrs. Logan that "they'll not shoot Joe"

2. See my critical history of the Irish novel (1988, 291–93) for an overview of Johnston's career. Christine St. Peter (1994) has usefully critiqued most of the criticism on Johnston, noting that most scholars have either ignored her work or failed to appreciate her point of view as a woman.

(16). Pulling from his pocket money obtained from Mrs. Logan's job at a café, Joe's father "waved the note with remarkable vigour for one so ill" (13). Habitually, "his father didn't come in until after he had gone to bed" (29).

Joe's parents are like O'Casey's Juno and the Paycock. The strongest character in the novel, Mrs. Logan, when she hears her husband's IRA "fairy tales" and blather about "freedom," bitterly replies: "Have they any more freedom in the south than we have? . . . Are those women down there scrubbing floors because stupid, useless old men are sitting around gassing about freedom?" (159). Mrs. Logan is continually worn down by work; on Saturday, her day "off," she scrubs the house from top to bottom, making her hands red and raw: "Her fingers absorbed her, the swollen joints, the scraped look of the skin, the white flecks on her ridged nails" (153–54). "Even the weight of her thin gold ring seemed too much for her" (39). Joe is aligned with his mother, whereas his older brother, Brendan—returned from England to drive cars for the IRA—sides with his father, unconvincingly telling Joe, "He's a great old skin . . . maimed by life" (34). Mrs. Logan would have preferred that Brendan stay in England— since there are no jobs, only Troubles, in Derry—and she is very attached to and perhaps overly protective of Joe. She "never really liked him going out to play with other children" (19–20).

Young Joe Logan spends much of his time enveloped in feelings of loathing for his father and his teacher, while some nights, "even if there was no trouble, were full of fear and waiting shadows" (69). Poetry is his only outlet early in the novel, though he has to wonder, "Was it poetry at all" (47). In his attempts at poetry, he is free to rage like Sylvia Plath against his father: "Father, it's time for you to go, / . . . Because I hate you so" (7). "I wish that you were bloody dead" (8). Like young Stephen Dedalus in Joyce's *Portrait,* Joe Logan would rather escape into his own mind, hiding from his parents' arguments, which "stripped him of his warmth . . . inescapable, like the stinging smell of smoke that lay night and day around the city" (25). *Shadows on Our Skins* is part Troubles novel, part bildungsroman. Rüdiger Imhof writes that "Johnston wants the reader to regard Joe Logan's frame of mind as somehow akin to that of Stephen Dedalus, for instance with regard to Joe's preoccupation with the sound and meaning of words" (1985, 139). Johnston also borrows the same little schooldays verse that Stephen writes down in *Portrait,* which is quoted by Kathleen earlier in the book (30) and then found by Joe in the copy of *A Golden Treasury of Verse* that she gives him at the end:

> Kathleen Doherty is my name,
> Ireland is my nation,
> Wicklow is my dwelling place,
> And heaven my destination. (191)

Joe is very glad to meet Kathleen Doherty, a young English teacher at a girls' school, who befriends Joe when they meet by chance after school, waiting in the street. Rakishly smoking cigarettes and joking with him, Kathleen takes an interest in his poetry, and she eventually confides to Joe her secret that she is engaged to a British soldier who is stationed in Germany. Lonely in his absence and unsatisfied with her job, she is glad to make a friend in Joe, whom she apparently sees (though Johnston never lets the reader into Kathleen's consciousness) as a sensitive and interesting young friend. She becomes understandably very upset when she witnesses the shooting of two British soldiers in a nearby Derry street, after which Joe's father obnoxiously sings the Irish nationalist song "A Nation Once Again" (153) in a loud voice.

Joe Logan is a boy who is irritated by other males—his father and brother and even his friend Peter—and much more attached to and moved by the two main women in his life. Seeing his mother and Kathleen react to the shooting of the two soldiers, Joe "was frightened by tears, not by children's tears of rage or pain, nor his father's blubbering of self-pity, but adult tears like hers and Kathleen's which made him feel that the world might crack open suddenly" (155).

But then Joe gets too jealous about his brother's interest in Kathleen: "She's my friend. That's what she is. . . . Not girl friend. Friend. Just that . . . and he has to go stick his nose in" (109). So Joe tells Brendan about her engagement to the soldier. The result is that Brendan's IRA friends beat up Kathleen and cut her hair, and she leaves for her native Wicklow, but not before Joe comes begging forgiveness, which she grants by kissing him and giving him her copy of the *Golden Treasury of Verse*. *Shadows on Our Skin* thus concludes with damning evidence of how the IRA ruins people's lives, but also some hope that Joe Logan has learned something from his friendship with Kathleen Doherty.

Cal was Bernard MacLaverty's second novel, following *Lamb* (1980), which dealt with a tragic relationship between a monk and one of his adolescent charges in a home for wayward boys. Born in Belfast, the Catholic MacLaverty worked for a decade as a medical laboratory technician before earning a degree at Queen's University, Belfast, and moving to Scotland. MacLaverty's three collections of stories *Secrets and Other Stories* (1977), *A Time to Dance* (1982), and *The Great Profundo* (1987) are striking for the variety of characters in them. MacLaverty's story "My Dear Palestrina," about a young boy and a music teacher he befriends, could be read as prefatory to both *Cal* and *Shadows on Our Skin.* In contrast to *Shadows on Our Skin,* a minor novel published after Johnston had already established herself as a fiction writer to be reckoned with, *Cal* was the big breakthrough in MacLaverty's career, largely due to the success of Pat O'Connor's 1984 film of the novel, which was released just a year after the book's publication and was one of the first Irish-made movies to achieve success outside Ireland, reaching a modest audience in the United States.

Cal attracted much attention, in both its book and film versions, for an imaginative plot structure in which the protagonist's crime is not revealed until midway through the work, by which time Cal is romancing his victim a year after the crime. MacLaverty makes effective use of both plot and characterization. Stephen Watt also credits him with a sharp sense of his characters' political, postcolonial plight: "The 'politics' of MacLaverty's fiction exists precisely within the tension between individual choice and the power of ideological state apparatuses to determine such choice well in advance. . . . MacLaverty's fiction is a fiction of subalterns struggling to secure moments of happiness" (1993, 144). Cal is older than Joe Logan—nineteen—and lives in a smaller town, near Magherafelt. But once again the woman with whom he falls in love, Marcella Morton, is quite a few years older: twenty-eight. *Cal* is something like *The Summer of '42* with civil war as aphrodisiac. The Catholic Marcella lost her Protestant husband, a policeman, in an IRA attack at their home a year earlier—in which, we eventually learn, Cal drove the car.

Once Cal realizes who Marcella is, he spends most of his time—fueled by a mixture of eros and guilt—obsessively thinking about her and plotting to get closer to her, at the same time that he tries to end his always reluctant IRA involvement. He borrows a Muddy Waters tape from the library where she works and then returns it the very next day, just so he can see her; later he checks out a copy of (appropriately enough) *Crime and Punishment.* When she drops her groceries in the street, Cal picks them up and carries them to her car, and after delivering some firewood to the house where she lives with her late husband's parents, he manages to get hired there as the Mortons' farmhand. After Cal and his father, who were the only Catholics left in a Protestant neighborhood, get burned out of their flat, Cal secretly moves into a dilapidated cottage behind the Mortons' house and, when discovered, is allowed to continue staying there. He has thus enhanced both of his goals with this single stroke: he now lives right next to Marcella, in a place removed from and unknown to the IRA men from whom he is trying to escape. However, at the end, after Cal and Marcella have become lovers, the police come and arrest Cal, leading him away as Marcella is presumably about to learn that he was involved in killing her husband.

The endings of both novels are abrupt and gratuitous, as if both Johnston and MacLaverty, after developing a young man's hopeful relationship with a woman, are saying, "It's too bad that the Northern men of violence inevitably have to destroy people's lives." Johnston's Joe Logan and MacLaverty's Cal McCrystal are both presented as sensitive characters—in pointed contrast to other, much cruder males such as Joe's friend Peter and his brother Brendan, and Cal's erstwhile schoolmate, the bullyboy Crilly. Cal's father, Shamie, is a more sympathetic character than Joe's father; it is just he and Cal living together, Cal's mother and older brother both having died years earlier. But Shamie goes mad after they get burned out, and ends up in an institution, an even more complete failure than Joe's father. Indeed, failed fathers are everywhere in Irish literature.

Whereas MacLaverty's title—just *Cal*—focuses everything completely on his male protagonist, Johnston's title, *Shadows on Our Skin,* opens out on a whole community rather than just one individual: it's not "shadows on *my* skin" or "*his* skin." In terms of sex, I can only say that MacLaverty's Cal is hot, whereas Johnston's Joe is not. If *Shadows on Our Skin* borrows from *A Portrait of the Artist as a Young Man,* then *Cal* is closer to Lawrence's *Lady Chatterley's Lover.* This is by no means to generalize and suggest that Irishmen write about sex and women don't: we shall soon see that Julia O'Faolain and William Trevor reverse such stereotypes, in terms of their main characters in *No Country for Young Men* and *Fools of Fortune.* Nor do I mean to suggest that the particular approaches to gender found in *Cal* and *Shadows on Our Skin* can be found in all of these authors' works. The protagonist of MacLaverty's latest novel and his first since *Cal, Grace Notes* (1997), is a female composer from Belfast—as if MacLaverty deliberately set out to counterbalance the male perspective of *Cal*. Johnston has also concentrated novels on female protagonists, as in *The Old Jest* (1979), about a teenage girl, and *The Invisible Worm* (1991), which explores incest between a father and his very young teenage daughter.

To be fair to Johnston, her protagonist is younger than Cal, too young to try to initiate an affair with Kathleen Doherty. Yet he is certainly not too young to think about sex. Remember John McGahern's *The Dark,* for example, with its otherwise equally young adolescent, male protagonist feverishly masturbating five times a day, inspired by ads of women in the *Irish Independent*. It is hard to believe that Johnston's boy likes spending time with Kathleen but never once thinks about sex, either with her or anyone else (of either gender)—even when the two of them take a bus outing to Grianan, the beautiful old Celtic fort outside and high above the city of Derry. And Joe's lack of credibility as a character is not limited to his lack of sex: it is also hard to believe an adolescent boy who feels guilty about sleeping with his socks on in the wrong bed in his room.

Sex is about *all* that MacLaverty's Cal thinks about, from early in the novel: "Beneath the stuff of her blouse he could see a faint laciness where her body touched it on the inside. . . . He wanted to reach out and touch her hand over the counter, to tell her that everything would be all right" (1983, 17). When he stoops to help Marcella pick up her groceries outside a shop, "Cal saw as she crouched that she wore no stockings. Her legs were tanned and shining" (27). Cal does have a legs fetish, noting that Marcella's are "hairless and tanned, as if she had been to the Continent" (31). He has typically vivid late-adolescent male sex dreams, such as one about a beautiful naked girl who is terrified when he goes to her room (36–37).

Cal's sexual feelings for Marcella are presented in microscopic detail, as in this representative example, when Cal finds himself squeezed up against Marcella, caught in the crowd's crush leaving church: "he could see the slope of her neck and the pin-holes of her pores and the slight down of hair that furred her spine" (41). Afterward "the firmness of her body still burned against the back of his hand" (42). Added to MacLaverty's sexual descriptions is his use of loaded metaphors, reminiscent of Joyce's fireworks in the "Nausicaa" chapter of *Ulysses*. When Marcella tries to rev up the water pump behind the cottage—before any literal lovemaking has occurred—Cal tells her, " 'Come on, put your back into it, Marcella.' He realised that he had said her name for the first time and it was like meat in his mouth" (114–15). Meanwhile, Marcella "was panting with the effort. A little rusted water squirted out and slapped on to the stone font" (115). "They both cheered. . . . In a way they had made a date" (115).

Such descriptive detail is this novel's strength as well as its problem. On the one hand, it grips the reader; when I taught both books, my students welcomed in *Cal* the visual details that they had found lacking in *Shadows on Our Skins,* where they complained that they were not able to "see" any of the characters. On the other hand, MacLaverty's Marcella Morton tends to be objectified as a series of body parts rather than allowed to be a real woman; there is even a scene in which Cal "peeps" at her from outside the house while she's taking her bath. He then fantasizes that Marcella becomes a Sleeping Beauty, the object of his necrophiliac desires. She would be "in a drugged coma and . . . he would kiss her and touch her without her responding" (137); the passive Marcella "would be displayed for him so that he could look at and touch any part of her" (137).

Cal is always trying to mentally "photograph" Marcella: "He tried to fix the picture, to snap the shutter" (102). "He shut his eyes and remembered her lifting arm and tilted breast in the bathroom, the touch of her haunch in church, the way she had held his hand by mistake and how she had looked long and hard into his eyes afterwards" (137). Cal snoops in Marcella's bedroom and even communes with her underwear (138). To be fair to MacLaverty, this is all presented through the eyes and mind of a nineteen-year-old, but one does have to wonder where the protagonist leaves off and the author picks up. MacLaverty does show a good sense of the gender differences between Cal and Marcella when they compare notes on their most guilty memories in life. For Marcella it had to do with refusing to go out with a boy, when she was younger, because he was unpopular: "I think that was bad—to go with the herd" (132). Since Cal cannot admit to Marcella his *real* worst memory (helping kill her husband), he tells her that it was when he joined Crilly at school in beating up a boy in the bathroom (132). Marcella's guilt has to do with feelings, with an interpersonal relationship, whereas Cal's guilt (both what he tells her and what he really feels most guilty about) concerns physical violence. Like Joe Logan, Cal feels Catholic guilt for having harmed the woman he loves with his crime; after informing on Kathleen Doherty, Joe thought to himself, "Father, I have sinned" (184). MacLaverty is able to develop a fuller Catholic theology of guilt for Cal than Johnston can do for Joe: Cal "knew that, because of what he had done, they could never come together. His sin kept them apart" (101). In an extended passage, Cal applies to himself the earlier admonition of a priest he knew: "A man damned himself" (101).

Edna O'Brien's indication that "very few writers have made the gender leap" (1997) is applicable to Jennifer Johnston in interesting ways. Shari Benstock perceptively notes concerning Johnston that although she often writes about male characters and the male-dominated world of political and military conflict, really Johnston's "world is not masculine, not open, accessible, social, a world of action, but rather specifically feminine: closed, suffocated, lonely, and inward-turning" (216). Joe Logan is really a female in the guise of a boy; Benstock notes that "there is little difference in tone or style, even in subject matter," between Johnston's young female and male characters, "between Minnie MacMahon and Nancy Gulliver's tales and Alexander Moore's or between Joe Logan's poetry and Diarmid's battle plans" (1982, 216).[3] Johnston's best character in *Shadows on Our Skin* is not Joe Logan, but his mother.

MacLaverty's Cal is a more believable male protagonist, but Marcella is Cal's wet dream rather than a believable woman; when they finally and inevitably make love, she immediately tells him that of course she had ceased loving her husband before he was murdered, anyway. If Johnston's Joe Logan is a woman's version of a boy, it is equally true that MacLaverty's Marcella Morton is an objectified, male-fantasy kind of woman. In light of Edna O'Brien's

---

3. Katie Donovan, who briefly compares Johnston and MacLaverty, argues that "the children and women who are the protagonists in Johnston's novels are more innocent and passive victims of public machinations which are out of their control and of which they are often scarcely aware. Theirs is more a calculated withdrawal into a private arena of self-definition, while McLaverty's [*sic*] heroes make more public, and thus more obviously punishable gestures of defiance" (1988, 30). I feel that Cal is rather passive himself about the IRA by the end of the novel, and that his differences lie elsewhere. Donovan believes that Johnston and MacLaverty are more similar than I do, writing that they "are unusual in their basic similarity of perspective" (31) and that "both writers tend to portray a similar situation, wherein two social outcasts from opposing backgrounds form a mutually supportive relationship based on shared visions of harmony, tolerance and love" (29).

point, it is not surprising that each author is better at portraying his or her own gender than the opposite gender. Moreover, the tradition in the Irish novel of seeking to represent political conflicts via male-female relationships is at least as old as John Banim's *The Boyne Water* (1826), in which an Englishman travels to Ireland and falls in love with an Irish woman, initiating a convention followed by many subsequent Irish novelists—including, with different twists, Julia O'Faolain and William Trevor.

Like *Shadows on Our Skin* and *Cal*, O'Faolain's *No Country for Young Men* (1980) and Trevor's *Fools of Fortune* (1983) are contemporary novels of the Troubles. However, these two novels, both set in the Republic of Ireland rather than the North, offer more complex perspectives than Johnston's and MacLaverty's novels, both in terms of their narrative points of view and in respect to history. Whereas *Shadows on Our Skin* and *Cal* are both focused almost entirely on the perspective of one young, male protagonist, O'Faolain's and Trevor's novels both elaborately and carefully balance female and male narrators whose lives are interconnected. The narrative intricacy of these two novels is increased by the fact that while each concentrates thoroughly on Ireland, each also reaches beyond Ireland to another key country from which some major characters (and, significant, many readers) come: the United States in *No Country for Young Men* and England in *Fools of Fortune*. Both novels relate Irish political conflicts of the early 1920s to parallel situations of the late 1970s, through characters whose contemporary problems are inherited from the earlier period, either from other characters related to them, or indeed because some of these 1970s characters came of age themselves in the 1920s.

For many Irish people, the 1920s and 1970s are not nearly so remotely separated as such a half-century gap would be for many Americans, for example. When the Irish critic Ann Owens Weekes refers to the 1920s and 1970s as "the two recent sequences of Troubles" (1990, 180), she reflects an Irish sense of the 1920s as still with us, still determining how many Irish people look at the world or at least how they view Ireland. The contemporary violence in the north of Ireland, which was at its worst during the 1970s—following the Catholic civil rights demonstrations of 1968 and the arrival of the British army in 1969—has its roots in the early

1920s. Following the Anglo-Irish or "Black and Tan" war between an English army wearing those colors and the guerrilla Irish republicans, the 1921 Anglo-Irish Treaty separated six Protestant-majority counties forming "Northern Ireland" within the United Kingdom from the other twenty-six counties of the "Free State" (which became the Republic of Ireland in 1949).

In the ironically named Free State, a conservative social code dominated by the narrowly Catholic 1937 constitution of Eamon de Valera, the dominant figure of the Republic, constrained citizens in the South just as surely as the Protestant-dominated apartheid state of Northern Ireland oppressed Catholics in the North. The shift from pre-Treaty British colonial status to the Free State was, in Christine St. Peter's words, "the replacement of one Master narrative, British Imperial history, with another totalizing plot, that of a hyper-masculine Irish nationalism" (1994, 154). As we shall see, *No Country for Young Men* and *Fools of Fortune* are both novels about history repeating itself, in very specific ways, from the 1920s to the 1970s. The 1921 partition remained the major source of conflict in the 1970s and indeed in the late 1990s.

In addition to the narrative and historical complexities of these two novels, several other parallels between *No Country for Young Men* and *Fools of Fortune* draw them together in ways that are perhaps even more striking than the similarities between *Shadows on Our Skin* and *Cal,* given the greater complexity of O'Faolain's and Trevor's novels; it is remarkable that two such labyrinthine books are similar in so many ways. In both novels, for example, the 1920s and 1970s are linked through the experiences of families so tightly intertwined that inbreeding is a problem. The major protagonists of both novels are cousins who marry or become lovers and produce children: Grainne and Michael O'Malley in *No Country for Young Men* and Willie Quinton and Marianne Woodcombe in *Fools of Fortune.* Their respective children, Cormac O'Malley and Imelda Quinton, experience problems as a result of these interfamilial unions; Cormac is an angry adolescent boy, and Imelda has lost her sanity and ability to speak, while the surrounding peasants see her as beatific and blessed with special powers.

In addition to inbreeding, sexual repression and perversion, often associated with violence, generally run rampant in these novels. For example, in *No Country for Young Men,* Patsy Flynn, whose knowledge of sex is limited to "stray dogs in alleys" (1980, 360), commits the crucial murder at the end, and sex between Grainne and her uncle, Owen Roe (who have had an inbred affair), turns into violence. Trevor painstakingly gender-balances sexual harassment in *Fools of Fortune:* Willie and Marianne are both bothered during their student days, Willie by Miss Halliwell and Marianne by Professor Gibbs-Bachelor. Both novelists follow the long-standing tradition in the Irish novel of seeing sexual relations between men and women as related to and emblematic of political relationships among nations and factions. In this respect, these novels are likewise comparable to *Shadows on Our Skin* and *Cal,* in which would-be romantic relationships are similarly played out along the grid of the sectarian divide in the north of Ireland. As I did with *Shadows on Our Skin* and *Cal,* here I want to examine *No Country for Young Men* and *Fools of Fortune* by first analyzing one novel and then the other, in some detail, and then turning to a comparison and contrast of the these two rich works.

No Country for Young Men has attracted more attention than any of O'Faolain's other works and is one of the most popular contemporary Irish novels among critics of the genre.[4] It was reviewed as "a stunning performance" in the *New York Times Book Review* and short-listed in England for the Booker Prize (Weekes 1997, 333). Like Jennifer Johnston, O'Faolain is the daughter of both a famous Irish literary father, Seán O'Faolain (1900–91), the celebrated fiction writer and tremendously influential editor and critic, and also an accomplished literary mother, Eileen O'Faolain (1900–88), author of children's books of myths and folktales. Julia was therefore "always aware," as she remarked in an interview, "that what the house produced was books" (quoted in Maddox 1984, 8). Her mother kept her at home until she was eight, filling her with the kinds of Gaelic legends that she would draw on in *No Country for Young Men* (Weekes 1990, 174). Her parents' influences were pervasive at the same time that she also went her own way: "They had this romantic thing about Ireland that I've reacted against. . . . They put me off Ireland. . . . I've inherited not the romanticism but the disillusion with it" (quoted in Maddox 1984, 8). As her father remarked, "She has no inhibitions. It helps that she's such a realist, interested in the material composition of everything, clothes, hats, shoes" (quoted in Maddox 1984, 9). She chose to leave Ireland, living in Italy and

4. See these six studies of *No Country for Young Men:* Weekes 1986 and 1990 (174–90); T. Moore 1991; Van Dale 1991; St. Peter 1994; and T. O'Connor 1996a.

the United States, and marrying an Italian-American history professor in Los Angeles.

O'Faolain had established solid credentials as a feminist writer for at least a decade before the appearance of *No Country for Young Men*. Her irreverently entitled first novel, *Godded and Codded* (1970), published in the United States as *Three Lovers*, was a frank account of women's sexual experiences, whereas her second novel, *Women in the Wall* (1975), examined the place of women in the religion of medieval Gaul. Collaborating with her husband, Lauro Martines, she also published *Not in God's Image: Women in History from the Greeks to the Victorians* (1973). Having done so, as she later told Ann Owens Weekes, she felt that she could then move beyond feminism per se, writing about women "without being bound by their political concerns" (Weekes 1997, 333). At the same time, issues of gender and politics are certainly all bound up together in O'Faolain's magnum opus, *No Country for Young Men*.

This novel begins by immediately interlacing the early 1920s and the late 1970s and establishing a conflict of genders. We cut straight from the opening March 1922 clipping from the New York *Gaelic American* newspaper, about Irish-American republican activist Spark Driscoll's death (1980, 7–8)—to "1979," with Judith Clancy (seventy-five years old now, seventeen in 1922) half-remembering and upset by "A knifing? There was a gap in her brain" (8). In 1922 as well as 1979, "both Judiths were clammy and terrified inside their clothes" (9). A doctor has advised Judith to "let go" of the half-lost memory that tortures her; she fears "more electro-shock" (9). " 'The past can kill,' she told him" (9). "She dreamed of a man who held his guts in his hand" (10)—a dream that for fifty-seven years has been troubling Judith (11), who sees "blood . . . in all my dreams" (11) and also gets "a fizzle in my extremities whenever I watch an axe or sword murder" on television (10–11).

The reader is thus well prepared, from the beginning of the novel, for the fact that is explicitly revealed more than 300 pages later: that Judith stabbed and killed the Irish-American IRA activist Sparky Driscoll in 1922 (342). Sparky had upset Judith as well as her brother Seamus and his IRA henchmen because he was about to run off to America with Kathleen, the sister of Judith and Seamus; he had unhooked a bayonet from the wall to playfully demonstrate it to the unhinged Judith, who ended up plunging it into his stomach. Like his carefully paralleled counterpart in 1979, James Duffy, Sparky thereby participates in his own *self*-destruction. As for Judith, Seamus sees to it that her crime is concealed, and Owen O'Malley subsequently has her committed to a convent. As Laura Van Dale notes, Judith "is punished for stepping out of bounds, not only those of femininity but also those of political correctness. The crime is not so much that she killed Sparky, but that she did not disguise the murder as an accident" (1991, 23).

Judith is not only a key agent in the plot of the novel, but also a richly symbolic female character. "My memory is a bog" (12), she remarks. O'Faolain glosses for her non-Irish readers the fact that " 'bog' was the Gaelic word for 'soft' " (12). Similarly, through James Duffy, the visiting American academic, she clarifies, especially for her U.S. readers, that "the Gardai were the Irish police" (28), " *fáil* is the Gealic for "destiny"—it rhymes with boil' " (67), and Grainne O'Malley's name was pronounced "Grawnya. . . . 'Graw' is the Gaelic for 'love' " (170) and was "the name of one of the love heroines of pre-Christian Irish saga. She was betrothed to the ageing warrior-leader, Finn Macool, but forced one of his fighting men to run off with her" (170). As she recollects it from Mucklea, her girlhood boarding school, Judith's "bog" is a wonderfully evocative symbol of the lost spaces of women and myth in the past: "This region was as active as a compost heap and here the millenial process of matter recycling itself was as disturbing as decay in a carcass. Phosphorescent glowings, said to come from the chemical residue of bones, exhaled from its depths" (12). This was a place where a person "could be sucked without trace" (12), much as Judith has been removed for decades to the convent.

At the center of *No Country for Young Men* is not the mysterious Judith, however, but the younger woman who takes Judith in when the convent closes down, Grainne O'Malley, and the American who becomes Grainne's lover, James Duffy. This novel is dominated by alternating sections utilizing the related but quite different narrative points of view of Grainne and James. James has come to Ireland to make a documentary, to be called *Four Green Fields,* about his American predecessor, Sparky Driscoll, for an organization called "Banned Aid" (a clear parody of the actual NORAID, the U.S. fundraising arm of the IRA). He is a burnt-out English professor who failed to get tenure, speaking to many readers of the novel by freely spouting Yeats and Joyce.

O'Faolain herself is likewise involved in marking her novel with the words of the Scylla and Charybdis of Irish literature, Yeats and Joyce. Her title, *No Country for Young Men,* is an obvious revision of Yeats's speaker's opening dismissal of Ireland in "Sailing to Byzantium": "That is no country for old men." To shift from "old" to "young" is not only to bring Yeats up to date, but to underscore the novel's extensive attention to the ways in which the dominant, archaic power structure of the old Republican Free State—embodied in such characters as Owen Roe O'Malley, Grainne's nasty uncle and a clone of de Valera—inhibit the development of young men like James Duffy and Cormac O'Malley, Grainne's son, not to mention young women such as Grainne. For Owen Roe and Michael O'Malley, O'Faolain also borrowed the names of Yeats's "two warring personae: the wild dreamer Michael Robartes and the worldly Owen Aherne, the public man who sets about the task of building a new Ireland" (Theresa O'Connor 1996a, 133).

James Duffy was similarly the name of the protagonist of "A Painful Case," Joyce's grim story of how an extramarital affair, as in O'Faolain's novel, is doomed to failure in the midst of personal and cultural repression; in Joyce's story, the affair is broken off and results in the death of one of its participants. Theresa O'Connor, who argues that *No Country for Young Men* is partly a revision of Joyce's *Finnegans Wake*—with Judith's violent, recurrent dream as its controlling metaphor—notes that James Duffy was also "the name of Joyce's Prankquean" (1996a, 126) and that Duffy's friend Larry O'Toole, who sends him to Ireland to make his movie, "bears the name of the *Wake*'s masterbuilder, Laurence O'Toole" (128).

A thoroughly modern woman, Grainne O'Malley has a name that is even more laden with meanings that draw us back into older Irish traditions. Best known is her aforementioned source in the ancient Irish legend of Grainne and Diarmuid, running off together much to the chagrin of Finn, who finally kills Diarmuid and virtually enslaves Grainne, who returns to Finn so that her children will be spared. Lady Gregory had been attracted to Grania's "power of will" in writing her play *Grania* (1910); O'Faolain felt a similar attraction. Here Diarmuid corresponds to James Duffy, and Finn to Grainne's husband Michael and perhaps even more to their controlling uncle, Owen Roe. Like Sparky Driscoll, James is murdered at the end of the novel—by Patsy Flynn, Owen Roe's pathetic yet despicable messenger—because he is on the verge of leaving for America with a woman with IRA connections, in this case Grainne.

Despite the misogynist streak in the old legend, O'Faolain sees Grainne as one of the remarkably strong women populating ancient Irish myth. As Grainne tells James, "in Celtic tales, it was the

woman who rode by on a white horse and bade [a man to] leap up
behind her" (171). The leading authority on Irish goddesses, Rosalind
Clark, describes Grainne as a "sovereignty figure" (1991, 198).
O'Faolain's use of the ancient myth has been extensively examined by
Ann Weekes, who notes that Finn "tricked Grainne into living with
him by promising to protect her children," as similarly, Grainne
O'Malley pledges to stop seeing James Duffy in return for Owen
Roe's promise not to take her son, Cormac, to dangerous republican
gatherings" (1990, 187). But Owen Roe, a nastier man than Finn,
refuses. Most optimistically, Weekes nonetheless believes that at the
end of the novel, "return to Michael and her old pattern is not
inevitable. The text falls from Grainne, not she from the text" (101).

There are further intertextual links to Grainne's name (both
first and last). As noted in chapter 2, Grainne O'Malley was the
name of a real woman, a remarkable late-sixteenth-century feminist
pirate of sorts called Grainne (or "Grace") O'Malley. In 1583 Sir
Henry Sidney described her as "a most famous feminine sea captain" and noted that his son, the poet Sir Philip Sidney, was en-
thralled with her (Sawyer 1993, 21). Furthermore, we already know
that Emily Lawless had formerly borrowed the name of this actual
historical "Sea Queen," as she was called, Grainne O'Malley, as the
name of her own protagonist of her earlier feminist (or protofeminist)
novel, *Grania* (1892), who lives and dies as courageously and independently as she can on the island of Inis Meáin, in the Aran
Islands off the west coast of Ireland. Either O'Faolain, who as we
have seen was extremely well steeped in Irish literature, had read
Lawless's novel, or this is an amazing coincidence whereby both
novelists borrowed the name and the example of the "Sea Queen."

In any case, we now have an elaborate intertextual set of relationships among the ancient Irish myth, the late-sixteenth-century
woman, and the novels of Lawless and O'Faolain, concerning which
a whole chapter unto itself could be written. My purpose, however,
is to return to the gender relationships in *No Country for Young Men,*
especially as they can then subsequently be compared with those in
Fools of Fortune. Therefore, let me limit myself here to noting that
a comparison of Lawless's Grania O'Malley with O'Faolain's is very
suggestive about both what they have in common and how much
things changed for Irish women from the late nineteenth century
to the late twentieth century. Both novelistic Grainnes are strong
women who struggle against the patriarchy of the family, and both
experience catastrophic loss at the end: the impending death of

Grania's sister, Honor, and finally Grania's own death, in Lawless; and James Duffy's death, in O'Faolain. Unlike Lawless's Grania O'Malley in late-nineteenth-century rural Ireland, however, O'Faolain's urban, late-twentieth-century Grainne O'Malley has a much wider range of experiences, including marriage, a son, and extramarital affairs.

Returning even earlier back into Irish women's literary tradition, one might also note that like *The Wild Irish Girl* (1806) by Sydney Owenson ("Lady Morgan")—*No Country for Young Men* involves a male protagonist identified with the reader's country (Mortimer the profligate Ascendancyman in the case of *The Wild Irish Girl*) who falls in love with a passionate Irishwoman with a myth-laden name: Glorvina in the earlier novel, and now Grainne. Both therefore make use of the woman-as-Ireland tradition and its landscape potentialities, though in terms of setting and style, *The Wild Irish Girl* and Lawless's *Grania* are more similar to each other than to O'Faolain's novel with its grittier urban and more contemporary, postmodern features.

Nonetheless, O'Faolain's Grainne O'Malley remains a woman frustrated by the constrictions of her society and by her marriage to her husband. We first meet her when she is returning to Dublin from several months of work in London at a center for battered women. She has been on sabbatical from her marriage to Michael, her cousin whom she married as a very young woman. Michael had been a brilliant man and a great singer, the only man she had ever loved, but then he turned into an alcoholic and half-impotent spouse. After he learns of her affair with James and her plan to leave him, Michael asks Grainne, "What right have you to be unhappy? . . . What more am I supposed to do?" (156). Grainne does not directly answer him, but in a remarkable and unique intrusion, it appears to be the voice of the author herself that does parenthetically but clearly answer him: "(Cleave to her. Be one flesh with her.)" (156).

But Michael can only remain limply under the sway of Owen Roe and his political friends; Michael actually would like to write the biography of his own Free State grandfather, Owen O'Malley. It was for good reason that when people had first heard of the earlier engagement of Michael and Grainne, "cracks had been made. . . . One was: 'the fellow couldn't marry his hero grandfather so he did the next best thing' " (46). That old joke about the true Irishman being the one who will step across the bodies of ten naked women to get to a pint of Guinness was based on men like Michael O'Malley.

When Grainne meets James Duffy, she is quickly attracted to him, even though "she remembered when she had last been looked at this way. It had been in Italy and she had hated it" (100). Of course it had been in Italy—not Ireland—and it has to be a foreigner, James Duffy, who will make love to her now, not an Irishman like her husband. As James's Polish-American wife, Therese, had told James before he went to Ireland, "Irishmen were all priests or homosexuals or both and their women driven to the ruthless entrapment of foreign men" (15). Therese released James to his own sabbatical from marriage, and he later sends long, frank, confessional letters to her, California-style, about his relationship with Grainne.

In contrast to the other novels examined in this chapter, where women tend to be either sexual objects (as in *Cal* and *Fools of Fortune*) or sexually dormant (in *Shadows on Our Skin*), Grainne is very much an active sexual agent: "She wanted a wanton love affair" (124). When Grainne and James make love, O'Faolain's language is more graphic than that of Johnston (who avoids sex), MacLaverty (whose heated descriptions deal more with the fantasy of sex than with its reality), or Trevor (to whom we are coming shortly). Afterwards, Grainne "glanced at the tongue which had just now been sliding in her vulva, like a neat, tail-flirting fish" (208). Later she thinks, "Sex was the merry-go-round. She did and didn't want to get off" (294). "She enjoyed but was suspicious of her enjoyment" (297).

O'Faolain also reverses sexual stereotypes. It is *James,* not Grainne, who wants to know where their relationship is going, whereas Grainne, he feels, is more content to just simply make love for an hour each day. James complains to Grainne, "I'm being treated like a goddamn nineteenth-century whore. You won't be seen in the street with me. I'm a penis" (228). He wants to marry her (230), whereas Grainne tries to simply enjoy the moment.

At the same time, however, James is caught in all too typically male ways of looking at women and the world. He was set up to come to Ireland by Larry O'Toole, a former football teammate on the college team that James quarterbacked. At the end of the novel, when he is deported but his plane develops a problem and turns back to Dublin, James decides to return to Grainne, take her away, and thus "win this game in overtime" (356). He has a classically male, football player's way of viewing the world. When he first meets Grainne, he mentally compares her body to that of Therese, his wife: "He was like a dog-breeder encountering a specimen of his breed" (106).

Although in some ways she is sexually liberated, Grainne is well aware of the ways in which her sexuality is constrained by the society that threatens her. Through Grainne we encounter perhaps the frankest, clearest assessments, outside of Edna O'Brien's, of the challenges faced by contemporary Irish women. Grainne remembers when she got married: "She had been eighteen. . . . Men defined you. Men talked. Other men listened and what was said could decide a girl's future. Then" (101). Indeed, de Valera's 1937 constitution declared that the "State shall . . . endeavour to ensure that mothers shall not be obliged by economic necessity to engage in labour to the neglect of their duties in the home" (quoted in St. Peter 1994, 156). As Christine St. Peter notes, "The mother, constitutionally unable to obtain abortion and divorce, and until 1979 unable to obtain legal contraception, remains in the home as financial dependent of her husband. And thus is the patriarchal family *textualized* as 'the necessary basis of social order' in the Irish Republic (Article 41.2)" (1994, 157).

In 1922, Sparky had asked Judith, "What about the women? They'll have a say now too, won't they?" Judith replies, "The men in this country would never let the women have a say" (213). From girlhood Judith had experienced that "Home was *male* territory. . . . What bound the family together was their Republicanism" (20). At Mucklea School in 1921, Judith and "History pupils were reminded that it was an Irishwoman's frail morals which led to the English first coming here in 1169. Women bore inherited guilt" (34).

In Ireland in 1979, Grainne thinks to herself and to us,

> laws here had not changed, nor people's attitudes underneath. Not for women. . . . Ireland moved with the times but stayed in the rear. Women could now live openly with lovers but legal protection lagged. There was no divorce. . . . Caught between canons, you could go wrong. The old said: "Thou shalt not be promiscuous nor basely sensual." The new: "Thou shalt have orgasms and enjoy God's good gifts to the full." The old, being old, had been eroded by custom. An ill-married woman might, it conceded, have a discreet fling if nobody got hurt in the process. The new was rigid: be honest, it bullied, be frank. . . . It demanded that women be true to themselves and break up a bad marriage instead of trying, hypocritically, to smooth things over. Unsatisfactory mates should be replaced. (101–2)

Grainne is prevented, however, from replacing her husband with her new lover, by Patsy Flynn, who, shortly before he pushes James's car into the River Liffey, calls Grainne a "whore" in his own mind and wonders about Grainne and James, still upstairs in her flat: "Could sexual congress be taking place up there this minute?" (363). Sparky Driscoll and James Duffy have thus both been murdered by virgins who are opposed to sex: Judith and Patsy, two misguised tools of a hegemonic, perverted Irish Republic. Some things never change, O'Faolain suggests.

In view of the many similarities and points of comparison between *No Country for Young Men* and *Fools of Fortune,* it is not surprising to learn that William Trevor reviewed O'Faolain's novel in 1980, the year in which it appeared and during the period when he was presumably working on his own novel. He praised it in *Hibernia* as "illuminated by a seriousness that is refreshing to encounter; though entertaining and rich in comedy, it eschews the trivial and is actually *about* something" (quoted in Weekes 1997, 335). Indeed, *No Country for Young Men* and *Fools of Fortune* are *about* many of the *same* serious things (or similar themes): the entrapment of Ireland circa 1980 in many of the same Troubles of the early 1920s, the ways in which a single murder from the earlier period continues to haunt characters during the later time, the distressed connections between Ireland and the United States and England, the interactions of women and men in the midst of these Troubles, the resulting difficulties of the love relationships of the main characters, and the diverse misfortunes (including madness) of many other characters as well.

These two novels are also parallel in their popular and critical success. *Fools of Fortune* won the Whitbread Award as the best novel of 1983, and in 1990 it was made into a successful film (starring Julie Christie as Willie's mother). Trevor (whose full name is William Trevor Cox) is one of the most celebrated contemporary Irish fiction writers, but as an émigré to England who has written a good deal of fiction set there, his reputation as an Irish (rather than English) writer was slow to develop, though it is now very solid. Collections of stories such as *The News from Ireland* (1985) and novels such as *Felicia's Journey* (1994), a powerful study of the victimization of a young Irish woman in England, have cemented

Trevor's status. Like O'Faolain, Trevor set his first novels outside of Ireland and, while he has written more and more frequently about Ireland, he continues to live away from his native County Cork. Whereas O'Faolain's background was middle-class and Catholic, Trevor came from upper-middle-class, Protestant stock, just a few steps away from the Big House. He is a Protestant who writes perceptively about Catholics, and a man who writes compassionately about women; indeed, Mary Fitzgerald-Hoyt rightly points out that Trevor has not received sufficient critical appreciation for the "realistic, sympathetic portrayals of Irish women in his fiction" (1993, 28).

Whereas *No Country for Young Men* opens with a clear insistence on the direct linkage of 1922 and 1979, *Fools of Fortune* begins by connecting and contrasting Ireland and England with equal precision, from its first sentences: "It is 1983. In Dorset the great house at Woodcombe Park bustles with life. In Ireland the more modest Kilneagh is as quiet as a grave" (1983, 9). O'Faolain's theme of history repeating itself is stated even more directly by Trevor, on his first page, as he explains how three generations of English, Woodcombe daughters united in sequence with three generations of Ascendancy-Irish, Quinton sons, with each of the Woodcombe women coming to live at Kilneagh, in County Cork. Somehow these events "caused history again to repeat itself, as in Anglo-Irish relationships it has a way of doing" (9). Whereas history repeats itself twice in *No Country for Young Men,* through the likes of Sparky Driscoll and James Duffy as well as Kathleen Clancy and Grainne O'Malley, it happens *three* times in *Fools of Fortune,* and the third time—the story of Willie Quinton and Marianne Woodcombe, the main plot of this novel—is not the charm, at least not in any conventional sense.

Much as *No Country for Young Men* alternates narrative sections aimed at Grainne, James, and Judith, *Fools of Fortune* is even more clearly divided into sections labeled (in the table of contents) "Willie," "Marianne," and "Imelda" (their daughter), with the sequence repeated twice, the sections growing shorter each time; the first "Willie" section is just over half the length of the book, whereas the second "Willie" section is just a few pages long, and the other sections become similarly abbreviated, with the second, final "Imelda" chapter just two pages in length. Thus, what starts out as a leisurely Anglo-Irish novel speeds up into an abrupt, disorienting, postmodern narrative. Such is the late-twentieth-century, Anglo-Irish, Big House inheritance explored by Trevor: stately, dignified, and inert in its past, yet complicated, disjointed, and painful in its present.

In view of the repeated marriages between the Quintons and Woodcombes, incest is even more of a problem in *Fools of Fortune* than in *No Country for Young Men,* and one can only wonder to what extent Imelda's insanity is a result not only of the troubled relationship, or lack of relationship, between her parents, but also of their already interwoven gene pool. Such themes as history repeating itself, inbreeding, insanity, and other often Gothic motifs can also be found in many earlier Irish Big House novels, such as the original one, Maria Edgeworth's *Castle Rackrent* (1800), in which four generations of landlords bring themselves to ruin; Somerville and Ross's *The Big House of Inver* (1925), a neo-Gothic tale of dispossesion and sex; and Elizabeth Bowen's *The Last September* (1929), so closely related to *Fools of Fortune* that the central catastrophe in both novels involves the burning of the Big House. Indeed, Trevor has remained fascinated with the Big House subgenre, following up *Fools of Fortune* with another Big House novel, *The Silence in the Garden* (1988).

Most of *Fools of Fortune* is written in the form of long letters of sorts between the two main cousins, Willie and Marianne. Willie's description of their first meeting in late adolescence is both aloof and loaded, in light of what happens later, with a lovestruck but repressed Willie introducing Marianne: "I simply said you were a cousin I had forgotten I possessed. . . . For my last two terms at school you continued to possess me" (101). Each comes from a genteel, liberal family. Anna Woodcombe, Marianne's ancestor and the first Woodcombe woman to marry a Quinton and live at Kilneagh, involved herself in Famine relief efforts in the middle of the nineteenth century. Willie Quinton's father sympathized and gave aid to Michael Collins (who appears in the novel) and his IRA rebel forces during the Anglo-Irish War of 1919–20; at the same time, he has an acute sense of the hopelessness of history that will be well borne out by succeeding events: " 'Oh, fool of fortune,' my father commented. . . . It was his favourite expression" (30).

The first tragedy at Kilneagh comes when Doyle, an employee of the Quintons who is suspected of informing to the English Black and Tan forces, is found murdered, hanging from a tree, his tongue cut out. The English Sergeant Rudkin and his men then take misdirected revenge on the Quintons by burning their house and shooting Mr. Quinton to death; Mrs. Quinton makes it out alive and Willie, hiding in the arms of their maid Josephine, survives, but his two sisters perish in the fire. Willie then moves to Cork City with his mother and Josephine, but his mother is never again the same, and she ends up committing suicide. Marianne Woodcombe meets Willie at his mother's funeral, and then, in love with him and offering him solace, goes to his bed in the middle of the night. In contrast to O'Faolain's graphic accounts of the sexual encounters of Grainne and James, Trevor's narrative is very indirect about the crucial tryst of Marianne and Willie. Marianne, as she narrates, simply "placed the lamp on your dressing-table and spoke your name" (113). That is the only time they make love in the whole book, but it is enough to produce Imelda. Marianne then leaves for boarding school in Switzerland, and by the time she returns to Kilneagh, pregnant with his child, Willie has left under mysterious circumstances, and Marianne does not see him again for a half-century. Only later do we (and Marianne) learn that Willie went to England and killed Sergeant Rudkin in revenge, and has remained out of Ireland in exile. He does not return to County Cork until 1971, for Josephine's funeral, and then again in 1982, for good. "Truncated" is Trevor's own word, via Marianne, for the experiences of Willie and Marianne: "Truncated lives, creatures of the shadows. Fools of fortune, as his father would have said; ghosts we become" (187).

Celeste Loughman notes how much is *not* said in this novel, as for example when Willie and Marianne barely speak before (or after) making love: "Though Trevor has said, 'I think that *Fools of Fortune* was entirely about chance,' the novel leads the reader elsewhere—to the destructive force of language and the mercy and healing power of silence" (1993, 95). After Imelda collapses at school and enters her life of madness or sainthood (depending on one's point of view), she chooses not to speak. Trevor has remarked that resilience and revenge were both crucial to Willie:

> Willie can recover from such an awful experience as the fire, whereas his mother can't, and she hasn't really lost more than he has lost. . . . What interests me is that human beings are made like that. Willie has the resilience and the toughness, as anyone, I think, of that age would (he is about eleven at the time of the fire) react with such resilience. . . . After his mother takes her life, his need for vengeance must have become impossible to ignore. After that, he just couldn't *live* a normal life, and it seems to me to be understandable that he couldn't—there's a sort of guilt and a dreadful shame that he would have felt. . . . You know

all this was sort of very chancy stuff, but that's the way life is.
(Trevor 1986, 7–8)

The narratives of Willie and Marianne are their attempts to explain themselves to each other across lifetimes in which each has barely seen or communicated with the other. Each narrative proceeds rather obliquely, not in actual epistolary form as letters sent between the two, though eventually direct address does creep in: "You were aware of my existence then," we learn from Willie in his account of his adolescence, "and I, without interest then, of yours" (67). Indeed, this is a book chock-full of unrequited love. Beyond Willie and Marianne, we meet Mr. Derenzy, the chief of staff at Mr. Quinton's mill, who loves Willie's Aunt Patsy, but does not marry her because he feels beneath her station; the proletarian Catholics Tim Paddy and Johnny Lacy, both of whom love (but cannot have) Josephine; and another aunt of Willie whose husband dies in World War I after just one month of marriage. As Willie stresses in his opening narrative, "All around us there seemed to be this unsettling love" (31).

The only sex we find in this novel seems perverse or furtive: the Cork schoolteacher Miss Halliwell's unwanted kisses on young Willie's neck, Professor Gibbs-Bachelor's groping of Marianne in Switzerland, Timmy Paddy and "the Sweeney girl" in the Quinton's garden, and indeed Marianne and Willie's quick rendezvous just after his mother's funeral. In this respect, *Fools of Fortune* is just the opposite of Johnston's *Shadows on Our Skin* with its platonic presentation of the teacher Kathleen Doherty and young Joe Logan; in Trevor's novel, Miss Halliwell, as recounted by Willie, kisses him "on the side of my face, her fingers stroked my wrist. . . . I knew she was wearing violet-coloured underclothes" (1983, 64), and Gibbs-Bachelor later whispers maniacally to Marianne, "You are my little wife" (122).[5] The all-male boarding school outside Dublin to which Willie is sent after his instruction in Cork by Miss Halliwell is all very phallic: "Mr. and Mrs. Scrotum" are the boys' nicknames for the headmaster and his wife (68), and there is an extended account about a teacher who was fired for sodomy and urinates through a window onto the sleeping man who terminated him. Moreover, much as in *Cal,* where violence and eros are intertwined, "references to love and war are often juxtaposed in *Fools of Fortune*" (Morrison

5. See Morrissey's perceptive article (1990) about these relationships.

1987, 494). For example, Willie imagines at first that he sees English Black and Tan soldiers outside Kilneagh, but then it actually turns out to be "ferrety" Tim Paddy with "the Sweeney girl" (37). Everyone is linked in love and war in this novel, and the "mix of these two realities will literally become incarnate in [Willie's] own child, conceived in love and born into war" (495). It is partly this disjunctive mixture of love and war that drives Imelda mad.

For young Willie growing up in the Big House, it is not only love, but life in general, that seems detached and distant. He memorizes, appropriately enough, Oliver Goldsmith's poem "The Deserted Village," that nostalgic, late-eighteenth-century, Anglo-Irish hymn to the superiority of past over present times. He learns his Irish history from Fr. Kilgarriff, a Catholic priest who was defrocked (reportedly because he was involved with a young woman) and then employed as family tutor by Mr. Quinton. "Will we tackle a bit of history?" (12), Fr. Kilgarriff asks Willie. Indeed they do, in the course of this novel. The great nonviolent nineteenth-century Irish leader Daniel O'Connell, the "Liberator," is the hero of Fr. Kilgarriff, who is crushed by the violence that befalls Kilneagh and the Quinton family.

As noted earlier, Julia O'Faolain is interested in the contrast between earlier and contemporary times for Irish women—as evidenced in Grainne's trenchant observations about changing "canons," and in the equally sharp contrast between men's and women's different ways of conceptualizing the world, exemplified by James Duffy, who thinks like the football player he was and looks at women like a dog breeder, and in Grainne O'Malley, who perceives sex in fish imagery. Trevor's Willie Quinton and Marianne Woodcombe, in contrast, seem nearly as alike—as two genteel young people thrown into chaos by events—as they are different, with Willie going off to enact violent, male revenge on Rudkin and Marianne staying behind at Kilneagh to raise their child. Willie and Marianne follow these different trajectories in their lives, but they tend to think and to tell their stories rather similarly, in rather detached styles for such turbulent tales. "I would love to remember you," remembers Willie at the beginning of the novel, "in the scarlet drawing-room, so fragrant in summer with the scent of roses, warmed in winter by the wood Tim Paddy gathered" (10). "We both wore black"—Marianne recalls at the beginning of her first narrative, linking herself to Willie in her account of his mother's funeral—"a fact that had been noted by our fellow-travellers. The consideration for our mourning implied that it rendered us delicate" (107). Indeed, O'Faolain and Trevor reverse gender stereotypes, not only in how they present the sexual encounters of their major characters, but in some other respects as well. Shari Benstock's assessment of Jennifer Johnston's world, cited earlier, as "not masculine, not open, accessible, social, a world of action, but rather specifically feminine: closed, suffocated, lonely, and inward-turning" (1982, 216) seems truer to Trevor's novel than to O'Faolain's. Likewise reversing stereotypes, Weekes notes O'Faolain's "no-holds-barred approach to sensitive political topics, to male territory in fact" (1997, 175).

At the end, when Willie and Marianne are finally reunited, "Fingers touch. One hand grasps another, awkwardly in elderliness" (191). Rather than dramatic and resolved, the final reunion of Willie and Marianne seems perhaps too little, too late:

> He smiles the smile of the photograph, and in the band of her straw hat the girl he loves wears an artificial rose. They are aware that they exist so in the idyll of their daughter's crazy thought. They are aware that there is a miracle in this end. . . . They are grateful for what they have been allowed, and for the mercy of their daughter's quiet world, in which there is not ugliness. (192)

Describing the lost Big House, the Anglo-Irish, Protestant Trevor uses Yeats even more poignantly than does the middle-class, Catholic O'Faolain, with Trevor making particular use of Yeats's poem "The Lake Isle of Innisfree," which functions as a symbolic lens through which Imelda imagines a happy life for her parents, with an evening "full of the linnet's wings" (192).

The endings of both novels are open—with O'Faolain's readers wondering what Grainne will do next, and Trevor's readers puzzling over whether or not Willie and Marianne are really together and will stay that way. *Fools of Fortune,* a depressing novel most of the way through, has a more upbeat ending, suffused with Imelda's beatific final vision, whereas *No Country for Young Men,* generally a more vibrant and livelier work, concludes more dishearteningly, with the murder of James Duffy. The difference in tone between these two novels' endings may be linked partly to their divergent rhetorics of readership, especially their intended non-Irish readerships. *No Country for Young Men* seems addressed partly to U.S. readers, by an author who married an American and moved to the United States, and indeed this novel has been met with a warm critical reception in the United States. In light of long-standing and ongoing Irish-American financial support for the IRA, O'Faolain seems to be warning American readers, through her accounts of the murders of Sparky Driscoll and James Duffy, to beware of such involvement.

The secondary readership of *Fools of Fortune,* beyond Ireland, seems to be more England than the United States, as constructed by an author who settled in Devonshire. In contrast, and in the context of eight centuries of ongoing conflict between England and Ireland, Trevor seems to hold out hope at the end of the novel that peace might yet be found. This attitude is reinforced by his deliberate construction of an English-Irish allegory through the repeated marriages between the English Woodcombe women and the Irish Quinton men. Lest his readers miss this allegory, Trevor even has Marianne remark to the Quintons' attorney that "when you looked at the map Ireland and England seemed like lovers. 'Don't you think so, Mr Lanigan? Does the map remind you curiously of embrace?' " (162). Within this allegorical framework, therefore, at novel's end Willie and Marianne represent Ireland and England meekly coming back together at peace with each other after many years of separation, in some sort of painful reconciliation, and Imelda is their confused but visionary future. It is curious and notable that Trevor chooses to reverse the long-standing Irish novelistic tradition of sending an English*man* to Ireland to fall in love with an Irish *woman,* a convention that in turn responds to the older cultural symbols of England as male (John Bull) and Ireland as female (Cathleen ni Hoolihan), and one that O'Faolain adapts by sending an American (James Duffy as Uncle Sam) to Ireland to fall in love with an Irish woman (Grainne O'Malley as Cathleen ni Hoolihan as well as the mythical Grainne). Trevor's gender reversal further problematizes these old, inherited cultural constructs.

❧

Many of the other differences between *No Country for Young Men* and *Fools of Fortune*—and they are not as stark in these two sophisticated and parallel novels as the contrasts between *Shadows on Our Skin* and *Cal*—may have as much to do with O'Faolain's and Trevor's different class backgrounds as with their genders. O'Faolain's main characters tend to be earthier, and Trevor's more detached, not so much because of their genders, but because O'Faolain writes of middle-class Dubliners and Trevor of Ascendancy gentry. Working-class peasants also populate *Fools of Fortune,* but only as secondary characters, in the distance, as contrasted with Willie, Marianne, and Imelda, whose narratives dominate the novel. In terms of gender, the contrasts between *No Country for Young Men* and *Fools of Fortune* seem less complete than the ones found in Johnston's and MacLaverty's two novels, for both O'Faolain and Trevor carefully balance the perspectives of their leading male and female characters, whereas Johnston and MacLaverty focus univocally on the point of view of a single male adolescent (as different as Joe and Cal are from each other).

Nonetheless, all four of these novels reflect Ireland and perhaps the world in general by showing how violence and war function as male preoccupations—particularly for Johnston's Joe Logan and his brother and father, for MacLaverty's Cal and the other males around him, for O'Faolain's Owen Roe O'Malley and his IRA cohorts, and for Trevor's Willie Quinton and the men involved in his revenge plot. Women tend to stand apart from the violent Troubles and to be victimized: Joe's mother and Kathleen Doherty in *Shadows on Our Skin,* Marcella Morton in *Cal,* Judith Clancy and Grainne O'Malley in *No Country for Young Men,* and Willie's mother as well as Marianne and Imelda in *Fools of Fortune.* Even Judith, who commits a murder, seems more a tool and victim of the Troubles than a real participant in them. All four novels expose the evils of violence, and all four authors thus seem to oppose violence, but there does seem to be a more righteous side to violence in *Fools of Fortune:* the torching of Kilneagh and the murder of Willie's father and sisters are so brutal that many readers may not blame Willie too much when, after his mother's suicide, he takes vengeance on Sergeant Rudkin by surprising him in his home in England in the middle of the night and stabbing him to death.

In the women's novels, violence is almost entirely externalized—something the other people (men) do, except when Judith kills Sparky after being driven to it by the IRA men who surround her, and when Grainne bites Owen Roe, an action in the war between the sexes, which he has coming to him because of how badly he's treated her. The males to whom Johnston and O'Faolain give primary attention—Joe Logan and James Duffy—are not participants in violence. In the men's novels, in contrast, violence is internalized; both *Cal* and *Fools of Fortune* offer detailed accounts of the consequences of the guilty involvement in violence on the part of their protagonists, Cal and Willie. In MacLaverty's and Trevor's novels, the central question about violence is much more "Why do we do this?" In Johnston's and O'Faolain's novels, it's more "Why do *you* do this?" Yet all four novels show how the Troubles did great damage to both women and men.

6

Conclusion

Fictional treatments of the Troubles, as discussed in my last chapter, have been continued in more recent Irish fiction and film.[1] Edna O'Brien's *House of Splendid Isolation* (1994) and Seamus Deane's *Reading in the Dark* (1996) are two more recent novels that extend the concerns of the ones discussed in my last chapter. Several Irish films have presented the Troubles to a wider public over the past several years, further exploring gender differences. These novels and films provide additional, more recent examples of works by women and men in need of further study in the ways that I have more closely examined the dozen authors and their works treated in my previous chapters. After describing these works, I offer some final observations about the authors and works examined in my earlier chapters, and suggest a few more authors and texts by women and men that would reward comparison and contrast. I hope that others will take up this task of reading women and men, together.

Edna O'Brien's *House of Splendid Isolation* is set in the Republic of Ireland and shows how the older Troubles continue to ravage the lives of women and men, as already seen in Julia O'Faolain's *No Country for Young Men* and William Trevor's *Fools of Fortune*. McGreevy, an IRA man on the run, hides out in the house of Josie O'Meara, who is ostensibly his hostage but comes to sympathize with him; as in the other novels, a man brings violence to a woman. McGreevy and Josie have more in common than they expect, however: McGreevy's wife was murdered by Protestant paramilitaries, and Josie's abusive husband was shot by the police. Like the characters of Trevor's Big House, McGreevy and Josie have many stories, which O'Brien interweaves, such as Josie's earlier clandestine

---

1. There are many other Troubles novels and related fiction dating from the 1960s and earlier; for studies of these works, see Cronin 1969b; D. E. S. Maxwell 1973; Deutsch 1976; McMinn 1980; Titley 1980; Imhof 1985; and Sloan 1993.

affair with a priest. But in the end, their peculiar idyll is inevitably doomed: the police come and in a big shootout, Josie is killed and McGreevy captured. Thus, O'Brien links two characters very different in their female versus male (and other) experiences—and then appears to suggest that the differences win out over the linkages.

Reading in the Dark is the remarkable first novel of a writer best known as a highly influential critic of Irish literature: Seamus Deane, native of Derry, for many years a professor at University College, Dublin, and now a distinguished professor at the University of Notre Dame. Like Jennifer Johnston's *Shadows on Our Skin* and Bernard MacLaverty's *Cal,* this novel is set in Northern Ireland and closely examines the effects of sectarian conflict from the point of view of a Catholic boy. Presented as a series of sharply drawn autobiographical vignettes of a boy growing up in Derry City, it builds suspense around a hard-kept set of family secrets divulged only late in the novel: that the boy's mother's IRA father had ordered the killing of the boy's father's brother, Uncle Eddie, mistakenly thinking that he was an informer; that the boy's mother had once dated a man involved in killing Eddie; and that his mother had learned the reason for Eddie's death only years later, at her father's deathbed, and had chosen never to tell her husband about the roles played by her father and the man she dated. The boy figures it all out, but finally respects his mother's desire to keep it secret.

Reading in the Dark is striking in its many vivid, realistic details. If Johnston's *Shadows on Our Skin* was an outsider's novel—a Protestant woman's novel about a young Catholic boy in Derry—then *Reading in the Dark* is the insider's story, with Deane naturally much truer to the facts about what it was like growing up as a young Catholic boy in Derry than Johnston was able to be. Like Johnston's Joe Logan, however, Deane's protagonist also hides a gun that he finds in the family home, frustrating policemen who then come and search the house, and as in Johnston's novel, the old Celtic fort of Grianan is a key secondary setting beyond Derry itself, suggesting a refuge from the world of guns in the city below. Deane's novel offers a more vivid account than *Shadows on Our Skin,* one that includes the boy's believable and entertaining thoughts about sex and seems true to the life of the city with all its class distinctions and complications.

The treatment of the Troubles and the continuation of these problems of gender and history in recent Irish films is a subject that

would require a book unto itself. This topic is worth briefly out-
lining here, however, for these themes are not limited to the hand-
ful of novels that I have examined, but are also echoed throughout
many works (including, of course, texts outside of my scope here,
in poetry and drama). The Troubles remain embedded throughout
Irish culture and its artifacts, functioning also as a site for exploring
how political and gender conflicts are interwoven with each other.
It seems natural to connect novels with films, partly because two of
the novels I discussed in my last chapter were made into films: *Cal*
(1984) and *Fools of Fortune* (1990), both effectively adapted by the
same director, Pat O'Connor, who later achieved wider commercial
success with the film *Circle of Friends* (1995). Paul Simpson and
Martin Montgomery have published an excellent study of *Cal* in its
film version, pointing out, for example, that Cal's voyeurism is
undercut or challenged more in the film than in the novel. For
instance, in the film the bathroom scene in which Cal is a Peeping
Tom watching an unsuspecting Marcella is cut in favor of two
shorter scenes where Cal watches Marcella but is spotted by her
doing so (1995, 158). Pat O'Connor thus nicely reverses expecta-
tions we might have about filmmakers missing the complexities of
a novel in order to simplify them for voyeuristic viewers of their
films. O'Connor, who also filmed Trevor's *The Ballroom of Romance,*
is fairly faithful to *Fools of Fortune,* while he experiments with chronology and takes some interesting liberties. For example, Willie
does not exile himself to Italy and Central America as in the novel,
but to the Aran Islands—adding to the Irish cultural contrasts that
the film can concisely offer in visual terms.

   Neil Jordan and Jim Sheridan are the two best-known creators
of contemporary Irish films that explore some of the gender issues
wrapped up in the Troubles, particularly in Jordan's *The Crying
Game* (1992) and Sheridan's *In the Name of the Father* (1993), *Some
Mother's Son* (1996), and *The Boxer* (1997). It makes sense for us to
link literature and film here just as naturally as they themselves
did: Jordan was first a fiction writer and Sheridan a stage director.
My own critical history of the Irish novel, published in 1988 before
Jordan became so much more famous as a filmmaker, included a
late section that moved directly from MacLaverty to Jordan (author
of such novels as *The Past* [1980] and *The Dream of the Beast* [1983]).
Jordan's and Sheridan's Troubles films are part of the amazing Irish
film industry, which emerged seemingly out of nowhere in the early
1980s. It gathered pace beginning with Jordan's early, melodra-

matic film about the Troubles, *Angel* (1982) and moved from one striking success to the next, peaking with Sheridan's *My Left Foot* (1989), for which Daniel Day-Lewis won the Best Actor Oscar and Brenda Fricker Best Supporting Actress.

Jordan's *The Crying Game*—whose title entered the popular vocabularly so much that an computer search brings up many unrelated articles about other subjects in which this phrase has been used—was a huge popular and critical success. Its success was due not only to its bold and artful representations of IRA characters, but even more to a vigorously promoted yet initially well-kept secret having to do with gender: the true, transvestite identity of one of the main characters. This film's popularity extended well beyond Ireland and Britain to the United States, where questions about sexual identities, the rights of homosexuals in the military, and so forth, were very much in the popular air in 1992. In *The Crying Game* a Black, British soldier is taken hostage by IRA terrorists outside of Belfast. With Jordan playing off Frank O'Connor's classic 1931 story "Guests of the Nation" and Brendan Behan's famous 1958 play *The Hostage,* a bond in captivity grows between the soldier (Forest Whitaker) and his IRA guard, Fergus (Stephen Rea, an actor and key member of Deane's Field Day Theatre Company). Later, in England, Fergus finds Dil (Jaye Davidson), the soldier's beautiful sweetheart, who turns out to be a man. *The Crying Game* thus manipulates several binary oppositions—male/female, black/white, Irish/British—each of which is called into question. Jordan's characterizations of his leading men, however, are better than those of such women as Jude, the cruel IRA sidekick played by Miranda Richardson; similarly, in his later film about the earlier Troubles leading up to 1922, *Michael Collins* (1996), the main focus is a male one on the title character (played by Liam Neeson) and his tragic friendship with Harry Boland and rivalry with Eamon de Valera, whereas Julia Roberts' role as Collins's lover Kitty Kiernan is a comparatively minor, marginalized one. In *The Crying Game,* Fergus fits into much the same subgenre of character as Cal—the reluctant IRA operative struggling to escape the IRA and achieve a fuller humanity—one with which Sheridan also works.

Indeed, as played by Daniel Day-Lewis, the protagonist of Sheridan's *In the Name of the Father*—a film whose popular and critical success equalled or even exceeded that of *The Crying Game*— is the most reluctant IRA man possible, since he was apparently innocent of such activity. His story was based on the true story of Gerry Conlon and three other young northern Irish natives (the "Guilford Four") wrongly convicted and imprisoned for some fifteen years for an IRA pub-bombing near London in 1974. Sheridan's film concentrates on the solid relationship between Gerry and his father (who ends up joining his son in prison); as in *The Crying Game,* the core of this film is about how men relate to other men, with women comparatively on the periphery, though Sheridan does try to develop the role of Gerry's female attorney. As if to compensate for such a male focus, Sheridan's next film (with Terry George) about the Troubles, *Some Mother's Son,* centered on the consciences of two women, both mothers of convicted Republican activists, as they try to sort out their different points of view on the difficult situations in which they and their families find themselves when their sons join the 1981 IRA prisoners' hunger strike led by Bobby Sands. Here the violence of the Troubles is only a precursor to a bigger story, as it is also in his latest collaboration with Daniel Day-Lewis, *The Boxer,* in which Day-Lewis plays a Belfast fighter struggling to make a new life for himself after fourteen years in prison as an IRA man.

For each of these films that has achieved wide commercial success, there are numerous other Irish films that have never or seldom been seen by any large audiences, especially in the United States or elsewhere outside Ireland, and some of those films similarly grapple with the gender issues of the Troubles. Two of them are women's films: Margo Harkin's *Hush-A-Bye Baby* (1989) and Orla Walsh's *The Visit* (1992). With Emer McCourt in the lead and Sinéad O'Connor playing one of her friends, *Hush-A-Bye Baby* forcefully presents the dilemma of a teenage girl in Derry whose boyfriend is interned by the British just as she discovers that she is carrying his baby. Walsh's short film tells the story of Sheila, the wife of a Republican prisoner in the Maze prison outside Belfast. Sexually separated from her husband for seven years, Sheila has an affair, thereby breaking the code of behavior for IRA wives, and she has to go tell her husband that she is pregnant. These important but neglected films provide new feminist spins on the general pattern that we have seen in both fiction and film: that the Troubles are presented chiefly through the experiences of its victims and nonparticipants, who include women like these ones (and Johnston's Kathleen Doherty, MacLaverty's Marcella Morton, and O'Faolain's Grainne O'Malley) as well as men like Gerry Conlon (and

MacLaverty's *Cal* and his father, Trevor's Willie and his father, and others).[2]

Another excellent but neglected film is Cathal Black's *Korea* (1995), which shows how the older Troubles still haunt contemporary characters, in a somewhat similar vein as in *No Country for Young Men* and *Fools of Fortune*. Black's visually beautiful and powerfully lyrical film, set around Lough Neagh in the North, is an adaptation of a story by John McGahern about a young Irishman who emigrated to the United States and then died in the Korean War. Like Sheridan's plot in *In the Name of the Father,* Black's storyline is riveted on a father-son relationship: an old fisherman who bears a grudge, rooted in the old Troubles, against a more prosperous family whose son has died in Korea, and his own son, who struggles to convince his father to overcome his old animosities so that both of them can get on with their lives. It is regrettable that films like these ones have not reached a wider audience.

We can find in these films some of the same kinds of differences that we discovered in the novels. For example, the female protagonists of both Harkin's *Hush-A-Bye Baby* and Sheridan and George's *Some Mother's Son* depend on other women for mutual support; *Some Mother's Son* follows a "double-female" pattern much like the one we observed in Somerville and Ross's lives as well as in the novels of Lawless and Kate and Edna O'Brien. The closest instance of mutual male support comes in *In the Name of the Father* when the protagonist's father joins him in prison, and in *Korea* when the son finally begins to break down his father's oppressive isolation. Otherwise, the males at the center of such films as *The Crying Game* and *Michael Collins* move largely in isolation.

Close attention to such texts suggests that male-female differences may run even deeper in Ireland, at least in these works, than do the Catholic-Protestant divisions that have received much more attention. At the same time, such gender distinctions are thoroughly interwoven with issues of class and sect, for as in the rest of the world, Irish women and men do not live in a vacuum, but

2. In her 1996 article "Reimagining the Nation: Gender and Subjectivity in the New Irish Cinema," Aine O'Healy critiques the tendency of Irish films to marginalize female characters but notes that some more recent films try to overcome this tendency. O'Healy discusses, among other films, *In the Name of the Father, The Crying Game, Hush-a-Bye Baby,* and *Some Mother's Son.* See also Megan Sullivan on Walsh's *The Visit.*

wholly within the society that they make up. The Troubles endured by these novelists' and filmmakers' characters are many, yet there is also much to learn from the courage and perseverance of the best of them.

❦

In my previous chapters, I devoted considerable attention to the distinctions of class and sect apparent among the dozen writers whose works I examined. In chapters 2 and 3, I emphasized how remote Emily Lawless was from Liam O'Flaherty, and Somerville and Ross from James Joyce, in the class and sectarian terms of these Protestant Ascendancy women versus the Catholic working- and middle-class men. O'Flaherty is unique among my dozen writers as the only writer whose background was working-class as well as Irish-speaking. In chapter 4, in contrast to chapters 2 and 3, I focused on three contemporaneous writers from fairly similar, middle-class, Catholic backgrounds: Edna O'Brien, John McGahern, and Brian Moore. Even the authors of the earlier novels that I outlined as providing male versus female models for the Irish bildungsroman—Joyce and Kate O'Brien—were also from middle-class Catholic backgrounds (though O'Brien's family was better off than that of Joyce's failed father). Yet the gender differences evident in these novelists, as discussed in chapter 4, suggest that as a form of difference in Irish fiction, gender does indeed appear to cut as deeply as—or in some ways even more deeply than—religion and class.

In terms of religion and class, chapter 5 included my most diverse and complex set of authors: the Ascendancy Protestant woman Jennifer Johnston, the middle-class Catholic man Bernard MacLaverty, the middle-class Catholic woman Julia O'Faolain, and the Ascendancy Protestant man William Trevor. In fact, they represent the four basic possible combinations of gender and religion within the middle class and the upper-class Ascendancy. In respect to class and religion, the pairings would be Johnston and Trevor, from the Protestant Ascendancy, versus MacLaverty and O'Faolain, from the Catholic middle class. Some similarities and differences follow these alternative pairings. For example, the novels by Johnston and Trevor are more reticent concerning their depictions of sex, in contrast to the much more graphic ones by MacLaverty and O'Faolain. It would be dangerous to say the least, however, to conclude that the Protestant Ascendancy is typically more repressed about sex and middle-class Catholics more liberated. In fact, in Ireland most people would assume that historically, the reverse has been the case, and even within the relatively small number of writers cited in my chapters, a counterexample is provided by Kate O'Brien (a middle-class Catholic who was taciturn about sex, at least in *The Land of Spices*).

To concentrate on gender, class, and religion is not to ignore other important distinctions within Ireland, such as region and language. On the one hand, in chapters 2 and 3 I pointed out how crucial authors' native places were to their consciousnesses: O'Flaherty the native of the Aran Islands versus Lawless the non-native, and Somerville and Ross from rural counties Cork and Galway versus Joyce the quintessential Dubliner. I deliberately included Brian Moore in chapter 4 in order to examine how adolescence in urban Belfast compared with rural upbringings in Edna O'Brien's County Clare and John McGahern's County Roscommon. The contrasts traced in chapter 5 between Johnston and MacLaverty also have to do with the fact that Johnston is from Dublin and MacLaverty from Belfast, and those between Trevor and O'Faolain are doubtlessly also linked to Trevor's background in small-town County Cork versus O'Faolain's in urban Dublin (as well as the even more cosmopolitan cities to which her famous father took her, such as London and Boston). However, such regional roots are complicated by the fact that each of these authors wrote the novels I discuss from other places of expatriation: Derry for Johnston, Scotland for MacLaverty, Los Angeles for O'Faolain, and England for Trevor. As with the expatriated Joyce, dislocation and emigration are important parts of the narrative points of view of these and many other Irish authors.

Nonetheless, despite these many complexities of class, religion, region, and language, it is clear that gender continues to cut across and to intertwine with these other distinctions in persistent, powerful ways. The fact that gender has clearly made big differences for the more diverse contemporary novelists treated in chapters 4 and 5, just as much for the two pairs of Anglo-Irish women versus Catholic men examined in chapters 2 and 3, shows just how tenacious gender is. The distinctions traced in chapters 2 and 3 that one might be tempted to ascribe to class and sect show up just as persistently in chapter 4 (in the cases of novelists sharing the same class and religious background) and chapter 5 (with four novelists marked by a complex set of different class and religious experiences).

I hope that this book encourages others to take up the comparative study of Irish (and other) female and male writers. We need to gender-balance literary studies, to continue to bring women writers into the mainstream, and to attend to gender in male authors just as much as we tend to do when writing about women. I have deliberately limited myself here to a relatively small set of authors, so that I could select a few especially logical pairings and read these writers and their texts as closely as possible. What other Irish authors might similarly reward attentive comparison and contrast? Katie Donovan (1988) outlines several other such pairings, such as Maria Edgeworth and William Carleton, Molly Keane and John Banville, and Val Mulkerns and Desmond Hogan. We would also do well to think this way about the other genres of Irish writing. Why not compare and contrast Augusta Gregory's plays with Yeats's, rather than continue to neglect her work or subsume it to that of her more canonical contemporary? Similarly, instead of examining women's and men's poetry always separately, as is generally the case, would it not be useful also to compare and contrast, across gender lines, the work of Eavan Boland and Thomas Kinsella, or Medbh McGuckian and Derek Mahon, or Nuala Ní Dhomhnaill and Seán Ó Ríordáin? The best such pairings are perhaps others that will occur to future critics, I hope.

In my introduction, I asked this question: What do Irish women and men want? My answer is that they want what people everywhere want: to find their way in the world. In most cases, this means trying to grow up—and not only in the bildungsromans analyzed in chapter 4, where coming of age is the defining feature of the novels. An important part of maturity is the ability to interrelate meaningfully with other women and men. Maturity, that most traditional of values, provides a very useful ground for evaluating all of the works discussed in this book—not only the traditional ones, but also the nontraditional ones. For example, when James Joyce appears to forgive his brother in *Finnegans Wake* (even as masked beneath his linguistic games), he achieves a new level of maturity in terms of their relationship, just as Stanislaus Joyce did when he too forgave his brother, remorsefully trying to heal the rift after James Joyce's death.

Maturity is a yardstick that distinguishes characters who fail from those who succeed. For example, O'Flaherty's Fergus O'Connor, the Stranger, is immature; Martin and Mary Delaney in "Spring Sowing" are more mature. Joyce's Stephen Dedalus is one of the most famous immature characters in literature, and Leopold Bloom has been held up as a (peculiar) model of maturity as often as any other literary character. Somerville and Ross's Francie Fitzgerald is tragically immature; their Mrs. Knox, comically mature.

Women sometimes achieve maturity only at the price of their freedom or even their lives—as in the cases of Lawless's Grania O'Malley and Edna O'Brien's Kate Brady. Especially given that Irish violence is traditionally focused on men, it is striking how many more women than men die in these novels, at least among the major characters. Francie Fitzgerald is another example. Somerville and Ross's Charlotte Mullen, O'Faolain's Grainne O'Malley, and MacLaverty's Marcella Morton all survive, but each has lost the man she loved and faces a difficult future, as does Johnston's Kathleen Doherty.

Except for the obvious exception of *Finnegans Wake,* these are predominantly realistic works of fiction. Yet McGahern's *The Dark* and Trevor's *Fools of Fortune* offer ironic endings that seem to place the ideal of maturity under some kind of postmodern question mark. When the protagonist of *The Dark* calls in his father, drops out of the university, and decides to join the Civil Service in Dublin, is that maturity? When after many years in exile, Willie Quinton rejoins Marianne Woodcombe and their insane, out-of-wedlock daughter Imelda, can we confidently believe that they will live happily ever after? Of course, maturity is not simply a status to be achieved; it involves a lifelong process of struggle. The most mature characters may be the ones who are struggling the most, such as Joyce's Bloom or the Grania/Grainne of both Lawless and O'Faolain.

The Troubles of Ireland's history are intermixed with the troubles of these kinds of characters. We come to maturity in struggle at the end of some of the best of those Troubles films, as in *Korea, The Crying Game,* and *Some Mother's Son. Korea* reminds us that maturity is not just a matter of age, for the father in Black's film has to learn from his son how to move beyond his grudges in order to find peace of mind. In *The Crying Game,* Dil teaches the secret for escaping isolation—loving and being loved—to Fergus. Fergus finally understands the power of love only at the end, when he is in prison and Dil visits him repeatedly, exemplifying loyalty and utter dedication. It takes the sexually aberrant Dil to teach this lesson, and it takes a woman in *Some Mother's Son* to begin to break down the Troubles. Appropriately enough, the same actress, Helen Mirren, who played Marcella Morton, a younger woman largely defeated by the Troubles, in O'Connor's *Cal,* plays a mature mother in *Some Mother's Son* who finally rises above the Troubles. At the end of the film she stands listening to men arguing over her hunger-striking son's life and trapped in their sectarian disagreements. Finally, their words become a meaningless blur of verbiage to this mother, and she walks out and signs the release form breaking her son's hunger strike. Her mature message is that human life is more important than political conflict.

"It's time to grow up," is the message of such works. Like many countries in terms of their historical divisions of gender, class, religion, and race, Ireland has often seemed still stuck in adolescence. It is no accident that the bildungsroman has remained so popular in Irish fiction. Growing up, a difficult and lifelong process, may be the only way out of Ireland's Troubles—North and South, male and female.

I keep thinking back to the woman and the man on the island of Inis Meáin in whose house I was a guest for five weeks in the summer of 1976. A short woman twenty years younger than she looked, the woman of the house worked her fingers to the bone. The tallest man on the island, the man of the house still made pampooties (the Aran moccasins) and fished, though he was in semiretirement by then. Both wore traditional clothes; a lot has changed on Inis Meáin since 1976, when most homes still did not have electricity. The woman and the man moved in separate worlds, in some respects, yet they were as close as could be, and clearly loved each other and their family and friends. One could not begin to understand or appreciate either person without some sense of their clearly demarcated gender roles. At the same time, they reversed gender stereotypes: she was reserved and rather taciturn, especially in the company of a foreigner such as myself, while he was very outgoing and warm. Both treated me—a vegetarian American who was learning their language—very kindly. I could not imagine one without the other. They had come of age long ago, and they had found their way within their own world.

Those two people on Inis Meáin exemplified maturity. So too do an elderly Quaker couple, from outside Dublin, who also confound stereotypes. Good friends of mine, they come into my mind still more forcefully now, in the present tense. He sits at one end of their large dinner table, jovially dishing out magnificent foods that he has prepared. She is at the other end, dominating conversation in the most positive sense, entertaining everyone, asking the right questions, saying the most splendid things; she reminds me of Somerville and Ross's Mrs. Knox, but is even more warmly impressive—and real. There is never a dull moment in their large house, which is filled throughout with laughter and good company. If they sit at opposite ends of the table, it is only to enclose their lucky guests within their warmhearted companionship; their great meals and wonderful lives represent a joint project. They embody kindness, wisdom, and peace.

As I hope has become apparent in this book, there are many kinds of women and men in Ireland, which is a more diverse country than many outsiders think. Yet I choose to remember these individuals, and to offer this book to readers who want to understand people like them as well as the characters and the authors of Irish fiction.

Works Cited

Index

Works Cited

Abel, Elizabeth, ed. 1982. *Writing and Sexual Difference*. Chicago: Univ. of Chicago Press.

Anonymous. 1781. *The Triumph of Prudence over Passion; or, The History of Miss Mortimer and Miss Fitzgerald*. 2 vols. Dublin: S. Colbert.

Ap Hywel, Elin. 1991. "Elise and the Great Queens of Ireland: 'Femininity' as Constructed by Sinn Féin and the Abbey Theatre, 1901–1907." In *Gender in Irish Writing*, edited by Toni O'Brien Johnson and David Cairns, 23–39. Buckingham: Open Univ. Press, Philadelphia: Milton Keynes.

Arensberg, Conrad. 1959. *The Irish Countryman: An Anthropological Study*. Gloucester, Mass.: Peter Smith.

Banim, John. 1826. *The Boyne Water*. 1976. Reprint, Lille, France: Université de Lille.

Banville, John. 1973. *Birchwood*. 1984. Reprint, London: Panther.

Barreca, Regina, ed. 1988. *Last Laughs: Perspectives on Women and Comedy*. New York: Gordon and Breach.

Bate, Jonathan. 1991. *Romantic Ecology: Wordsworth and the Environmental Tradition*. New York: Routledge.

Beale, Jenny. 1987. *Women in Ireland: Voices of Change*. Bloomington: Indiana Univ. Press.

Begnal, Michael H., and Grace Eckley. 1975. *Narrator and Character in "Finnegans Wake."* Lewisburg, Pa.: Bucknell Univ. Press.

Behan, Brendan. 1958. *The Hostage*. 1978. Reprint. In *Brendan Behan: The Complete Plays*, 127–237. New York: Grove Press.

Benstock, Bernard. 1965. *Joyce-again's Wake: An Analysis of "Finnegans Wake."* Seattle: Univ. of Washington Press.

Benstock, Shari. 1982. "The Masculine World of Jennifer Johnston." In *Twentieth-Century Women Novelists*, edited by Thomas F. Staley, 191–217. Totowa, N.J.: Barnes and Noble.

Black, Cathal. 1995. *Korea*. Cathal Black Films and Black Star Films.

Blount, Marcellus. 1990. "Caged Birds: Race and Gender in the Sonnet." In *Engendering Men: The Question of Male Feminist Criticism*, edited by

Joseph A. Boone and Michael Cadden, 225–38. New York and London: Routledge.

Bohan, Janice S. 1993. "Regarding Gender: Essentialism, Constructionism, and Feminist Psychology." *Psychology of Women Quarterly* 17: 5–21.

Boone, Joseph A., and Michael Cadden, eds. 1990. *Engendering Men: The Question of Male Feminist Criticism.* New York and London: Routledge.

Bowen, Elizabeth. 1929. *The Last September.* 1964. Reprint, New York: Alfred A. Knopf.

Boyd, Ernest. 1922. *Ireland's Literary Renaissance.* Revised edition of original 1916 book. 1968. Reprint, New York: Barnes and Noble.

Brewer, Betty Webb. 1983. " 'She Was a Part of It': Emily Lawless (1845–1913)." *Éire-Ireland* 18, no. 4: 119–31.

Brown, Terence. 1981. *Ireland: A Social and Cultural History, 1922–85.* 1985. Reprint, London: Fontana.

Cahalan, James M. 1979. "Tailor Tim Buckley: Folklore, Literature, and *Seanchas an Táilliúra.*" *Éire-Ireland* 14, no. 2: 110–18.

———. 1983. *Great Hatred, Little Room: The Irish Historical Novel.* Syracuse: Syracuse Univ. Press; Dublin: Gill and Macmillan.

———. 1988. *The Irish Novel: A Critical History.* Boston: Twayne; Dublin: Gill and Macmillan.

———. 1991a. "Edward Garnett and the Making of Early Modernist Fiction." *Lamar Journal of the Humanities* 17.2 (Fall): 41–52.

———. 1991b. "Forging a Tradition: Emily Lawless and the Irish Literary Canon." 27, no. 1: 27–39.

———. 1991c. *Liam O'Flaherty: A Study of the Short Fiction.* Boston: Twayne.

———. 1993a. " 'Humor with a Gender': Somerville and Ross and *The Irish R.M.*" *Éire-Ireland: The Journal of Irish Studies* 28, no. 3: 87–102.

———. 1993b. *Modern Irish Literature and Culture: A Chronology.* New York: G. K. Hall / Macmillan.

———. 1997. "Liam O'Flaherty." In *Modern Irish Writers: A Bio-Critical Sourcebook,* edited by Alexander G. Gonzalez, 344–48. Westport, Conn.: Greenwood Press.

Cahalan, James M., and David Downing, eds. 1991. *Practicing Theory in Introductory College Literature Courses.* Urbana, Ill.: National Council of Teachers of English.

Cairns, David, and Shaun Richards. 1988. *Writing Ireland: Colonialism, Nationalism, and Culture.* Manchester: Manchester Univ. Press.

Campbell, Joseph, and Henry Morton Robinson. 1961. *A Skeleton Key to "Finnegans Wake."* New York: Viking.

Castle, Gregory. 1989. "The Book of Youth: Reading Joyce's Bildungsroman." *Genre* 22: 21–40.

Chen, Bi-ling. 1998. "De-mystifying the Family Romance: A Feminist Reading of Somerville and Ross's *The Big House of Inver.*" *Notes on Modern Irish Literature* 10: 17–25.

Chodorow, Nancy. 1978. *The Reproduction of Mothering: Psychoanalysis and the Sociology of Gender*. Berkeley and Los Angeles: Univ. of California Press.

Cixous, Hélène. 1976. *The Exile of James Joyce*. Translated by Sally A. J. Purcell. London: John Calder.

———. 1987. "Reaching the Point of Wheat, or A Portrait of the Artist as a Maturing Woman." *New Literary History* 19, no. 1: 1–21.

Claridge, Laura, and Elizabeth Langland, eds. 1990. *Out of Bounds: Male Writers and Gender(ed) Criticism*. Amherst: Univ. of Massachusetts Press.

Clark, Rosalind. 1991. *The Great Queens: Irish Goddesses from the Morrígan to Cathleen ní Houlihan*. Savage, Maryland: Barnes and Noble.

Collis, Maurice. 1968. *Somerville and Ross: A Biography*. London: Faber.

Cook, Bruce. 1974. "Brian Moore: Private Person." *Commonweal* 100 (23 Aug.): 457–59.

Cotter, Denis. 1982. "Irish Novels of the Developing Self, 1760–1960." Ph.D. diss., University College, Dublin.

Cronin, Anthony. 1982. *Heritage Now: Irish Literature in the English Language*. Dingle, County Kerry: Brandon.

Cronin, John. 1969a. " 'The Dark' Is Not Light Enough: The Fiction of John McGahern." *Studies* (winter): 427–32.

———. 1969b. "Ulster's Alarming Novels." *Éire-Ireland* 4, no. 4: 27–34.

———. 1972. *Somerville and Ross*. Lewisburg, Pa.: Bucknell Univ. Press.

Cross, Eric. 1942. *The Tailor and Ansty*. London: Northumberland.

Cullingford, Elizabeth. *Gender and History in Yeats's Love Poetry*. 1993. New York and Cambridge: Cambridge Univ. Press.

Cummins, Geraldine. 1952. *Dr. E. OE. Somerville: A Biography*. London: Andrew Dakers.

Curtin, Christopher, and Anthony Varley. 1987. "Marginal Men? Bachelor Farmers in a West of Ireland Community." In *Gender in Irish Society*, edited by Christopher Curtin, Pauline Jackson, and Barbara O'Connor, 287–308. Galway: Galway Univ. Press.

Dahlie, Hallvard. 1969. *Brian Moore*. Toronto: Copp Clark.

———. 1981. *Brian Moore*. Boston: Twayne.

Deane, Seamus. 1986. *Short History of Irish Literature*. South Bend, Ind.: Univ. of Notre Dame Press.

———. 1996. *Reading in the Dark*. 1997. Reprint, New York: Alfred A. Knopf.

Deane, Seamus, Andrew Carpenter, and Jonathan Williams, eds. 1991. *The Field Day Anthology of Irish Writing*. 3 vols. Derry: Field Day.

Denvir, Gearóid. 1989. "The Living Tradition: Oral Irish Language Poetry in Connemara Today." *Éire-Ireland* 24, no. 1: 99, 107.

DeSalvo, Louise, Kathleen Walsh D'Arcy, and Katherine Hogan. 1989. Introduction. *Territories of the Voice: Contemporary Stories by Irish Women Writers*, xi–xxii. Boston: Beacon Press.

Deutsch, Richard. 1976. " 'Within Two Shadows': The Troubles in Northern Ireland." *Cahiers Irlandaises* 4–5: 131–54.

Devine, Paul. 1979. "Style and Structure in John McGahern's *The Dark*." *Critique* 21, no. 1: 49–58.

Doherty, J. E., and D. J. Hickey. 1989. *A Chronology of Irish History since 1500*. Dublin: Gill and Macmillan.

Donovan, Katie. 1988. *Irish Women Writers: Marginalised by Whom?* Dublin: Raven Arts Press.

Donovan, Katie, A. Norman Jeffares, and Brendan Kennelly, eds. 1994. *Ireland's Women: Writings Past and Present*. Dublin: Gill and Macmillan.

Dowling, Colette. 1981. *The Cinderella Complex: Women's Hidden Fear of Independence*. New York: Pocket.

Doyle, Roddy. 1987. *The Commitments*. 1989. Reprint, New York: Vintage.

Eckley, Grace. 1974. *Edna O'Brien*. Lewisburg, Pa: Bucknell Univ. Press.

Edgeworth, Maria. 1800. *Castle Rackrent*. 1995. Reprint, New York: Oxford Univ. Press.

Ellmann, Richard. 1958. Introduction. *My Brother's Keeper: James Joyce's Early Years,* by Stanislaus Joyce, x–xxii. New York: Viking.

———. 1982. *James Joyce*. Revised edition of original 1959 biography. New York: Oxford Univ. Press.

Fehlmann, Guy. 1979. "The Composition of Somerville and Ross's *Irish R. M.*" In *The Irish Short Story,* edited by Patrick Rafroidi and Terence Brown, 103–11. Lille, France: Univ. of Lille Press; Gerrards Cross, England: Colin Smythe; Atlantic Highlands, N.J.: Humanities Press.

Fitzgerald, Laurie. 1992. "Multiple Genres and Questions of Gender in Maria Edgeworth's *Belinda*." *Studies on Voltaire and the Eighteenth Century* 304: 821–23.

Fitzgerald-Hoyt, Mary. 1993. "De-Colleenizing Ireland: William Trevor's *Family Sins*." *Notes on Modern Irish Literature* 5: 28–33.

Flanagan, Thomas. 1966. "The Big House of Ross-Drishane." *Kenyon Review* 28: 54–78.

Flood, Jeanne. 1974. *Brian Moore*. Lewisburg, Pa.: Bucknell Univ. Press.

Foster, John Wilson. 1974. *Forces and Themes in Ulster Fiction*. Dublin: Gill and Macmillan.

———. 1987. *Fictions of the Irish Literary Revival: A Changeling Art*. Syracuse: Syracuse Univ. Press.

Franklin, Miles. 1902. *My Brilliant Career*. 1980. Reprint, London: Virago.

Friberg, Hedda. 1990. "Women in Three Works by Liam O'Flaherty: In Search of an Egalitarian Impulse." In *Homage to Ireland: Aspects of Culture, Literature, and Language,* edited by Birgit Bramsbäck, 45–61. Uppsala, Sweden: Uppsala Univ. Press.

Fuderer, Laura Sue. 1990. *The Female Bildungsroman in English: An Annotated Bibliography of Criticism*. New York: Modern Language Association.

Gardiner, Judith Kegan. 1982. "On Female Identity and Writing by Women." In *Writing and Sexual Difference,* edited by Elizabeth Abel, 177–92. Chicago: Univ. of Chicago Press.

Gilbert, Sandra M., and Susan Gubar, eds. 1985. *The Norton Anthology of Literature by Women: The Tradition in English*. New York and London: Norton.

————. 1988. *The War of the Words*. Vol. 1 of *No Man's Land: The Place of the Woman Writer in the Twentieth Century*. New Haven and London: Yale Univ. Press.

Gilligan, Carol. 1982. *In a Different Voice: Psychological Theory in Women's Development*. Cambridge. Harvard Univ. Press.

Glotfelty, Cheryll Burgess, and Patrick D. Murphy. 1993. "Introduction." *ISLE: Interdisciplinary Studies in Literature and Environment* 1, no. 1: 1–4.

Goodman, Charlotte. 1993. "Cinderella in the Classroom: (Mis)Reading Alice Munroe's 'Red Dress—1946'." *Reader* 30: 49–61.

Green, Robert. 1982. "The Function of Poetry in Brian Moore's *The Emperor of Ice-Cream*." *Canadian Literature* 93: 164–72.

Grubgeld, Elizabeth. 1986. "The Poems of Emily Lawless and the Life of the West." *Turn-of-the-Century Women* 3, no. 2: 35–41.

————. 1987. "Emily Lawless's *Grania: The Story of an Island*." *Éire-Ireland* 22, no. 3: 115–29.

Haberstroh, Patricia Boyle. 1996. *Women Creating Women: Contemporary Irish Women Poets*. Syracuse: Syracuse Univ. Press.

Hall, Wayne E. *Shadowy Heroes: Irish Literature in the 1890s*. 1980. Syracuse: Syracuse Univ. Press.

Hardin, James, ed. 1991. *Reflection and Action: Essays on the Bildungsroman*. Columbia: Univ. of South Carolina Press.

Hargreaves, Tamsin. 1988. "Women's Consciousness and Identity in Four Irish Women's Novelists." In *Cultural Contexts and Literary Idioms in Contemporary Irish Literature,* edited by Michael Kenneally, 290–305. Totowa, N.J.: Barnes and Noble.

Harkin, Margaret. 1989. *Hush-A-Bye Baby*. Derry Film and Video Workshop, in association with British Screen and Radio Telefís Éireann.

Haule, James. 1987. "Tough Luck: The Unfortunate Birth of Edna O'Brien." *Colby Quarterly* 23, no. 4: 216–24.

Heath, Stephen. 1987. "Male Feminism." In *Men in Feminism,* edited by Alice Jardine and Paul Smith, 1–32. New York and London: Methuen.

Heilbrun, Carolyn. 1988. *Writing a Woman's Life*. New York and London: Norton.

Henke, Suzette. 1983. "James Joyce and Women: The Matriarchal Muse." In *Work in Progress: Joyce Centenary Essays,* edited by Richard F. Peterson, 117–31. Carbondale: Southern Illinois Univ. Press.

Hirschberg, Stuart. 1975. "Growing up Abject as Theme in Brian Moore's Novels." *Canadian Journal of Irish Studies* 1, no. 2: 11–16.

Hogan, Desmond. 1976. *The Ikon Maker*. Dublin: Irish Writers' Cooperative.

————. 1980. *The Leaves on Grey*. 1981. Reprint, London: Pan.

Imhof, Rüdiger. 1985. " 'A Little Bit of Ivory, Two Inches Wide': The Small World of Jennifer Johnson's Fiction." *Études Irlandaises* 10 (Dec.): 129–44.

Innes, C. L. 1993. *Woman and Nation in Irish Literature and Society 1880–1935.* Athens: Univ. of Georgia Press.

James, Kilroy. 1976. "Nineteenth-Century Writers." In *Anglo-Irish Literature: A Review of Research,* edited by Richard Finneran, 24–47. New York: Modern Language Association.

Jardine, Alice. 1987. "Men in Feminism: Odor di Uomo or Compagnons de Route?" In *Men in Feminism,* edited by Alice Jardine and Paul Smith, 54–61. New York and London: Methuen.

Jeffares, A. Norman. 1980. "Yeats and the Wrong Lever." In *Yeats, Sligo and Ireland: Essays to Mark the 21st Yeats International Summer School,* 98–111. Totowa, N.J.: Barnes and Noble.

———. 1982. *Anglo-Irish Literature.* London: Macmillan.

Jehlen, Myra. 1981. "Archimedes and the Paradox of Feminist Criticism." *Signs* 6, no. 4: 575–601.

Johnson, Toni O'Brien, and David Cairns, eds. 1991. *Gender in Irish Writing.* Buckingham: Open Univ. Press; Philadelphia: Milton Keynes.

Johnston, Denis. 1929. *The Old Lady Says No!.* 1990. Reprint. In *Irish Drama 1900–1980,* edited by Cóilín D. Owens and Joan N. Radner, 346–404. Washington, D. C.: Catholic Univ. Press.

Johnston, Jennifer. 1972. *The Captains and the Kings.* London: Fontana.

———. 1974. *How Many Miles to Babylon?.* 1984. Reprint, London: Fontana.

———. 1977. *Shadows on Our Skin.* London: Hamish Hamilton.

———. 1979. *The Old Jest.* London: Fontana.

———. 1984. *The Railway Station Man.* 1986. Reprint, London: Fontana.

———. 1987. *Fool's Sanctuary.* London: Hamish Hamilton.

———. 1991. *The Invisible Worm.* 1992. Reprint, New York: Penguin.

Jordan, Neil. 1980. *The Past.* London: Abacus.

———. 1982. *Angel.* Motion Picture Co. of Ireland.

———. 1983. *The Dream of the Beast.* London: Chatto and Windus.

———. 1992. *The Crying Game.* Palace Pictures, Paramount.

———. 1996. *Michael Collins.* Geffen Pictures, Warner Brothers.

Joyce, James. 1901. "The Day of the Rabblement." 1959. Reprint, New York: Viking.

———. 1914. *Dubliners.* 1967. Reprint. In *The Portable James Joyce,* edited by Harry Levin, 19–242. New York: Penguin.

———. 1916. *A Portrait of the Artist as a Young Man.* 1993. Reprint. Corrected ed. New York: St. Martin's Press.

———. 1922. *Ulysses.* 1986. Corrected ed. New York: Random House.

———. 1939. *Finnegans Wake.* 1959. Reprint, New York: Viking.

———. 1944. *Stephen Hero.* 1963. Reprint, New York: New Directions.

———. 1963. *A First-Draft Version of "Finnegans Wake."* Edited and annotated by David Hayman. London: Faber and Faber.

————. 1966. *Selected Letters of James Joyce*. Edited by Richard Ellmann. New York: Viking.

Joyce, Stanislaus. 1941. "James Joyce: A Memoir." Trans. by Felix Giovanelli. *Hudson Review* 2: 487–514.

————. 1949. "Early Memories of James Joyce." *The Listener* 41: 896–97.

————. 1958. *My Brother's Keeper: James Joyce's Early Years*. Edited by Richard Ellmann. New York: Viking.

————. 1971. *The Complete Dublin Diary of Stanislaus Joyce*. Edited by George H. Healey. Ithaca: Cornell Univ. Press.

Keane, Molly. 1981. *Good Behaviour*. 1982. Reprint, London: Sphere.

Kearney, Richard. 1984. *Myth and Motherland*. Derry: Field Day.

Kelleher, Margaret. 1997. *The Feminization of Famine: Expressions of the Inexpressible?* Cork: Cork Univ. Press.

Kelly, Angeline A. 1976. *Liam O'Flaherty the Storyteller*. London: Macmillan.

————. 1978. "Afterword." *The Ecstasy of Angus,* by Liam O'Flaherty, 59–62. Reprint of 1931 O'Flaherty book. Dublin: Wolfhound Press.

Kelly, Gary. 1994. "Class, Gender, Nation, and Empire: Money and Merit in the Writing of the Edgeworths." *Wordsworth Circle* 25, no. 2: 89–93.

Kennedy, Eileen. 1983. "The Novels of John McGahern: The Road Away Becomes the Road Back." In *Contemporary Irish Writing,* edited by James D. Brophy and Raymond J. Porter, 115–26. Boston: Twayne.

Kiberd, Declan. 1985. *Men and Feminism in Modern Literature*. New York: St. Martin's.

————. 1995. *Inventing Ireland: The Literature of the Modern Nation.* Cambridge: Harvard Univ. Press.

Kiell, Norman. 1983. Introduction. In *Blood Brothers: Siblings as Writers,* 3–48. New York: International Universities Press.

Kiely, Benedict. 1949. "Liam O'Flaherty: A Story of Discontent." *The Month* 2, no. 5: 185.

Kilfeather, Siobhan. 1986. "Beyond the Pale: Sexual Identity and National Identity in Early Irish Fiction." *Critical Matrix* 2, nos. 4–6: 1–31.

Kilroy, James, ed. 1976. *Anglo-Irish Literature: A Review of Research*. New York: Modern Language Association.

Kimball, Jean. 1983. "James and Stanislaus Joyce: A Jungian Speculation." In *Blood Brothers: Siblings as Writers,* edited by Norman Kiell, 73–113. New York: International Universities Press.

————. 1988. " 'Lui, c'est moi': The Brother Relationship in *Ulysses*." *James Joyce Quarterly* 25, no. 2: 227–35.

Kimball, Meredith M. 1995. *Feminist Visions of Gender Similarities and Differences*. New York and London: Harrington Park Press.

Kirkpatrick, Kathryn. 1995. Introduction to *Castle Rackrent* [1800], by Maria Edgeworth, vii–xxxvi. Oxford and New York: Oxford Univ. Press.

Kolodny, Annette. 1980. "A Map for Rereading: Or, Gender and the Interpretation of Literary Texts." *New Literary History* 11, no. 3: 451–68.

Lawless, Emily. 1882a. *A Chelsea Householder*. 3 vols. London: Sampson Low.

———. 1882b. "Iar-Connaught: A Sketch." *Cornhill Magazine* 45: 319–33.

———. 1885. *A Millionaire's Cousin*. London: Macmillan.

———. 1886. *Hurrish: A Study*. 2 vols. Edinburgh and London: William Blackwood.

———. 1887. *The Story of Ireland*. With some additions by Mrs. A. Bronson. London: T. Fisher Unwin.

———. 1889. *Plain Frances Mowbray and Other Tales*. London: John Murray.

———. 1890. *With Essex in Ireland*. London: Isbister.

———. 1892. *Grania (The Story of an Island)*. New York: Macmillan.

———. 1894. *Maelcho: A Sixteenth-Century Narrative*. 2 vols. London: Smith and Elder.

———. 1897. *Traits and Confidences*. 1979. Reprint, New York: Garland.

———. 1901. *A Garden Diary: September, 1899–September, 1900*. London: Methuen.

———. 1902. *With the Wild Geese*. London: Isbister.

———. 1904. *Maria Edgeworth*. London: Macmillan.

Lawrence, D. H. 1913. *Sons and Lovers*. 1981. Reprint, Harmondsworth, Eng.: Penguin.

Lewis, Gifford. 1985. *Somerville and Ross: The World of the Irish R. M.* Middlesex, Eng.; New York: Viking.

Lloyd, Richard. 1989. "Memory Becoming Imagination: The Novels of John McGahern." *Journal of Irish Literature* 18, no. 3: 39–44.

Loughman, Celeste. 1993. "The Mercy of Silence: William Trevor's *Fools of Fortune*." *Éire-Ireland* 28, no. 1: 87–96.

Lover, Samuel. 1842. *Handy Andy*. London: F. Lover.

Ludwig, Jack. 1962. "Brian Moore: Ireland's Loss, Canada's Novelist." *Critique* 4: 5–13.

MacCurtain, Margaret, and Donncha Ó Corrain. 1978. *Women in Irish Society: The Historical Dimension*. Dublin: Arlen House.

MacLaverty, Bernard. 1977. *Secrets and Other Stories*. Belfast: Blackstaff Press.

———. 1980. *Lamb*. 1981. Reprint, Middlesex, England: Penguin.

———. 1982. *A Time to Dance and Other Stories*. London: Jonathan Cape.

———. 1983. *Cal*. London: Jonathan Cape.

———. 1987. *The Great Profundo and Other Stories*. London: Jonathan Cape.

———. 1997. *Grace Notes*. London: Jonathan Cape.

Madden-Simpson, Janet. 1984. "Anglo-Irish Literature: The Received Tradition." Introduction to *Women's Part: An Anthology of Short Fiction by and about Irishwomen 1890–1920*, 1–19. Dublin: Arlen House.

Maddox, Brenda. 1984. "The Romantic and the Realist." *London Sunday Times Magazine,* 1 Apr.: 8–9.

Mahoney, Rosemary. 1993. *Whoredom in Kimmage: Irish Women Coming of Age.* Boston: Houghton Mifflin.

Manganiello, Dominic. 1980. *Joyce's Politics.* London: Macmillan.

Martin, Augustine. 1980. *Anglo-Irish Literature.* Dublin: Government of Ireland.

Mason, Ellsworth. 1955. "Mr. Stanislaus Joyce and John Henry Raleigh." *Modern Language Notes* 70 (Mar.): 187–91.

Maxwell, D.E.S. 1973. "Imagining the North: Violence and the Writers." *Éire-Ireland* 8, no. 2: 91–107.

Maxwell, W. H. 1832. *Wild Sports of the West.* London: D. Bryce.

McCourt, Frank. 1996. *Angela's Ashes.* New York: Scribner's.

McGahern, John. 1963. *The Barracks.* 1966. Reprint, London: Panther.

———. 1965. *The Dark.* 1977. Reprint, London: Quartet.

———. 1974. *The Leavetaking.* Rev. ed. Boston: Little, Brown, 1975.

———. 1979. *The Pornographer.* 1980. Reprint, London: Quartet.

———. 1984. "Q. and A. with John McGahern." Interview by Eileen Kennedy. *Irish Literary Supplement* 3, no. 1: 40.

———. 1987. "*An tOileánach / The Islandman.*" *Canadian Journal of Irish Studies* 13, no. 1: 7–15.

———. 1990. *Amongst Women.* London: Faber.

———. 1991a. "Me among the Protestants: A Bookish Boyhood." *New York Times Book Review,* 28 Apr.: 1, 25, 27.

———. 1991b. "*Dubliners.*" *Canadian Journal of Irish Studies* 17, no. 1: 31–37.

McHugh, Roger, and Maurice Harmon. 1982. *Short History of Anglo-Irish Literature, from Its Origins to the Present Day.* Totowa, N.J.: Barnes and Noble.

McMinn, Joseph. 1980. "Contemporary Novels on the Troubles." *Études Irlandaises* 5: 113–21.

McSweeney, Kerry. 1976. "Brian Moore Past and Present." *Critical Quarterly* 18, no. 2: 53–66.

———. 1983. *Four Contemporary Novelists: Angus Wilson, Brian Moore, John Fowles, V. S. Naipaul.* Kingston, Canada: McGill-Queen's Univ. Press.

Mead, Margaret. 1949. *Male and Female: A Study of the Sexes in a Changing World.* New York: William Morrow.

Mercier, Vivian. 1962. *The Irish Comic Tradition.* New York: Oxford Univ. Press.

Messenger, John C. 1969. *Inis Beag: Isle of Ireland.* New York: Holt, Rinehart, and Winston.

Meyers, Diana T. 1992. "The Subversion of Women's Agency in Psychoanalytic Feminism: Chodorow, Flax, Kristeva." In *Revaluing French Feminism: Critical Essays on Difference, Agency, and Culture,* edited by

Nancy Fraser and Sandra Lee Bartky, 136–61. Bloomington and Indianapolis: Indiana Univ. Press.

Miller, Jean Baker. 1976. *Towards a New Psychology of Women*. Boston: Beacon.

Mitchell [Robinson], Hilary. 1969. "Somerville and Ross: Amateur to Professional." In *Somerville and Ross: A Symposium*, 20–40. Belfast: Institute of Irish Studies.

Molloy, F. C. 1977. "The Novels of John McGahern." *Critique* 19, no. 1: 5–27.

Mooney, Shawn R. 1992. " 'Colliding Stars': Heterosexism in Biographical Representations of Somerville and Ross." *Canadian Journal of Irish Studies* 18, no. 1: 157–75.

Moore, Brian. 1955. *The Lonely Passion of Judith Hearne*. Boston: Little, Brown.

———. 1958. *The Feast of Lupercal*. 1983. Reprint, London: Granada.

———. 1960. *The Luck of Ginger Coffey*. Boston and Toronto: Little, Brown.

———. 1965. *The Emperor of Ice-Cream*. 1967. Reprint, London: Mayflower.

———. 1968. *I Am Mary Dunne*. New York: Viking.

———. 1975. *The Great Victorian Collection*. New York: Farrar, Straus, and Giroux.

———. 1981. *The Temptation of Eileen Hughes*. 1983. Reprint, London: Triad / Panther.

Moore, George. 1886. *A Drama in Muslin*. Rewritten as *Muslin* [1915]. 1922. Reprint, New York: Boni and Liverwright.

Moore, Thomas R. 1991. "Triangles and Entrapment: Julia O'Faolain's *No Country for Young Men*." *Colby Quarterly* 27, no. 1: 9–16.

Morrison, Kristin. 1987. "William Trevor's 'System of Correspondences'." *Massachusetts Review* 28, no. 3: 489–96.

Morrissey, Thomas. 1990. "Trevor's *Fools of Fortune*: The Rape of Ireland." *Notes on Modern Irish Literature* 2: 58–60.

Morse, J. Mitchell. 1954–55. "Jacob and Esau in *Finnegans Wake*." *Modern Philology* 52: 123–30.

Mulkerns, Val. 1986. *Very Like a Whale*. London: John Murray.

Murphy, Patrick D. 1988. "Introduction: Feminism, Ecology, and the Future of the Humanities." *Studies in the Humanities* 15, no. 2: 85–89.

Myers, Mitzi. 1988. "The Dilemmas of Gender as Double-Voiced Narrative; or, Maria Edgeworth Mothers the Bildungsroman." In *The Idea of the Novel in the Eighteenth Century*, edited by Robert W. Uphaus, 67–96. East Lansing, Mich.: Colleagues Press.

Nadel, Ira B. 1991. "The Incomplete Joyce." *Joyce Studies Annual*: 86–100.

Nash, Catherine. 1994. "Remapping the Body/Land: New Cartographies of Identity, Gender, and Landscape in Ireland." In *Writing Women and Space: Colonial and Postcolonial Geographies*, edited by Allison Blunt and Gillian Rose, 237–50. New York and London: Guilford Press.

Nelson, Cary. 1987. "Men, Feminism: The Materiality of Discourse." In *Men in Feminism,* edited by Alice Jardine and Paul Smith, 153–72. New York and London: Methuen.

Ní Chuilleanáin, Eiléan. 1985. "Women as Writers: Dánta Grá to Maria Edgeworth." In *Irish Women: Image and Achievement,* edited by Eiléan Ní Chuilleanáin, 111–26. Dublin: Arlen House.

O'Brien, Darcy. 1982. "Edna O'Brien: A Kind of Irish Childhood." In *Twentieth-Century Women Novelists,* edited by Thomas F. Staley, 179–90. Totowa, N.J.: Barnes and Noble.

O'Brien, Edna. 1966. *Casualties of Peace.* London: Cape.

———. 1970. *A Pagan Place.* 1971. Reprint, London: Penguin.

———. 1972. *Night.* London: Weidenfeld and Nicolson.

———. 1976a. *August Is a Wicked Month.* London: Cape.

———. 1976b. *Mother Ireland.* London: Weidenfeld and Nicolson.

———. 1984a. "The Art of Fiction: Edna O'Brien." Interview by Shusha Guppy. *Paris Review* 26, no. 92: 22–50.

———. 1984b. "Edna O'Brien." Interview by Philip Roth. *New York Times Book Review,* 18 Nov.: 38–40.

———. 1986a. *The Country Girls Trilogy.* Includes *The Country Girls* [1960], *The Lonely Girl* [1962], and *Girls in Their Married Bliss* [1964], and "Epilogue" [1986]. New York and London: Penguin.

———. 1986b. "Why Irish Heroines Don't Have to Be Good Anymore." *New York Times Book Review,* 11 May: 13.

———. 1994. *House of Splendid Isolation.* 1995. Reprint, New York: Penguin.

———. 1997. "On Tour: Edna O'Brien" (interview). *Hungry Mind Review: An Independent Book Review.* Accessed at http://www.bookwire.com/HMR/Review/tobrien.html

O'Brien, Kate. 1936. *Mary Lavelle.* 1984. Reprint, London: Virago.

———. 1941. *The Land of Spices.* 1982. Reprint, Dublin: Arlen House.

O'Brien, Peggy. 1987. "The Silly and the Serious: An Assessment of Edna O'Brien." *Massachusetts Review* 28, no. 3: 474–88.

O'Casey, Sean. 1925. *Juno and the Paycock.* 1981. Reprint. In *Three Plays,* 1–73. New York: St. Martin's Press.

O'Connell, Shaun. 1984. "Door into the Light." *Massachusetts Review* 25: 255–68.

———. 1988. "Brian Moore's Ireland: A World Well Lost." *Massachusetts Review* 29: 539–55.

O'Connor, Frank. 1931. "Guests of the Nation." 1956. Reprint. In *Stories by Frank O'Connor,* 3–16. New York: Vintage.

———. 1962. *The Lonely Voice: A Study of the Short Story.* Cleveland: World.

O'Connor, Pat. 1984. *Cal.* Enigma Films.

———. 1990. *Fools of Fortune.* Working Title, New Line.

———. 1995. *Circle of Friends.* Savoy Pictures.

O'Connor, Theresa. 1996a. "History, Gender, and the Postcolonial Condition: Julia O'Faolain's Comic Rewriting of *Finnegans Wake.*" In *The Comic Tradition in Irish Women Writers,* edited by Theresa O'Connor, 124–48. Gainesville: Univ. Press of Florida.

O'Connor, Theresa, ed. 1996b. *The Comic Tradition in Irish Women Writers.* Gainesville: Univ. Press of Florida.

O'Donnell, Peadar. 1928. *Islanders.* 1963. Reprint, Cork and Dublin: Mercier.

O'Donoghue, Jo. 1990. *Brian Moore: A Critical Study.* Dublin: Gill and Macmillan.

O'Dowd, Liam. 1987. "Church, State and Women: The Aftermath of Partition." In *Gender in Irish Society,* edited by Christopher Curtin, Pauline Jackson, and Barbara O'Connor, 3–36. Galway: Galway Univ. Press.

O'Faolain, Julia. 1970. *Godded and Codded. Three Lovers* in U. S. edition. New York: Coward, McCann, and Geoghegan.

———. 1975. *Women in the Wall.* New York: Viking.

———. 1980. *No Country for Young Men.* Middlesex, Eng.: Penguin.

O'Faolain, Julia, and Lauro Martines, eds. 1973. *Not in God's Image: Women in History from the Greeks to the Victorians.* 1979. Reprint, London: Virago.

O'Faolain, Nuala. 1985. "Irish Women and Writing in Modern Ireland." In *Irish Women: Image and Achievement,* edited by Eiléan Ní Chuilleanáin, 127–35. Dublin: Arlen House.

O'Flaherty, Liam. 1923. *The Neighbor's Wife.* Reprint, Dublin: Wolfhound Press.

———. 1924a. *The Black Soul.* 1996. Reprint, Dublin: Wolfhound.

———. 1924b. *Spring Sowing.* London: Cape.

———. 1925. "Mr. Tasker's Gods." *The Irish Statesman* 3 (7 Mar.): 827.

———. 1927. *The Life of Tim Healy.* London: Jonathan Cape.

———. 1928a. *The Assassin.* London: Jonathan Cape.

———. 1928b. "My Life of Adventure." *T. P.'s Weekly,* 120 October: 756.

———. 1929. *The Mountain Tavern and Other Stories.* New York: Harcourt.

———. 1930. *Two Years.* London: Cape.

———. 1931a. *I Went to Russia.* New York: Harcourt.

———. 1931b. *The Ecstasy of Angus.* 1978. Reprint, Dublin: Wolfhound Press.

———. 1932a. "Secret Drinking." *This Quarter* 2, no. 1 (July–Sept.): 109–14.

———. 1932b. *Skerrett.* 1982. Reprint, Dublin: Wolfhound Press.

———. 1933. *The Martyr.* New York: Macmillan.

———. 1934. *Shame the Devil.* 1981. Reprint, Dublin: Wolfhound Press.

———. 1937a. *Famine.* 1982. Reprint, Boston: David R. Godine.

———. 1937b. *The Short Stories of Liam O'Flaherty.* 1986. Reprint, Kent, Eng.: New English Library.

————. 1948. *Two Lovely Beasts*. 1950. Reprint, New York: Devin-Adair.

————. 1953. *Dúil*. Baile Atha Cliath [Dublin]: Sáirséal agus Dill.

————. 1956. *The Stories of Liam O'Flaherty*. New York: Devin-Adair.

————. 1973. *The Wounded Cormorant and Other Stories*. New York: Norton.

————. 1976. *Short Stories*. 1986. Reprint, Dublin: Wolfhound Press.

O'Healy, Aine. 1996. "Reimagining the Nation: Gender and Subjectivity in the New Irish Cinema." *Cinefocus* 4: 18–24.

O'Leary, Phillip. 1994. *The Prose Literature of the Gaelic Revival, 1881–1921*. State College: Pennsylvania State Univ. Press.

Onkey, Lauren. 1993. "Celtic Soul Brothers." *Éire-Ireland* 28, no. 3: 147–58.

Owens, Cóilín. 1980. "McGahern, John." In *Dictionary of Irish Literature*, edited by Robert Hogan, 399–401. Westport, Conn.: Greenwood.

Owenson, Sydney. 1806. *The Wild Irish Girl*. 1850. Reprint. 2 vols. Hartford, Conn.: Andrus.

Popot, Raymonde. 1976. "Edna O'Brien's Paradise Lost." *The Irish Novel in Our Time,* edited by Patrick Rafroidi and Maurice Harmon, 255–85. Lille, France: Lille Univ. Press.

Powell, Violet. 1970. *The Irish Cousins: The Books and Background of Somerville and Ross*. London: Heinemann.

Prosky, Murray. 1971. "The Crisis of Identity in the Novels of Brian Moore." *Éire-Ireland* 6, no. 3: 106–18.

Raleigh, John Henry. 1953. " 'My Brother's Keeper'—Stanislaus Joyce and *Finnegans Wake*." *Modern Language Notes* 68: 107–10.

Rees, David. 1991. *Brian Moore, Alasdair Gray, John McGahern: A Bibliography of their First Editions*. London: David Rees.

Reynolds, Mary T. 1988. "Joyce and His Brothers: The Process of Fictional Transformation." *James Joyce Quarterly* 25, no. 2: 217–25.

Robinson, Hilary. 1980. *Somerville and Ross: A Critical Appreciation*. Dublin: Gill and Macmillan; New York: St. Martin's Press.

Roth, Philip. 1979. *The Ghost Writer*. New York: Farrar, Straus, and Giroux.

Rynne, Andrew. 1982. *Abortion: The Irish Question*. Dublin: Ward River Press.

Sale, Richard B. 1969. "An Interview in London with Brian Moore." *Studies in the Novel* 1, no. 1: 67–80.

Sammons, Jeffrey. 1991. "The Bildungsroman for Nonspecialists: An Attempt at a Clarification." In *Reflection and Action: Essays on the Bildungsroman,* edited by James Hardin, 26–45. Columbia: Univ. of South Carolina Press.

Sampson, Denis. 1993. *Outstaring Nature's Eye: The Fiction of John McGahern*. Washington, D. C.: Catholic Univ. Press.

Sawyer, Roger. 1993. *"We Are but Women": Women in Ireland's History*. London: Routledge.

Scanlan, Margaret. 1985. "The Unbearable Present: Northern Ireland in Four Contemporary Novels." *Études Irlandaises* 10 (Dec.): 145–61.

Scheper-Hughes, Nancy. 1979. *Saints, Scholars, and Schizophrenics: Mental Illness in Rural Ireland.* Berkeley and Los Angeles: Univ. of California Press.

Schweickart, Patrocinio P. 1986. "Reading Ourselves: Toward a Feminist Theory of Reading." 1994. Reprint. In *Contemporary Literary Criticism: Literary and Cultural Studies,* edited by Robert Con Davis and Ronald Schleifer, 191–214. 3rd ed. New York and London: Longman.

Scott, Bonnie Kime. 1984. *Joyce and Feminism.* Bloomington: Indiana Univ. Press.

———. 1990. *The Gender of Modernism: A Critical Anthology.* Bloomington: Indiana Univ. Press.

Senn, Fritz. 1966. "Reverberations." *James Joyce Quarterly* 3: 222.

Shaffer, Julie. 1993. "Not Subordinate: Empowering Women in the Marriage Plot—the Novels of Frances Burney, Maria Edgeworth, and Jane Austen." In *Reading with a Difference: Gender, Race, and Cultural Identity,* edited by Arthur Marotti et al., 21–43. Detroit: Wayne State Univ. Press.

Sheeran, Patrick F. 1976. *The Novels of Liam O'Flaherty: A Study in Romantic Realism.* Atlantic Highlands, N.J.: Humanities Press.

Sheridan, Jim. 1989. *My Left Foot.* Granada, Miramax.

———. 1993. *In the Name of the Father.* Hell's Kitchen, Universal.

———. 1996. *Some Mother's Son.* Castle Rock, Columbia.

———. 1997. *The Boxer.* Universal.

Showalter, Elaine. 1982. "Feminist Criticism in the Wilderness." In *Writing and Sexual Difference,* edited by Elizabeth Abel, 9–36. Chicago: Univ. of Chicago Press.

———. 1987. "Critical Cross-Dressing; Male Feminists and the Woman of the Year." In *Men in Feminism,* edited by Alice Jardine and Paul Smith, 116–352. New York and London: Methuen.

———. 1989. *Speaking of Gender.* New York and London: Routledge.

Simpson, Paul, and Martin Montgomery. 1995. "Language, Literature, and Film: The Stylistics of Bernard MacLaverty's *Cal.*" In *Twentieth-Century Fiction: From Text to Context,* edited by Peter Verdonk and Jean Jacques Weber, 138–64. London and New York: Routledge.

Sloan, Barry. 1993. "Growing Up in a 'Sacrificial Society': Northern Ireland in Adolescent Fiction." *Éire-Ireland* 28, no. 4 (winter): 16–27.

Smith, Larry. 1986. "A Mirror of the Whole: Shaun in Book III, Chapters 1–3." *Modern Fiction Studies* 32, no. 4: 561–68.

Smyth, Ailbhe. 1982. *Women's Rights in Ireland.* Dublin: Irish Council for Civil Liberties and Ward River Press.

———. 1989. "The Floozie in the Jacuzzi." *Irish Review* 6: 7–24.

Snow, Lotus. 1979. " 'That Trenchant Childhood Route?' Quest in Edna O'Brien's Novels." *Éire-Ireland* 14, no. 1: 74–83.

Somerville and Ross: A Symposium. 1969. Belfast: Queen's University.

Somerville, E. OE. [Edith], ed. 1885. *The Mark Twain Birthday Book*. London: Remington.

———. 1917. *Irish Memories*. London: Longmans, Green.

———. 1944. *Experiences of an Irish R. M.* 1957. Reprint, London: J. M. Dent; New York: E. P. Dutton.

Somerville, E. OE. [Edith], and Martin Ross [Violet Martin]. 1889. *An Irish Cousin*. 2 vols. London: Bentley.

———. 1891. *Naboth's Vineyard*. London: Spencer Blackett.

———. 1893a. *In the Vine Country*. London: W. H. Allen.

———. 1893b. *Through Connemara in a Governess Cart*. London: W. H. Allen.

———. 1894. *The Real Charlotte*. 1982. Reprint, London: Quartet.

———. 1895. *Beggars on Horseback*. Edinburgh and London: Blackwood.

———. 1898. *The Silver Fox*. London: Lawrence and Bullen.

———. 1902. *A St. Patrick's Day Hunt*. Westminster: A. Constable.

———. 1903a. *All on the Irish Shore*. Leipzig: Tauchnitz.

———. 1903b. *Slipper's ABC of Fox Hunting*. London: Longsmans, Green.

———. 1911. *Dan Russell the Fox*. London: Methuen.

———. 1925. *The Big House of Inver*. New York: Doubleday.

———. 1928. *The Irish R. M.* [consisting of *Some Experiences of an Irish R.M.* (1899), *Further Experiences of an Irish R.M.* (1908), *In Mr. Knox's Country* (1915)]. 1989. Reprint, London: Sphere / Abacus.

———. 1989. *The Selected Letters of Somerville and Ross*. Edited by Gifford Lewis. London: Faber.

St. Peter, Christine. 1994. "Reconstituting the Irish Nationalist Family Romance: *No Country for Young Men*." In *Historicité et Métafiction dans le Roman Contemporain des Iles Brittanniques,* edited by Max Duperray, 151–66. Provence: Université de Provence.

Steinberg, Laurence. 1993. *Adolescence*. 3rd ed. New York: McGraw-Hill.

Stovel, Bruce. 1981. "Brian Moore: The Realist's Progress." *English Studies in Canada* 7, no. 2: 183–200.

Sullivan, Megan. 1998. "Orla Walsh's *The Visit* (1992): Incarceration and Feminist Cinema in Northern Ireland." *New Hibernia Review* 2, no. 2: 85–99.

Synge, John Millington. 1966. *Collected Works*. Volume 2, *Prose*. Edited by Alan Price. London: Oxford Univ. Press.

———. 1903. *Riders to the Sea*. 1987. Reprint. In *Irish Literature: A Reader,* edited by Maureen O'Rourke Murphy and James MacKillop, 174–83. Syracuse: Syracuse Univ. Press.

———. 1907. *The Playboy of the Western World*. 1990. Reprint. In *Irish Drama 1900–1980,* edited by Cóilín D. Owens and Joan N. Radner, 115–66. Washington, D. C.: Catholic Univ. Press.

Tannen, Deborah. 1990. *You Just Don't Understand: Women and Men in Conversation*. New York: Ballantine.

Thornton, Weldon. 1994. *The Antimodernism of Joyce's "Portrait of the Artist as a Young Man."* Syracuse: Syracuse Univ. Press.

Tindall, William York. 1959. *A Reader's Guide to James Joyce.* New York: Noonday.

Titley, Alan. 1980. "Rough Rug-Headed Kerns: The Irish Gunman in the Popular Novel." *Éire-Ireland* 15, no. 4 (winter): 15–38.

———. 1991. *An tÚrscéal Gaeilge* [The Gaelic novel] Baile átha Cliath: An Clóchomhar.

Toolan, Michael J. 1980. "Psyche and Belief: Brian Moore's Contending Angels." *Éire-Ireland* 15, no. 3: 97–111.

Trevor, William. 1972. *The Ballroom of Romance.* New York: Viking.

———. 1983. *Fools of Fortune.* London: Penguin.

———. 1985. *The News from Ireland.* London: Bodley Head.

———. 1986. "William Trevor: An Interview." Interview by Jacqueline Stahl Aronson. *Irish Literary Supplement* spring: 7–8.

———. 1988. *The Silence in the Garden.* New York: Viking.

———. 1994. *Felicia's Journey.* Harmondsworth, Eng.: Penguin.

Trotter, Elizabeth Stanley. 1922. "Humor With A Gender." *Atlantic Monthly* 130, no. 6: 784–87.

Valente, Joseph. 1994. "The Myth of Sovereignty: Gender in the Literature of Irish Nationalism." *ELH* 61: 189–210.

Van Dale, Laura. 1991. "Women Across Time: Sister Judith Remembers." *Colby Quarterly* 27, no. 1: 17–26.

Walker, Alice. 1982. *The Color Purple.* New York: Harcourt.

Walker, Nancy A. 1988. *A Very Serious Thing: Women's Humor and American Culture.* Minneapolis: Univ. of Minnesota Press.

Wall, Mervyn. 1948. *The Return of Fursey.* London: Pilot.

Walsh, Orla. 1992. *The Visit.* Róisín Rua Films.

Waters, Maureen. 1984. *The Comic Irishman.* Albany: SUNY Press.

Watt, Stephen. 1993. "The Politics of Bernard MacLaverty's *Cal.*" *Éire-Ireland* 28, no. 3: 130–46.

Weekes, Ann Owens. 1986. "Diarmuid and Grainne Again: Julia O'Faolain's *No Country for Young Men.*" *Éire-Ireland* 21, no. 1: 89–102.

———. 1990. *Irish Woman Writers, an Uncharted Tradition.* Lexington: Univ. Press of Kentucky.

———. 1997. "Julia O'Faolain." In *Modern Irish Writers: A Bio-Critical Sourcebook,* edited by Alexander G. Gonzalez, 332–35. Westport, Conn.: Greenwood Press.

———. 1998. "Trackless Roads: Irish Nationalisms and Lesbian Writing." In *Border Crossings: Irish Women Writers and National Identity,* edited by Kathryn Kirkpatrick. Tuscaloosa: Univ. of Alabama Press, forthcoming.

Wilde, Oscar. 1895. *The Importance of Being Earnest.* 1965. Reprint, New York: Avon.

Williams, Judith, and Stephen Watt. 1996. "Representing a 'Great Distress': Melodrama, Gender, and the Irish Famine." In *Melodrama: The Cultural Emergence of a Genre,* edited by Michael Hays and Anastasia Nikolopoulou, 245–66. New York: St. Martin's Press.

Winkler, Karen J. 1996. "Inventing a New Field: The Study of Literature About the Environment." *Chronicle of Higher Education* 9 Aug.: A8–9, A15.

Wolff, Robert Lee. 1979. "The Irish Fiction of the Honourable Emily Lawless." Introduction to *Traits and Confidences,* by Emily Lawless. New York: Garland. v–xv.

Woolf, Virginia. 1942. "Professions for Women." 1985. Reprint. In *The Norton Anthology of Literature by Women: The Tradition in English,* edited by Sandra M. Gilbert and Susan Gubar, 1383–88. New York and London: Norton.

Yeats, William Butler. 1989. *The Collected Poems of W. B. Yeats: A New Edition,* edited by Richard J. Finneran. New York: Macmillan.

———. 1902. *Cathleen Ni Hoolihan.* 1964. Reprint. In *Eleven Plays of William Butler Yeats,* edited by A. Norman Jeffares, 221–31. New York: Macmillan.

Index